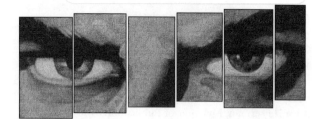

Changing Criminal Thinking: A Treatment Program 2nd Edition

Boyd D. Sharp, MS, LPC

FOUNDED 1870

Mission of the American Correctional Association

The American Correctional Association provides a professional organization for all individuals and groups, both public and private, that share a common goal of improving the justice system.

American Correctional Association Staff

Gwendolyn C. Chunn, President
James A. Gondles, Jr., CAE, Executive Director
Gabriella M. Klatt, Director, Communications and Publications
Harry Wilhelm, Marketing Manager
Alice Heiserman, Manager of Publications and Research
Michael Kelly, Associate Editor
Dana M. McCoy, Graphics and Production Manager
Joseph Fuller II, Graphics and Production Associate
Darlene Jones Powell, Graphics and Production Associate
Cover by Mike Selby

Printed in the United States of America by Graphic Communications, Upper Marlboro, MD

For information on publications and videos available from ACA, contact our worldwide web home page at: http://www.aca.org

ISBN: 1-56991-179-7

This publication may be ordered from:
American Correctional Association
206 North Washington St.
Alexandria, Va 22314
1-800-222-5646

Library of Congress Cataloging in Publication Data

Sharp, Boyd D.
    Changing criminal thinking : a treatment program / Boyd Sharp.-2nd ed.
        p. cm.
    Includes bibliographical references.
    ISBN 1-56991-179-7 (pbk.)
        1. Criminals-Rehabilitation-United States-Case studies. 2. Criminal
        psychology-United States-Case studies. 3. Criminal behavior-United States-Case
studies. I. Title.

HV9304.S43 2005
364.4'8-dc22   2005054587

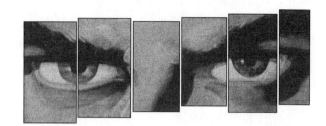

CONTENTS

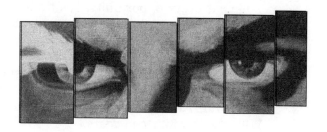

DEDICATION AND ACKNOWLEDGMENTS

This book is dedicated to the honor, excellence, commitment, and dedication of all the men and women who work in corrections in any capacity—including those who have gone before me in this field. It also is dedicated to any person who reads this book and gains insight into a loved one who is struggling with this thinking pattern and a criminal lifestyle.

I wish to thank the many people who have given me permission to quote and summarize their works. This book is only possible because of all the people who have had a hand in producing it, from the editors and reviewers, to the typesetters, bookbinders, order takers, delivery people, and the book sellers.

Many people directly and indirectly contributed to the first edition of this book and are listed in the references. However, others deserve a special note for their support and assistance, so special thanks go to:

- The Powder River Correctional Facility and staff in Baker City, Oregon, where this all began
- The Baker County Council on Alcohol and Drug Problems, Inc., the contract agency
- Kurt Lewis, who pioneered the development and early training of this model
- The Consortium Board of Directors and the Consortium staff, who were very supportive and encouraging of these efforts

- Dr. Richard Pohl, who has and continues to advocate for this idea at every opportunity. His tireless effort in promoting the development of these principles resulted in our teaching criminality classes in the Applied Psychology Department at the Oregon Institute of Technology
- Kelly Kiser, who spearheaded the first edition of this work
- Alice Heiserman, whose editing made this book readable
- My wife, Anne, who has listened to me rant and rave about this for the last fourteen years

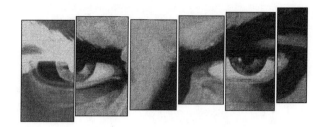

FOREWORD

Since publishing the first edition of this book in 2000, ACA has received positive responses to the ideas and content within the book. I believe this second edition will also garner positive feedback. It is valuable for both practitioners and for students in corrections. The author, Boyd Sharp, offers a treatment approach that has been tested and has proven its success. He uses popular examples from the news, media, and literature to illustrate the points he is making.

If offenders can be taught to think in a pro-social fashion then they may be able to make a successful transition back into society and our communities will be safer with productive and participating citizens. *Changing Criminal Thinking* provides some excellent suggestions for dealing with offenders whether they are in a therapeutic community or in the general population.

Sharp's book provides a tested, effective program for changing how offenders view themselves and the world around them.

James A. Gondles, Jr., CAE
Executive Director
American Correctional Association

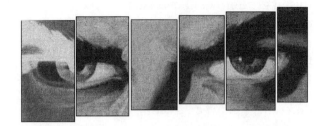

PREFACE

This edition discusses how criminal thinking allows criminals to commit crimes without remorse or guilt but when apprehended, criminals believe they are the victims. They can say they feel remorse because "they know the word but not its meaning." Hare, the guru of psychopathy, said he "once was dumbfounded by the logic of an inmate who described his murder victim as having benefited from the crime by learning 'a hard lesson about life'" (1993). Criminals' thinking allows them never to be held accountable nor responsible for their behavior, or at least minimizes the consequences of that behavior. This book examines how criminals think differently from prosocial thinking individuals. We view this along a thinking-pattern continuum. This book also addresses society's approach to and understanding of criminal thinking and behavior.

The theme of this book is that if the criminal's thinking is different from those of prosocial thinkers, then it makes sense that the treatment approach also must be different. We discuss this difference in some detail and outline ways to hold the criminal responsible and accountable.

The book outlines staff boundaries and relationships with the criminal client. We discuss how the criminal client attempts to compromise and set up the change agent to avoid accountability and responsibility. We use the word "criminal" the same way that we use the word alcoholic—not as a derogatory remark—but simply a term used to describe a particular behavior and activity that individuals have been engaged in for many years. However, some people object to this. They call it labeling and shaming and reject the need to label individuals as criminals. We discuss this in greater detail in a later chapter.

This second edition includes many additional sources of support for the ideas in the book. The book is rearranged to highlight its major themes: (1) cognitive behavior or thinking leads to behavior; (2) restructuring of the thinking pattern leads to changed behavior; (3) we can demystify the idea of causation and the denial system. This leads us to the differences between treating criminals and treating prosocial people. We also describe the characteristics of correctional change agents so those working with criminals can be effective at what they do.

This second edition has several new concepts: the development of a thinking-pattern continuum; discussion of contingency management (a reward/incentive program); and advice on change-agent detachment. We greatly expanded the therapeutic community chapter. The chapter on thinking errors and tactics presents them clustered into harmonious units. The section on thinking reports has a new discussion on affirmation writing as a method of changing thinking. Finally, another new chapter discusses the Klamath Falls Jail treatment program with updates on the Powder River and the Consortium programs.

Since the first edition of the book, Mr. Sharp has read and studied extensively the criminal behavior and the thinking patterns people have. This has contributed to the current edition. Some of the following reading and studying has influenced the update.

After the first book was published, Mr. Sharp examined *Your Erroneous Zone* by Dr. Wayne W. Dyer (1976). This book was a best seller for Mr. Dyer. Yet, Mr. Sharp had the mistaken notion that it was about sexual zones and enhancing sexual power. However, it was about thinking errors—and was addressed to the general public. This led him to Mr. Dyer's many other books: *Real Magic* (1992), *Your Sacred Self* (1995), *Manifesting Your Own Destiny* (1993), *10 Secrets to Inner Peace and Success* (2001); *There Is a Spiritual Solution to Every Problem* (2001), and his latest best seller *The Power of Intention* (2004). All of these books deal with thinking patterns and taking responsibility for one's own thinking.

Additional books from the criminal justice field that have influenced Mr. Sharp in his teaching and in using these philosophies are the following: *Without Conscience: The Disturbing World of the Psychopaths Among Us* by Robert Hare (1993), *Why They Kill* by Richard Rhodes (1999), *Game Over* by Bill Elliott and Vicki Verdeyen (2002), *Correctional Assessment, Casework and Counseling, 4th Edition,* by Anthony Walsh (2005); *Breaking Barriers: A Cognitive Reality Model* by Gordon Graham and Company (1999); *Becoming a Model Warden: Striving for Excellence* by Clemens Bartollas (2004); Frank J. Porporino's "Revisiting Responsivity: Why What Works? Isn't Working," in *What Works and Why: Effective Approaches to Re-entry* (2005); John Perry's *Repairing Communities through Restorative Justice* (2002); Vivian Gadsen's *Heading Home: Offender Reintegration into the Family* (2003); and numerous articles listed in the bibliography. Other influential books include: *Power vs. Force* by David Hawkins (1995, 1998, 2002); the *Bhagavad Gita*, the ancient Hindu scripture, translated for the modern reader by Eknath Easwaran, (1985); *The Tibetan Book of Living and Dying* edited by Sogyal Rinpoche, (1993); *The Legend of Bagger Vance* by Steven Pressfield, (1995); *The Heart of the Soul* by Gary Zukav and Linda Francis (2001); *The Way of the Peaceful Warrior* by Dan Millman (1984); and *The Fire From Within* by Carlos Castaneda (1984). The major themes of these works place full accountability on the client. These readings have contributed to the changes and additions in this edition.

At this juncture, a quote from Frank Wood, formerly a model warden in Minnesota, is appropriate. To be a model warden (change agent) in a correctional setting "it is important to continue your education through a broad range of reading on a wide variety of topics—history, philosophy, logic, ethics, treatment modalities, and, of equal importance, religion and theology," (Bartollas, 2004). Throughout this work, the author uses many quotes from a wide range of sources not normally associated with corrections. Yet, they make powerful comments and statements, which can provide insight and help in the correctional field. Hopefully, readers will not reject them simply because they have not come from within the field. Others have much to offer this discipline.

Workshops and training also have influenced the expansion of this work. Such training as Harvey Milkman's "Pathways To Self-Discovery and Change: Delinquency, Crime and Substance Abuse Treatment for Adolescents;" Ken Robinson's, "What Works in Treatment: Research Based on Cognitive Models and Their Use in Substance Abuse Treatment ("Moral Reconation Therapy (MRT)"); Gordon Graham's "Navigating Change: Charting Your Own Course," Al Cohen and Maxine Stitzer's "Contingency Management—The Evidence and Issues;" and The National Conference on Addiction and Criminal Behavior Training sponsored by GWC, Inc.—all these have been influential.

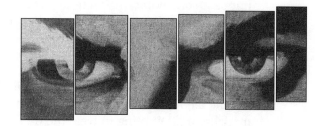

Introduction

Most criminal justice system and treatment programs that attempt to treat the criminal have failed because they have not understood the criminal mind. What they do not understand is that for the criminal, the crime makes absolute sense. Criminals think differently than we do. For this reason, the crime makes sense for male and female criminals but not for us.

This book shows how the criminals' thinking differs from that of prosocial people. To do this, we developed a thinking-pattern model, which we compare to the drinking-pattern model. We then describe the treatment model for substance-abusing criminals that we developed. Until recently, most treatment programs attempted to treat alcohol and other drug-addicted criminals by superimposing the prosocial models that they were using for noncriminal alcoholics and addicts. The gurus of new approaches, Andrews and Bonta (1998), call these inappropriate treatment approaches. They include in this group "non-directive client-oriented/ psycho-dynamic approaches, non-behavioral milieu, and intensive non-behavioral group interaction."

Additional problems with traditional approaches include the following:

- By superimposing a prosocial model on an antisocial population, correctional practitioners do not get significant changes in the long-term behavior of correctional clients.

- A good male model, often called the Minnesota model, is super-imposed on women. Belatedly, we have learned that a new model is necessary for women because they have different needs than men.
- We also made the mistake of taking the adult model and super-imposing it on youths. Again, we have learned that a new model for youths is needed. Recently, we have discovered that just taking the alcohol and drug treatment model and the mental health model and attempting to treat the dual-diagnosed is not enough. We need a brand-new model to treat this population.
- We also need a new model for treating the criminal population. This book demonstrates such a model and shows how to use it.

We believe that our model is more useful than previous models because criminals do not think like law-abiding prosocial people—much like alcoholics do not drink like social drinkers. Their thinking is different from that of prosocial persons—again in comparison to how the alcoholic's drinking is different from a social drinker's. The antisocial model states that criminals commit crimes because their thinking rationalizes and justifies their behavior, and that criminal behavior is the result of erroneous thinking (Dyer, 1976). Criminals' thinking leads to their feelings, their feelings lead to their behavior, and their behavior reaffirms their thinking. To use the words of Alcoholics Anonymous, the criminal is afflicted with "stinking thinking," which includes rationalizing, justifying, excuse-making, blaming, accusing, and being a victim.

Until the late 1980s, much of the research literature on criminals and society focused on causation. The studies of Yochelson and Samenow, *The Criminal Personality* (1976, 1977, 1987), were exceptions. Many theories have attempted to explain why an individual develops a criminal personality. Some of these explanations include: social inadequacies, lack of early childhood nurturing, family dynamics and dysfunction, addiction to drugs and alcohol, and so forth. Most focus on either the nurturing or the nature theory. Andrews and Bonta (1998) say that "labeling, conflict, and due process perspective do not contain well-formulated principles of behavioral influence." Thus, this work focuses on a third theory: choice or free will.

Since the 1990s, much evidence-based research on criminal thought patterns supports the cognitive-restructuring discussions in this book. Many writers suggest that the cognitive-restructuring treatment approach fits nicely for treatment in the general population.

However, many prosocial individuals continue to look at the atrocious crimes committed by criminals and cannot understand them because they do not understand the criminals' thinking. So, they respond in one of two ways. On the one hand, they reject the criminals as depraved and demand that we lock them up and throw away the keys. Andrews and Bonta (1998) call this "retributive or just deserts." They go on to say ". . . there is no evidence that a reliance on just deserts or deterrence-based sanctioning is followed by meaningful reductions in recidivism." The second response is to say no sane person could act that way. So, they begin to look for causes.

By contrast, the antisocial model discussed in this book does not address causation of crime or reasons criminals commit crimes other than to say that criminals commit crimes because of the way they think. In the antisocial model, the emphasis is on choice. Such choice occurs in the way the staff interacts with clients and the way clients interact with staff and with one another. We believe that all clients in the program made individual choices to get where they are. They did this despite their childhood or parents, their economic or social status, and their living or working conditions. In an antisocial treatment program, they also can make individual choices to change what they think and how they act.

Although it may appear insensitive and cold, it is essential that staff working with criminals maintain this attitude regarding free choice. To do otherwise results in not being successful with criminals. Criminals' chief survival mechanism is avoiding responsibility. One of their first refuges, as they try to avoid facing who they are and what they have done, is to blame others for their plight. To allow clients to excuse their criminal behavior by blaming an alcoholic mother or an abusive father gives them permission not to accept responsibility for their own actions. We believe that optimum opportunity for success in a treatment program requires that clients be held accountable for all their actions, past, present, and future.

A second reason for not factoring in causation, when dealing with the criminal personality, is that criminals are all too eager to buy into the idea that their criminal behavior is not their fault. This sets the stage for them to manipulate situations and exploit other people. For example, if the counselor were to agree with a client that abuse in childhood had led him to a life of crime, the resident would attempt to exploit the counselor's sympathies. He would try to manipulate every situation using his sorry history. The criminal would de-focus or attempt to focus attention on other people, situations, or circumstances to divert attention away from his problem to other areas to avoid changing his behavior. "One gets the impression from sociological criminology that everything is responsible for crime except the people who commit it" (Walsh, 2005).

An illustration of this type of thinking comes from a Calvin and Hobbes cartoon (1992). This cartoon provided some excellent examples of criminal thinking and behavior. Calvin, in a talk with his father says:

> I have concluded that nothing bad that I do is my fault. . . . being young and irresponsible, I'm a helpless victim of count- less bad influences. An unwholesome culture panders to my undeveloped values and it pushes me into misbehavior. . . . I take no responsibility for my behavior. I'm an innocent pawn in society.

Programs that focus on this idea of the criminal being a victim of society "tend to focus not on the individuals as the targets of service, but on development and strengthening of welfare agencies, neighborhood organizations and inborn leadership" (Andrews and Bonta, 1998, p. 277). We address the subject of avoiding causation more fully later.

In a cognitive-behavioral program, by contrast, the "criminal-think- ing" component is its therapeutic heart. We address criminal thinking in all group and individual counseling sessions, in leisure time, and in work activities. We help clients examine their criminal thinking and behavior in every treatment hour. In Dyer's words "we become like what we think about all day long." If all the criminals are thinking about is how to beat the man, how to get one over on others, how to take advantage of others, then that is how they will act. To take full advantage of the antisocial pro- gram, clients are asked to take responsibility for their thinking and to change that thinking pattern. As they remain drug, alcohol, and crime free and practice all of the activities of the program, they learn to iden- tify patterns in their thinking as a direct means of understanding themselves. As their thinking changes, their feelings change, and their behavior will change.

In this cognitive approach, we believe that if you change persons' thinking, their feelings and behavior will change. This approach is also very directive—far different from a Rogerian client-centered, nondirec- tive approach, where the theme is to change the feeling, allowing the clients to direct where they want to go in the session, and then expect that their behavior will change. It also is not a psychoanalytical approach.

"Psychoanalysis and client-centered therapy rarely are used in a correctional setting primarily because they are too nondirective" (Walsh, 2005).

This is not a behaviorist approach, even though the term "cognitive-behavioral" is used. It refers to the behavioral changes desired as effected by the thinking changes; the theme is if you change the behavior, the feelings and thinking will change. Experts agree that "cognitive-behavioral approaches consistently appear to be the most effective treatment therapy for substance abusers" (Montague, 2001). "Behavioral, cognitive-behavioral and social learning approaches to treatment provide the greatest likelihood of success" (Andrews and Bonta, 1998).

This cognitive approach is similar to the approaches of Transactional Analysis, Reality Therapy, and Rational Emotive Behavior Therapy. Walsh (2005), in a discussion of counseling theories, describes cognitive therapy this way: "What actually is practiced is cognitive therapy with some behavioral and modeling techniques applied, when possible. Changing maladaptive thought patterns takes on a central role in treatment."

The antisocial model we employ uses a variety of tools to guide clients in scrutinizing their criminal-thinking errors. Initially, clients are presented with Yochelson and Samenow's list of thirty-six "Thinking Errors Characteristic of the Criminal Personality" (1976) or a revised version of this. Clients focus on their thinking and address their thinking errors in group discussions, role plays, and in individually assigned papers. In similar fashion, we present the eighteen "Tactics Obstructing Effective Transactions in Treatment" and "Criminal Mask" (from Yochelson and Samenow, 1976). Thus, from the very beginning, clients are aware that we understand their thinking patterns and that they are unlikely to pull the wool over the eyes of any staff member of an antisocial model program. This is very important. It disarms the clients and makes them more receptive to treatment.

Other tools we employ are *A Framework for Breaking Barriers* (1999) by Gordon Graham and S. Hyrum, Hazelden's *Design for Living* (1993), and the Franklin Reality Model (Bennett and Smith, 1987), now included in *A Framework for Breaking Barriers*. The latter employs a structured video and workbook program for use in a group setting. At the beginning of treatment, clients are introduced to the concept of reframing their thought process. These models also can engage the clients in early hands-on material. If there is only a short time for work with the criminal, we recommend beginning with the Franklin Reality Model followed by *Design for Living*, then *Breaking Barriers*.

THE BEGINNING OF THE COGNITIVE RESTRUCTURING PROGRAMS

As we hired our staff, half went to two weeks of training at the Oregon Department of Corrections. After this, we spent one week planning. Then, we had our first fifteen inmates. The building was not yet completed, doors were not hung on the offices, and the remaining staff were attending their training for two weeks. When they finished training, we received another fifteen inmates. At this point, we had thirty inmates who were smarter and sharper than we were, and they ran the place for the next year. This caused the corrections staff annoyance and fear, and horror and frustration for the treatment staff. Staff quickly had to learn about criminals and how to treat them. It took us a year to develop the program and antisocial model discussed in this book.

Later, we implemented the antisocial program developed at Powder River in a day reporting/day treatment program at the Klamath County Treatment and Correctional Provider's Consortium in Klamath Falls, Oregon. This program received federal funding from the Center for Substance Abuse Treatment. The initial program design was developed as a prosocial treatment model, although the Powder River Program was the model for developing the grant. After two years of experience, this model was replaced with the antisocial model discussed here.

In addition, we developed a jail-treatment program in the Klamath Falls County Jail. This four-year program, funded by the Edward Byrnes Memorial Foundation, successfully employed the antisocial model (a cognitive-behavioral approach). This included strict use of sanctions for program rule violations, cognitive restructuring of criminal thought patterns, and a modified therapeutic community. Research has demonstrated that "cognitive, behavioral and therapeutic community approaches are more likely to result in changes in the behavior of your offender clients" (Montague, 2001).

Research also documented some things we learned during the first five years in developing the Powder River program and subsequently in the Klamath Falls Consortium, the jail treatment program. Gendreau says:

> . . . Evidence concerning effective treatment services for offenders has continued to accumulate at an impressive pace. This evidence is contained in a variety of literature reviews published since 1980 (Andrews and Bonta, 1994; Andrews, Bonta, and Hoge, 1990; Andrews, Zinger, et al., 1990; Antonowicz and Ross, 1994; Basta and Davidson, 1988; Borduin, in press; Cullen and Gendreau, 1989; Cullen et al., in press; Garrett, 1985; Gendreau, in press-a; Gendreau and Andrews, 1990; Gendreau, Cullen, and Bonta, 1994; Gendreau, Paparozzi, Little, and Goddar, 1993; Gendreau and Ross, 1981, 1987; Gottschalk, Davidson, Gensheimer, and Mayer, 1987; Greenwood and Zimring, 1985; Hollin 1993; Izzo and Ross, 1990; Kazdin, 1987; Lipsey, 1992; Losel, 1995, in press; Marshall and Pithers, 1994; Morris and Braukmann, 1987; Muvey, Arthur, and Repucci, 1993; Palmer, 1983, 1992; Quay, 1987; Roberts and Camasso, 1991; Ross, Antonowicz, and Dhaliwal, 1995; Ross and Fabiana, 1985; Ross and Gendreau, 1980; Van Voorhis, 1987; Whitehead and Lab, 1989, 1996b).

This book describes what worked for us. You might want to try it. It may work for you with some modifications based on your own clients, setting and staff. We would be interested in hearing from you about your experience. Please send your comments to bsharp@oregontrail.net.

chapter 1

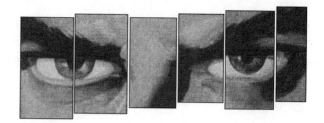

THE THINKING-PATTERN CONTINUUM VERSUS A DRINKING-PATTERN CONTINUUM

The literature increasingly reveals that human thinking follows a pattern of thought processes, which extend from internal thinking (where a person takes full responsibility for his or her thoughts and actions) to the other end of the spectrum, where individuals are psychopathic in their thinking and behavior. We compare this thinking-pattern continuum to the drinking-pattern continuum that is commonly accepted by the treatment community.

Drinking-Pattern Continuum

|25 percent|----------------------75 to 85 percent----------------------- |3 to 5 percent|
|NONDRINKING | SOCIAL DRINKING | BEGINNING PROBLEMS | ABUSIVE DRINKING | ADDICTION | CHRONIC SKID ROW

Estimates are that about 25 percent of the U.S. population does not drink for several reasons. Some do not drink because they are in recovery, some out of religious convictions, and others simply because they

1

have chosen not to drink. These people, of course, have no difficulty with drinking.

Social drinkers seem to be about 40 percent of the population. Social drinkers drink responsibly. They very seldom have more than two or three drinks at a time; most often they do not drink on a daily basis, and this is the way they drink until they die, with perhaps an occasional drunk thrown in. These folk also do not encounter any problems with their drinking.

Beginning problem drinkers make up about 10 percent of the population. They often drink too much; they have minor family, job, money, law, and sex problems. They may have hangovers that interfere with activities and often are embarrassed about things they have done while drinking. They often drink after a disappointment or argument.

About 10 percent of people are abusive drinkers. They encounter more serious problems such as arrests, separation, divorce, lawsuits, fights, beginning health problems, drinking alone or at inappropriate times, increased tolerance, and relief drinking. Here is the beginning of the alibi system. They begin to forget parts of the night before and are often in a hurry to get that first drink. They continue drinking after friends have quit.

Ten percent of our population is addicted to alcohol. Some signs are benders or binges, beginning to lose tolerance, severe blackouts, inability to predict how much one will drink, shakes, and need for a drink after prolonged absence. They are preoccupied with the idea of drinking. All activity centers on drinking. They hide bottles and sneak drinks. Their alibi system collapses and they have irregular eating habits while drinking.

Skid row alcoholics makes up about 3 to 5 percent of the population. They generally have lost their families, jobs, and health. They mainly live from drink to drink. Delirium tremors (DTs) are very common and include hallucinations. Generally, these people are homeless, sleeping wherever they can find a place.

THINKING-PATTERN CONTINUUM

Let us now consider the thinking-pattern continuum. There are at least three reasons to do this. The first is that the literature suggests that all human-thinking patterns follow a continuum of thought patterns, which affect all behavior. "It is true that correctional professionals are not pure and completely honest 100 percent of the time. All of us have engaged in a 'con' game or manipulated someone to get what we wanted" (Elliott and Verdeyen, 2002).

The second is that in teaching cognitive restructuring at the college level, students constantly begin to see, in their own thinking, some of the thought patterns attributed to criminals. They became concerned about whether they were or could be considered criminal. This thinking-pattern continuum should assist in quieting their concern and helping them become more ethical individuals.

The third reason is to help criminals understand their criminal-thought patterns, and subsequently to assist them in changing these patterns. If we see where criminals fall on the continuum and how that differs from prosocial thinking, we are better able to structure a treatment regime that fits the clients' needs. This regime should include the right intensity in terms of dosage, length of treatment, and response to misbehavior. "Offenders with more involvement in the criminal justice system are likely to require more external control on their behavior as compared to those with less prior criminal justice history" (Montague, 2001). We develop this idea more fully in a subsequent chapter.

Thinking-Pattern Continuum

	15 to 25 percent			------------------75 to 85 percent------------------		3 to 5 percent	

|Prosocial		Prosocial		Erroneous		Problem		Criminal	|Chronic
Internal		External		Thinking		Thinking		Thinking		Psychopathic
Thinking		Thinking					Thinking

Internal-thinking people can be compared to the nondrinker. According to Dyer (1976) and David Hawkins (1995), only about 15 to 25 percent of the human population are internal thinkers. Internal thinkers take full responsibility for all their thoughts and behaviors. In *Your Erroneous Zones* (1976), Dyer points out that the internal-thinking person puts the responsibility for how she thinks squarely on her own shoulders. When asked why she feels bad, this person responds with "I tell myself the wrong things." They change such thoughts of "You hurt my feelings" to "I hurt my feelings because of the things I told myself about your reaction to me." Or "you're embarrassing me" to "I'm embarrassing myself." Instead of saying "you make me mad," they say "I feel mad when you do such and such."

Hawkins (1995) has postulated a continuum of human consciousness; he says that only 15 percent of the population is above what he calls the line separating those whose thought patterns are positive and enriching the universe and those whose thought patterns are negative and inhibiting the universe. This first group easily can separate truth from falsehoods. He suggests the prosocial internal thinkers have thoughts of love, peace, joy, acceptance, and reason. They view the world as a hopeful, harmonious, and meaningful place. These people have the grand ability to be able to discern between those things that support life and those things that do not support life. They see the world as complete, benign, and perfect. It is an inspiring and safe place. These folk do not have thoughts of being a victim. They do not play the blame game; that is, they do not blame circumstances, neighborhoods, race, sexual orientation, or any other reason. They are able to be empathic and caring without any expectation of a return for their effort. For them, the past does not drive the present. These people live in the present moment.

Most prosocial people are external thinkers. This stage corresponds to the social drinker on the drinking continuum. They are about 40 percent of the population. People in this category begin to play the blame game even though they know it is not true. Though these people can distinguish between truth and falsehood, they occasionally use lies to get what they want. These people are still able to feel empathy, remorse, and guilt. They continue to be able to identify supportive life endeavors as opposed to destructive life activities. People at this point in the continuum talk about bad luck and complain that things do not break right for them. They often worry about keeping their jobs, mates, health, the weather, and other issues. Here is where you will see people who make statements such as "You make me mad," "He makes me sick," "She turns me on," "You make a fool of me." This places their thinking outside of themselves and places the blame on someone else. Their thinking does not get them in much trouble. Occasionally, their thinking will lead to arguments and unrest, but they get the situation corrected. They may have erroneous thinking 20 percent of the time; however, they have a system of internal/external deterrents present that keeps them out of trouble.

An example of this kind of prosocial thinking can be seen in Sally Forth by Francesco Marciuliano in the Sunday Comics, of October 24, 2004 as distributed by the *Eastern Oregonian*, Pendleton, Oregon.

Ted: See you later, Sal.

Sally: Where are you going?

Ted: I'm playing golf with Chris, Charlie and Cousin Jim, remember?

Sally: But it's not even 5 A.M.

Ted: We scored an early tee time.

Sally: But it's barely forty degrees outside.

Ted: We'll dress in layers.

Sally: But they're predicting a thunderstorm.

Ted: We could use a little challenge in our game.

Sally: But is it even worth it? You always play lousy against Chris, Charlie and Cousin Jim.

Ted: And now I'll be able to blame that on the miserable weather and appalling tee time. See you at lunch.

Reprinted with permission of © King Features Syndicate.

The erroneous thinking stage is parallel to the beginning problem-drinking phase. At this stage of the continuum, people begin to encounter difficulty because of their thinking pattern. This category is about 10 percent of the population. These people begin to rely more on the blame game. Their thinking embraces the thought of "it is not my fault." Others are to blame for their behavior and circumstances. Their excuse-making increases. They rationalize much of their behavior. It is more difficult for them to distinguish right from wrong or falsehood from truth. These people often think they are victims. In this stage, their thinking begins to get them in trouble with their friends and family, and they commit some illegal acts. At this juncture, one begins to confuse life-supportive and life-destructive behaviors. They even may come in contact with the law. They begin to believe the excuses and rationalizations they are thinking. They are easily offended, have to be right, and have to win. It is harder for them to feel remorse and guilt. They do not understand how their thinking and choices contribute to the "bad luck" in their lives. These thoughts comprise about 40 percent of their thinking pattern.

We now come to the point in the continuum (problem thinking) where people's thinking begins to get them in trouble with the law and arrested on a periodic basis. Like the abusive drinker, about 10 percent of the population falls into this category. Approximately 60 percent of their thinking excuses their behavior. They are beginning to lose any ability to feel remorse or guilt for their behavior. Their incidents of thinking that they are the victim and not the initiator of problems increases.

Most often they have a good explanation of why things happen as they do. They begin to lie on a regular basis when held accountable for their acts. Their ability to know the difference between lying and telling the truth is almost gone. They are unreliable, inconsiderate, late, and careless. You see good behavior only when it suits their purpose to get something they want. Their consideration of supportive actions and destructive actions depends on what they want to selfishly accomplish. They routinely turn conversations and disagreements back onto the other person. They attack when they believe they will be held accountable. Often, at this point in the continuum, the person will get others pitted against each other to take the focus off of them.

Now, we come to thinking patterns that routinely are considered criminal thinking. This thinking comprises 80 to 100 percent of their thoughts. Once in group while attempting to get a client to recognize his thinking errors, he, in exasperation, declared "Everything I think is a thinking error." Our response was "Now, you are beginning to get the picture." At least 10 percent of the population falls into this level of thinking. They match the alcoholic on the drinking continuum. These people have lost all ability to have thoughts of remorse even though they may express remorse to receive a lighter sentence or sympathy. Their thinking constantly puts them in the victim's role. The blame game is the only game they think of. Their thinking includes thoughts of "I have my own lifestyle."

They think they have little in common with others. Thoughts of conquest are uppermost in their minds. They are constantly thinking of how to get one over on others. They have lost the majority of the ability to distinguish between those things that support life and those that do not. Manipulation and control over others and situations is their modality. The moment is all that counts. Their past completely drives their present and how they project into the future. They think "I must keep others in their place if I am to succeed." They have thoughts of never being able to lose, a desire to be the center of all things, and they want to keep control at all cost. In addition, they cannot tell the difference between truth and falsehood. Lying has become a way of life. Lying is all they know. Their arrest record has many notations on it, many for petty crimes, that have led to more serious assaults that have led to armed robberies, rape, and so forth.

Last in line along this continuum is what can be called the psychopathic thinker. Like the skid row alcoholic, this is the end of the line. "Researchers in this area reserve the term psychopath for those whose antisocial behavior is considered to be primarily genetic in origin, and sociopath for those whose antisocial behavior is mostly environmental in origin (Walsh, 2005). Rhodes (1999) says the only difference in the label between psychopath and sociopath is whether you have a degree in sociology or psychology.

Hare (1993) believes that this group comprises at least 25 percent of the criminal population. His book is about psychopaths; however, it talks about the same behaviors and thinking we describe in this book. "An important question is whether psychopaths are qualitatively different from other criminals or whether all criminals are psychopaths, to some extent—some more so than others. Is psychopathy a discrete personality construct or a continuous dimension of personality? Or, could they be divided into primary and secondary groups? At what point does one become a psychopath? There is still no agreement" (Andrews and Bonta, 1998). In our experience, the percentage of psychopaths is much lower than 25 percent, probably about 5 percent of the population. Rhodes (1999) notes, "The serial killer as a deranged psychopath is a fiction. Ultra-violent criminals may kill multiple victims within a short enough period of time to qualify for designation as 'serial killers.' But they know what they are doing and do it consciously not compulsively and unconsciously."

In addition to having lost all ability to feel remorse or guilt, they actually become sadistic. Their thoughts are constantly on how to harm others, how to make them suffer. They get delight in watching other people squirm. These people no longer know the difference between action supportive of life and action destructive of life. They make statements such as "by killing him I was teaching him a lesson." When a man who seduced many women and stole their money was asked if he had a sense of guilt, he responded by saying, "Sure I took their money, but they got their money's worth out of me." He said, "I fulfilled their need. There were times we didn't even get out of bed," Hare (1993). Hare goes on to quote the following concerning another man: "When asked if he had ever committed a violent offense, a man serving time for theft answered, 'No, but I once had to kill someone.'"

chapter 2

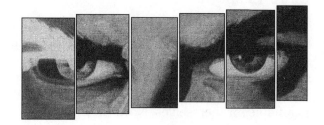

CRIMINAL THINKING IS DIFFERENT FROM PROSOCIAL THINKING

Now, we turn to specifics about how criminals think. When we talk about offenders and criminals, we are talking about people who do what they do as a process because of the way they think. We are not saying that these are ultimately terrible or evil people. We are talking about people who have chosen certain thinking patterns that lead to particular skills and methods of behaving. As we describe their thinking patterns and behavior, keep in mind that the criminals act the way they do toward everyone, not just toward therapists or change agents.

They interact and respond to everyone in the same way. Their behavior is not personal toward individuals—it is just the way they are. If you are hunting elk in the wilderness of some state and get attacked by a cougar "it makes no sense to be offended by the cougar, because the cougar is just doing what cougars do" (Dyer, 1995). The criminal, in some ways, is just doing what a criminal does. "If you can accept that, without being offended, then you can be motivated to make the correctional field a better place, without first needing to be offended" (Dyer, 1995). This is why in Chapter 4 on change agents, we emphasize the need to be completely unattached to the outcome of our work.

GOOD PERSONS

Criminals' thinking allows them to see themselves as good persons. They truly believe or see themselves as decent individuals. We have seen individuals with forty to fifty felonies on their record and when asked how they see themselves, they responded by stating that they see themselves as really good women and men. Most believe their actions are very justifiable for themselves. Now, they may not see how those same actions are okay for the next person, but they are okay for them.

Two individuals in one of our criminality classes had committed the same kind of crime—armed robbery. Both committed the robberies in a convenience store. One man identified the reason for his crime was his need for money to buy drugs. The other man said that he committed the robbery because his family was hungry. He stood up and looked at the one who robbed to buy drugs and confronted this individual. He told him what a low-life he thought he was for committing a robbery just to buy drugs. What he did was okay because his family was hungry. What he did not say was that he had spent all the money his family had to buy drugs as well.

These omissions are ways to see themselves as good individuals. We will address these lies of omission when we talk about the criminals' thinking errors. Another thinking error, minimization, is evident in this example. As we continue, we will analyze further examples of criminal thinking and suggest methods for helping criminals recognize and then stop such thinking.

Some criminals will attend church one day and burglarize a home the next day. Then, when they are caught, they will emphasize that they attended church the day before and their belief was that they were good guys, so their crime was okay.

A handout from the Institute for Integral Development (Samenow, nd), a premier training organization specializing in the addictions field, in discussing the criminal's view of himself as a good person, states:

> He holds this view regardless of how many crimes he has committed. Even an individual who has engaged in acts of tremendous brutality believes that he is inherently a decent human being. This is important for an interviewer to understand because it is a basic premise from which other beliefs of the criminal emanate.

1. Criminals may acknowledge that they are, in fact, criminals, but this may be to get others off their back or to feed people what they think they want to hear.
2. Criminals' acknowledgment of criminality may only be a reference to the obvious fact that they have broken a law. It is not an element of their appraisal of themselves as human beings.
3. Criminals base their view of themselves as good people on a number of considerations, including:
   - Their charitable acts
   - Their religious observance
   - Their talents (artistic, mechanical, and so forth)
   - Whatever can be documented of their willingness to fulfill requirements of others, such as holding a job
   - Their abhorrence of particular sorts of crimes

The previous example displays this thinking. Another example is one criminal saying that he only sold drugs to adults, but never sold drugs to kids as other criminals do. The criminal sees himself as a good person in this example, and he minimizes his behavior. This thinking error is discussed later in the book.

Other signs that criminals view themselves as good people include:

- Their acts of consideration to friends and strangers
- Their sentimentality toward animals, babies, elderly people, their own parents, a girlfriend or boyfriend, spouse, or child.

Most of their sentimentality is only window dressing to allow them to do what they have in mind. They can be walking down the street, see an injured animal, and take it to the veterinarian. They will spend their last dollar taking care of the animal and then go on to rob the elderly lady down the street. When confronted with their crime, they will refocus the conversation to tell you how they spent their last dollar taking care of the injured animal. It is important to realize that offenders' constant endeavor is to avoid accountability and responsibility for their behavior.

4. Fundamental to the criminals' view of themselves as good persons is that they know the difference between right and wrong. But the criminal approaches this issue with a completely different mentality from the responsible person: "I can make anything right wrong, and anything wrong right. Right is what I want to do at the time."

In this respect, offenders clearly can see how their fellow criminals are guilty and wrong in their thinking and behavior. They quickly will point this out. Simultaneously, though, their thinking will make the same thinking and behavior okay for them. They live by their own code.

5. When criminals are arrested, it is their view that they are the aggrieved party. Others have interfered with what they want to do. If what they thought they had done was wrong at the time, they would not have done it. (They go on with what they want to do because they can shut out deterrent considerations of right and wrong.)

Coincidentally, this is one reason our prison systems do not work in and of themselves. Punishment alone is not a deterrent for criminals.

There is not, to our knowledge, a single review of controlled studies on the effects of the criminal penalty (diversion, probation, custody, restorative justice) that has found evidence of consistent effects on recidivism. From the earliest to the latest reviews of the research literature, only the studies on the delivery of direct human service have shown promise—promise evident across a variety of settings, including nonjustice settings, diversion programs, probation, and custody (Andrew and Bonta, 1998). "The promise resides not in the 'heat' but in the human service" (Gendreau, Cullen, and Bonta, 1994).

While criminals sit in jail or prison, they are building elaborate cases for why they are the victims. Thus, they come out of prison convinced they have been wronged. Punishment without confronting their thinking errors allows them to delude themselves into believing they were justified in their behavior. Punishment works for prosocial people who can feel real guilt, remorse, fear, and so forth. It works on you and me, not on criminals. Criminals should be put in prison; however, we need to add the element of treatment, or when they are released from incarceration, they just will commit a new crime.

The following examples show how criminals see themselves as good persons in spite of their criminal behavior. In Powder River, we managed to save some money in our budgeted expenses and were going to use this money to carpet part of the dayroom. During a community meeting, we explained this to the residents. One resident interrupted the explanation to strongly state his objection to using the money for this purpose. He stated that we should return this money to the state coffers. When the client was questioned as to his objection, he quickly informed us that he felt he was a guardian of society's resources. Too many bureaucrats spend the tax dollars foolishly; they squander and waste the people's money, and his role was to insure that this did not happen. He stated all of this although he was in prison for his third charge of aggravated assault. This was his way of appearing to be a good person in spite of his crimes. He also was attempting to refocus off his situation onto something else to escape accountability and responsibility for his crimes.

Another illustration of a criminal portraying himself as a good person comes from an article about the sentencing of a thirty-three-year-old man for "the kidnapping, beating and raping of a seventeen-year-old girl before leaving her . . . on a snow bank" to die. The man had offered to give her a ride to find her boyfriend. On the way to the boyfriend's, he requested a kiss as some payment. When she refused, he went on to commit the aforementioned crimes. The judge called him a "predator" as he had a prior rape conviction and was "suspected in two other rapes, but the victims declined to testify." At his sentencing he "unremorsefully . . . called the victim a liar who convinced him to give her a ride to a party . . . by claiming she desperately needed to get home." He claimed "she . . . offered him sex for the ride but he forced her out of the car." He goes on to say "I am sorry I tried to be a helpful person" (Craig, 1996).

On the stand in his own behalf, he called himself a "people person." This is an excellent example of a criminal who sees himself as a good person. You also can begin to see how the criminal twists the circumstance to make himself the victim. He comes across very clearly as the aggrieved individual. "He cannot consider that he has created destructive consequences. . . . He lives in a fantasy. In his fantasy, all is for the best" (Zukav and Francis, 2001). Zukav and Francis appear to be writing about people who are erroneous thinkers and problem thinkers. At times, they even may be discussing criminal-thinking people.

Without an antisocial treatment program, as we are discussing here, the individual will sit in prison perfecting his victim stance—coming back out to rape again. There will be more discussion of the victim stance later.

EXCITEMENT

Another difference between antisocial and prosocial people is in the area of excitement. Criminals see us as Joe Lunch Buckets. We are boring. They perceive us as without excitement in our lives. Much of what criminals do is for the excitement of it. They get excited when committing crimes—breaking rules—"getting something over on the man." This excitement is different from bungee jumping, mountain climbing, or car racing. It only can come from breaking the rules, committing crimes.

In the mid-seventies our alcohol and drug program admitted a client, "Joe," into our detoxification center. Joe became detoxed and was admitted to our halfway house. His progress was excellent. Because of the money shortage, we did what many programs did then—we offered Joe a night watchman's job in exchange for room and board. As he continued to progress, we sent him to training and were promoting him as he developed. We became close to Joe. We got to know him well. After about a year of being clean and sober and working in the program, he told us that he did not miss the heroin anymore. He said what he did miss was setting up the heroin buy, getting into the alley, making the buy, and getting out without being caught. Back then, we did not know about the criminal mind, and we wrote this off as a fascination with drug paraphernalia.

Some months later, Joe ran off with a woman client. They went to a small Idaho town, set up a buy, got into the alley, made the buy, got out, and used the drugs. Later, needing more money and under the influence, he and the woman attempted to rob a 7-11 store. Police arrived on the scene. They shot the women through the throat—she recovered. They shot Joe between the eyes and he died, all because of the excitement of breaking the rules.

The television film *The Outside Woman* (1989) is another example of this excitement. The film, based on a true story in Tennessee, involves a woman who commandeers a helicopter to break a man out of jail. The film also shows why it is so important for us as helping agents not to need anything from the criminals who we are treating.

This woman, who belonged to a church choir, had an unsatisfactory relationship with a boyfriend and was completely bored. One night after choir practice, the director asked her to go into the local prison the following Saturday night with the group. She had no interest in doing so. However, as she was leaving the church, her boyfriend asked her for a date the next Saturday night. In an impulsive decision, to avoid the date, she declined, stating she had to take the message to prisoners that night. Now, trapped into this commitment, she went. The film is the story of how one prisoner began to set her up, con, manipulate, and convince her to break him out of prison.

At a place in her town, helicopter rides were available for a price. She arranged for a ride. While in the air, she pointed a gun at the pilot and commanded him to fly the plane to the prison where they helped three prisoners to escape. This woman had never even had so much as a traffic ticket.

After landing, they released the pilot (she paid him for the ride after they landed—an example of the good person syndrome—"I may have forced you to fly into the prison, but at least I paid you for the ride") and they were on the run for five days. They were caught and arrested at the end of five days and subsequently tried. Each of the three prisoners received additional sentences. The woman received seven years in prison. A reporter asked her if it was worth it as she was leaving the courthouse on her way to prison. Her reply was that those were the most exciting five days of her life and she would do it all over just for those five days.

In Powder River, we gave each person twenty pushpins so that they could mount family pictures on their individual bulletin boards. Because pushpins could be used as weapons if fastened to the end of a broom handle or any such item (they make excellent weapons to put out an eye), we frequently counted them to insure that they had not been misappropriated. Council members and a staff member conducted the inventory. Another resident, knowing they were going to perform this inventory went ahead of them and confiscated five pushpins from the first five rooms. He then went and sat in the dayroom. He watched as the staff went into the first room and noticed the missing pins. He began to get excited as they went to the second room and came out with five pins missing. As they went into the third room, he could not sit still. He was beside himself because by this time, the resident council member and the staff person were becoming concerned. By the time they reached the fifth room, he was so excited he could not keep still and had to let other residents in on his adventure. Of course, his actions were revealed and we dealt with the situation. But this is an example of the excitement criminals receive as they break the rules of any society they live in, despite the seriousness of the rule. This is another example of the importance of enforcing all the rules, a topic we will return to in a later chapter. However, keep in mind, criminals break rules just for the fun of it!

This also is an example of spinning the change agent. The change agent is anyone who attempts to hold the criminal accountable and responsible.

Another example comes from a feature article on teens carrying guns to school. A fifteen-year-old youth found guilty of attempted murder says: "My little brother showed me where my dad's guns were hidden. There was a .38 and a .357. I got excited loading and unloading them. Once I found the guns, they were mine. I took one to school the next day" (Boss, 1994). (We will come back to the statement "they were mine" under the topic of ownership).

In another feature article Boss wrote: "Today, Robert's hands are wrapped around a cheeseburger. Not long ago, they were clenching a .22 derringer . . . the derringer was his gun of choice . . . he took it out from under his pillow and slipped it into his gym bag . . . his folks thought he was just packing a change of clothes. At school, he'd wave the gun in kids' faces, take their lunch money and feel a rush of butterflies in his gut . . . 'I thought I was unstoppable'" (Boss, 1994). Both the excitement and something we will describe later as the "God state" are evident here.

We can illustrate the criminal way of thinking by drawing from numerous examples, our own experiences, and those in the popular culture. Readers probably can think of several examples based on their own experience with criminals. Here is an example from Jack Higgins' book *Angel of Death* (1996), an espionage story about the peace efforts in Ireland in the early nineties and attempts at sabotaging them. In the book, a character becomes a contract hit man—not for money or cause— but for the excitement of it. He discusses his first killing with a friend:

> He lit a cigarette and sat back, shaking with excitement. He had never felt like this in his life before, not even in the Paras in Ireland. Every sense felt keener, even the colors when he looked out at the passing streets seemed sharper. But the excitement, the damned excitement (Higgins, 1966, p. 58)!

One last illustration comes from a client attending our group. Clients write and present a criminal autobiography in group therapy. They are instructed to include all their crimes, both those they have been arrested for and those they have not. By the way, most criminals only get arrested for approximately one out of ten crimes.

One client, "Dick," began to get animated as he shared his story about a crime for which he had not been arrested. He described stabbing a man. He talked about feeling the knife enter the body, seeing the blood begin to run down his arm, and the tremendous charge this gave him. Of course, the other clients began to confront him on this, not because they, too, did not get excited committing their crimes, but because what might be right for them is not okay for others, as we mentioned earlier. They can all talk the talk. (We did not say this treatment approach was quick.)

Dick came back in defense with minimization. He did not stick the knife in deep—he could have killed the guy. His crime was not as bad as others in the group—at least he had not raped anyone or sold drugs to children. We will discuss the minimization defense later.

When dealing with criminals in treatment, they present so many thinking errors, you have to choose which ones to address at the moment. Anyway, Dick's example illustrates the excitement criminals get from committing crimes. It cannot be compared to the excitement prosocial people get from white water rafting, seeing a good play, or watching a beautiful sunset.

The oldest bank robber in prison died at the age of ninety-two just recently. He did not begin robbing banks until he was in his eighties. By his own admission, he started robbing banks for the excitement it brought into his life. This is much like the movie *Going in Style* mentioned in the next section.

Anthony (1998) gives another example:

> End to end, arranged carefully upon banquet tables, they crowded the second floor of the Wadpole fire hall: thousands upon thousands of items, the stuff of people's lives. Cameras and jewelry; guns and rare coins; autographed balls, cordless drills, porn videos, fishing rods, teapots, and even women's underwear. It looked like a flea market. But the rummage carted out of Jake Hunter's cellar didn't belong to him; it came from scores of homes up and down western New Hampshire. He stole it, and he hid it all away. For two decades, on and off,

he'd park his truck and make his move. *Just for the thrill.* [emphasis ours]. What he took, he removed not for profit but for keepsake, a souvenir or two for mere adventure—enough to sate his urges but often too little for his victims to notice they'd been violated.

THE THOUGHT IS THE DEED

Another area where criminals are different from prosocial persons is in the connection they make between the thought and the deed. Prosocial people realize that just thinking something does not make it true. They may like to shorten the distance between the thought and the action, but they realize that planning and making decisions must occur before action can be taken.

For the criminals, this time lag does not exist. When they think a thought, the action has taken place. The seed of the thought planted in the criminal's mind produces the oak tree. The thought makes the action or behavior completed or true. There is no time lag between thought and action for criminals in their thinking. The action just exists. This is why it is important to get the criminal to change his thoughts. If the thought changes, then so does the behavior.

One of our clients, "Larry," recalled walking by the house of an elderly couple on his way to a party. The male was suffering from cancer, and there were many narcotics on a tray as his wife cared for him. As Larry walked by the house, he glanced through the window and spotted the drugs. He knew the couple and knew the man had cancer. He kept on walking and all he could think about were all the drugs that were on the table. At that point, he had not decided for sure (he says) that he was going to do something.

As he returned home that night, he burglarized the house and assaulted the lady as he obtained the drugs. The seed (thought) was planted when he saw the drugs through the window. The thought continued until the action was taken. The drugs were his. In the next subsection, we address the issue of ownership that is also in evidence here.

Another client, "Leroy," talked of driving down the street in his hometown and began to think that he really should go to college. Without any further ado, he headed his car across the state to the state college to enroll. On the way, he did not consider that he had no transcripts, no registration information, and especially no money. Finally, he thought about the need for money as he was passing a Burger King. He thought to himself, they have money. So he drove in and attempted to rob the place. He was apprehended and became one of our clients.

When criminals think about what they want, it is already an accomplished fact. That gets to be very dangerous as we saw in the examples, but it is dangerous also in terms of their behavior with friends, family, employers, and especially with the opposite sex. If they see someone they want to be with, in their mind, the act is accomplished. They just need to complete it.

A young man in the criminal-thinking range of the continuum had a casual conversation with the owner of a business about getting a job with the company. The owner made no commitment nor were any specifics discussed. Yet, when the young man shared this with other people, he already had the job; it would start Monday morning and would pay him $25.00 an hour. None of this had been discussed, but in his mind, it was so because he had the thoughts and they became real. The irony of this is that when none of this came to pass, the young man blamed the owner for going back on his word. "You can't trust anyone these days."

Prosocial people can and do have thoughts that could lead to actions and behavior that would get them in trouble or for which they are not proud. However, because for them the thought does not automatically lead to action, they have time to examine and discard most unhealthy thoughts. This is not true for the criminal. Thus, criminals cannot even entertain thoughts that would be harmless for prosocial people. A similar situation exists for alcoholics and nonalcoholics. Nonalcoholics can think about drinking and even decide to have a drink. They will not get in trouble with their thoughts. The alcoholics cannot afford to even begin to think about drinking. If they do, they either are on the road to or in relapse.

We cannot emphasize enough that for the criminal, the thought is the deed. The minute the criminal thinks—it is! As we treat offenders, it is important to teach them that they cannot even allow certain thoughts to come into their minds. If these thoughts do enter their minds, they must have some tool or mechanism to replace the thoughts with the right thoughts. We teach criminals "brakes to thoughts" and replacement thoughts.

Wayne Dyer (2001, 2004) in his books says "we become what we think about all day long." Gordon Graham in his training manual and tapes called *A Framework for Breaking Barriers: A Cognitive Reality Model* (1999) talks about how the inmate is always walking the big yard: talking and thinking about what he is going to do, how he was set up, complaining that he is the victim, and how he is going to get even. He is constantly thinking about how to set up the man. Both men say that to change behavior the thinking has to change. Dyer (2004) says "that if you change the way you look at things, the things you look at will change." Graham teaches criminals to make positive affirmations to replace the criminal talk or thinking.

The thought is the first sign of relapse, and criminals have a relapse process very much like alcoholics or addicts. It is important to teach them brakes and positive affirmations. Later, we will discuss the importance of addressing and challenging each and every thought criminals have and the steps in making and following new affirmations. Remember, with criminals, the thought will become the deed.

OWNERSHIP

There is a natural progression from the thought is the deed to what I see or what I want is mine. The thought makes it so. Like the two-year-old child, everything around him is his.

Ann Landers printed an anonymous article sent in by a reader that described a two-year-old child's response to life. It not only described the toddler but very adequately described the criminal.

Toddler's Creed

If I want it, it's mine.

If I give it to you and change my mind later, it's mine.

If I can take it away from you, it's mine.

If I had it a little while ago, it's mine.

If it's mine, it will never belong to anybody else, no matter what.

If we are building something together, all the pieces are mine.

If it looks just like mine, it is mine.

This describes criminals. They have a strong sense of entitlement. "Entitlement is the belief that [they] have a right to what [they] desire, regardless of what others desire. It is the feeling that [they] are not subject to rules that limit others. [They] see [themselves] above others. [Other's] activities are unworthy of [them], and boring. Entitlement is a perception that [they] are fundamentally superior" (Zukav and Francis, 2001). Everything belongs to them. They are the centers of their universe. What they see or want belongs to them as a matter of thinking. Remember, earlier we were discussing the excitement of the boy who found his dad's guns? He said that when he saw them "they were mine!" The client in prison for stealing the elderly couples' cancer medication owned the drugs the minute he decided he wanted them. "[Their] ego insists that all you have to do is want it and that [their} specialness entitles [them]. [They] don't even have to earn it, only want it" (Dyer, 1995).

When prosocial people walk by a bank, they may think about what interest rate they could get on their money. Could they get a loan from the bank? What is the bank's policy on check writing? The criminal walks by the bank and wonders how they are taking care of his money. Now, he has never even been in the bank let alone deposited any money in the bank, but because he would like to have the money in the bank, it belongs to him. He just has not made a withdrawal yet.

We asked an individual in our program to begin keeping a daily log on his thinking process. We asked him to do this every day at a certain time. He began keeping his log by writing down what he saw across the roadway on a ranch. What he observed was a couple of horses and some nice farm equipment that he really took a liking to. As he kept his log each day, he would comment on the animals and equipment. As his log continued, he began to personalize the things he saw. He began to move from how he admired the animals and how much he liked them to referring to the horses as "my horses." The client started talking about the ranch equipment as if it belonged to him.

During an individual session, he admitted that he had planned on how he was going to obtain that (his) property. He had friends who lived in another community, and he knew that he could get them to come and get his property. By this time, the horses and equipment really had come to belong to him. For him, the process moved from commenting on the horses and equipment, to admiring them, to believing they belonged to him, to how he could recover his property.

Another client, "George," was in prison for assaulting a male friend of his estranged wife. During group, he explained his actions to other group members—he was in jail because another man had been sleeping with his wife. As his story unfolded, we learned that he and his wife had separated because he had taken up with another woman. One day, he and his girlfriend were driving by his estranged wife's house, and he noticed that a guy's truck was parked out front. He took a baseball bat out of his rig and told his girlfriend to remain in the car. George went into the house and beat the sleeping man almost to death. His justification was that it was his wife, and no man had the right to her except him. When he was asked to discuss the difference between his girlfriend and his wife's boyfriend, he kept repeating "she is my wife."

The criminal's attitude about life is that it is my wife, my children, my car, my dog, my money, with no difference in his or her attitude between inanimate objects and human beings. When a prosocial person talks about "my wife" or "my kids," it is not about ownership but of people of equal value who share equal responsibilities in the home and in their relationship. When criminals use the terms "my wife" or "my children," they talk about them as if they are objects like a stereo. Hare (1993) says, "If they do maintain ties with their spouses or children, it is only because they see their family members as possessions, much like their stereos or automobiles."

As you get criminals to explain what their family means, they will describe them the same way that they would describe a stereo, a dog, or a piece of equipment around the house. Consequently, since people are their property, they have the right to treat people as they want to, and they do not see that as bad. IT IS THEIR RIGHT. They can go home and kick their dog or throw out the stereo and buy a new one. Their thinking operates the same with their family. Criminals all will claim to love and appreciate their wife and children. They even cry tears because they cannot be with them on their birthdays. Yet, they treat them as objects.

To a prosocial person, this thought process seems irrational and ridiculous. However, to the criminal, this thought process is very rational behavior. This illustrates what we having been saying. Criminals' thinking is far different from that of prosocial persons, and they can commit crimes with the belief that they are entirely entitled to do what they do. If we do not change this thinking process, they will continue to commit crimes no matter what we do because they believe they have the right.

Much abuse of women is based on this thinking by the male criminal. If he sees or wants a woman, she belongs to him. If he has lived with her or if he has been married to her and gotten a divorce, she still belongs to him. She will belong to him the rest of her life.

CENTER OF THE UNIVERSE

The criminals' world revolves around what they want, when they want it. They demand immediate gratification. They have no appreciation of other people's needs, schedules, or situations.

Another Calvin and Hobbes cartoon illustrates this point. Calvin says to Hobbes, "I'm at peace with the world. I'm completely serene. . . . I've discovered my purpose in life. I know why I was put here and why everything exists. . . . I am here so everybody can do what I want. . . . Once everyone accepts it, they'll be serene too." Criminals believe that if other people would just realize their importance and respond accordingly, everything would be all right.

We had the resident council members at Powder River submit written reports to us on the activities of the community. They were our pulse on how the community was functioning. They had a far better handle on the atmosphere of the community than we did. All staff read these reports and could use them in individual or group sessions. They proved to be excellent ways to address criminal thinking by the residents. Supervisors reviewed the reports each week with the six-member coordinating council.

Part of one report illustrates this self-centeredness by a client who was a department head. The report concerns the community service of ten of the residents in the prior week.

COMMUNITY SERVICE REPORT

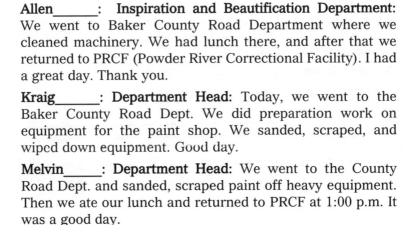

Allen_____: Inspiration and Beautification Department: We went to Baker County Road Department where we cleaned machinery. We had lunch there, and after that we returned to PRCF (Powder River Correctional Facility). I had a great day. Thank you.

Kraig_____: Department Head: Today, we went to the Baker County Road Dept. We did preparation work on equipment for the paint shop. We sanded, scraped, and wiped down equipment. Good day.

Melvin_____: Department Head: We went to the County Road Dept. and sanded, scraped paint off heavy equipment. Then we ate our lunch and returned to PRCF at 1:00 p.m. It was a good day.

Michael_____: Department Head: I went to Baker County Road Dept. I worked on a D-7 cat scraping grease and sanding after sanding a rock crusher. After that, came back to PRCF.

Note how Allen, Kraig, and Melvin all used the word "we" as they describe their activities. When Michael describes his activities, it is with the word "I." You might remark, so what? Remember, every word, every deed, every action that criminals say or do, which allows them to support their uniqueness, must be addressed for them to put brakes on their thinking. The use of the word "I" here reinforces the individual's self-centeredness. Unaddressed, it allows him to remain in this thinking mode that allows him to continue to believe, like Calvin, that the world revolves around him. The change agent's task is to point this out to him. Criminals believe they have been given permission to continue with the thought process if the change agent remains silent about this thought process.

Another example of this "I" self-centeredness comes from another client's report. In reviewing this report, note that unlike the previous report, this report mainly comes from crew members not department heads or coordinators. Crew members generally have less time in the program and would be expected to have more thinking errors than department heads and coordinators.

INSPIRATION AND BEAUTIFICATION WEEKLY DEPARTMENT REPORT

COORDINATOR: Allen_____

DEPT. HEAD: Kraig_____

CREW CHIEF: Lester_____

CREW MEMBER: Rodger_____

CREW MEMBER: Tim_____

CREW MEMBER: Ken_____

Misconduct

Mr._____: Problem Sheet for missing I and B meeting.

Comments

CREW MEMBER: I watered the plants outside and planted some flowers and watered the plants inside. Also put up the phone list.

CREW MEMBER: I opened the library and tonight will enter four new books into the inventory and library. Had a good week and enjoyed my responsibility.

CREW MEMBER: I outlined a design for the new Verbal Warning Board. Did the Thought for the Week, and helped plant some flowers outside.

CREW CHIEF: I went through and checked the plants to see if they were ready for water, then had Mr._____water them (when we examine the thinking errors we will see some power to control issues in the statement "Then had Mr._____water . . ."). I stopped in at the library to see how Mr._____was doing and if he needed anything . . .

DEPT. HEAD: I got most of the crew involved (again power to control issues here) in planting flowers. We all enjoyed doing it. I have been communicating with everyone making sure they know their jobs, and if they have any suggestions or questions to let me know.

COORDINATOR: It was a real good week this week. We had no problems this week. I had a talk with Mr. O'Quin (staff member) about the new Verbal Warning Board, and he is going to take the new idea to be approved.

Note how all of the crew members, even the department head, center in on the "I" of self-centeredness. When you come to the coordinator, who has progressed in treatment, you see more of the "we" idea. He is beginning to move out of his self-centered position.

Prosocial people know that they are connected to others. They have a group consciousness and often even a universal consciousness. Prosocial people know that what they do affects others and what others do affects them. There is a butterfly effect. "If a butterfly flutters its wings in Oregon, the air moves in Japan."

The following report from the inspiration and beautification department emphasizes the idea of criminals being self-centered.

INSPIRATION AND BEAUTIFICATION WEEKLY DEPARTMENT REPORT

COORDINATOR: Allen_____

DEPT. HEAD: Kraig_____

CREW CHIEF: Lester_____

CREW MEMBER: Rodger_____

CREW MEMBER: Timothy____

CREW MEMBER: Kenneth____

CREW MEMBER: Steve_____

Comments

CREW MEMBER: I Rodger did Mike's certificate as well as Allen's. Also did the 'Thought for the Week' and the Calendar Board for June.

CREW MEMBER: I Timothy opened the library. Also did the inventory again. Everything is running smoothly.

CREW MEMBER: I Kenneth watered the plants and I put up the phone list.

CREW MEMBER: I Steve am still waiting to find out what my job is going to be on the Inspiration and Beautification Dept.

In this statement, there may be some attack on the change agent—whether department head, coordinator, or staff. You stupid people still have not told me my job yet. How do you expect me to be in compliance if you do not do your job? This, at least, should be explored with Steve.

CREW CHIEF: I Lester am training Mr.____ for the Crew Chief position and I have received two graduation certificates for Mr.____ and Mr.____.

DEPT. HEAD: The inventory is done. We got a new crew member, Mr.____. It's been a very good week.

COORDINATOR: The crew got all the inventory done. I talked with Mrs. Graham (staff) and she wanted me to get with Mr.____ and go over the inventory in the library again.

From this example, you can see that the crew members continue to use the self-centered "I." However, it is good to note that Kraig, the department head, has joined the coordinator in eliminating the "I" word. They are inclusive with "we" and are rephrasing their statement to avoid self-centeredness.

By this time, you might be asking how is this any different from prosocial people? There are many prosocial people who are self-centered and constantly use "I" in their discussions. You are right. It is a matter of degree and intention. Most prosocial people use thinking errors, but not in the same manner or to the same degree. Criminals are much further along the continuum of thinking-error use. It is much like social drinking versus chronic alcoholism. Many people drink socially without any problems. Then, there are people who are problem drinkers; some are drinking abusively, some move on to mild addictive drinking, others to severe addictive drinking, and some to chronic addiction.

Many, maybe most, people use thinking errors. It would be great if they did not, and people may want to work at eliminating these errors from their personality. However, like the social drinker, their use does not get them into deep trouble except on occasion. As outlined on the thinking-pattern continuum, some people use thinking errors problematically. Others are abusive in their use of thinking errors. Then, there is the criminals' use of thinking errors. Debate occurs over the question of when does this pattern move from prosocial abuse to criminal behavior, to psychopathic behavior?

This is a major gap in our development of the antisocial theory. We need to develop instruments that can give us a better assessment tool for knowing when a person has moved into the criminal/antisocial mindset. When is a person antisocial and not just a creep or an alcoholic who commits crime? Much like alcoholics who are alcoholics from their first drink, there may be people who by the age of four on up have developed an antisocial personality. One is referred back to the "Thinking-Pattern Continuum." We hope this continuum assists in assessing people. Hare (1993) says, ". . . modern research has an even more vital goal—the development of reliable ways to identify these individuals in order to minimize the risk they pose to others. This task is of immense importance to the general public and individuals alike." Hare has developed a Psychopathy Checklist, which many people have been trained to use, to assist in identifying the psychopath. Many community correctional agencies use the "Level of Service Inventory-Revised" (LSI-R) as developed by Andrews and Bonta (1998) to determine the level of supervision and treatment.

However, let us get back to the subject at hand—criminals being the center of their universe. An example comes from a fantasy book by Terry Brooks, *The Tangle Box* in a description of the wizard.

> Mostly, Horris was an opportunist. To be an opportunist one needed an appreciation for the possibilities, and Horris knew about possibilities better than he knew about almost anything. He was forever considering how something might be turned to his advantage. He was convinced that the wealth of the world—of any world—had been created for his ultimate benefit. Time and space were irrelevant; in the end, everything belonged to him. His opinion of himself was extreme. He, better than anyone, understood the fine art of exploitation. He alone could analyze the weaknesses that were indigenous to all creatures and determine how they might be mined. He was certain his insight approached prescience, and he took it as his mission in life to improve his lot at the expense of almost everyone. He possessed a relentless passion for using people and circumstances to achieve this end. Horris cared not a whit for the misfortune of others, for moral conventions, for noble causes, the environment, stray cats and dogs, or little children. These were all concerns for lesser beings. He cared only for himself, for his own creature comforts, for twisting things about when it suited him, and for schemes that reinforced his continuing belief that all other life-forms were impossibly stupid and gullible (Brooks, page 12).

This is an excellent example of a criminal mindset, which we discuss in detail later in this chapter. It definitely addresses the issue of self-centeredness. In addition, it touches on many other issues of the criminal's thinking—entitlement, ownership, God state, and grandiosity, to mention a few. We can hear echoes of Calvin in the description of Horris. We who have worked with the antisocial can hear echoes of each and every criminal with whom we have worked.

ANTISOCIAL/NARCISSISTIC PERSONALITIES

The antisocial personality description tells what a criminal does. The narcissistic personality description explains who the criminal is. A narcissistic description is a closer fit with the self-centeredness of the criminals. It describes their thinking process as opposed to the antisocial description that defines their behavior. However, remember, it is the criminals' thinking that leads to their behavior and allows the behavior, in the criminals' mind, to be justified.

The *Diagnostic and Statistical Manual of Mental Disorders* (2000) of the American Psychiatric Association lists the following for Narcissistic Personality Disorder, 301.81.

A pervasive pattern of grandiosity (in fantasy or behavior), need for admiration, and lack of empathy, beginning by early adulthood [we would suggest that these are present much before adulthood, but masked by childhood and adolescent development characteristics] and present in a variety of contexts, as indicated by five (or more) of the following:

(1) has a grandiose sense of self-importance (e.g., exaggerates achievements and talents, expects to be recognized as superior without commensurate achievements)

(2) is preoccupied with fantasies of unlimited success, power, brilliance, beauty, or ideal love

(3) believes that he or she is "special" and unique and can only be understood by, or should associate with, other special or high-status people (or institutions)

(4) requires excessive admiration

(5) has a sense of entitlement, i.e., unreasonable expectations of especially favorable treatment or automatic compliance with his or her expectations

(6) is interpersonally exploitative, i.e., takes advantage of others to achieve his or her own ends

(7) lacks empathy: is unwilling to recognize or identify with the feelings and needs of others

(8) is often envious of others or believes that others are envious of him or her

(9) shows arrogant, haughty behaviors or attitudes

Reprinted with permission from the *Diagnostic and Statistical Manual of Mental Disorders*, Copyright 2000, American Psychiatric Association.

The diagnostic criteria from the DSM IIIR (1987) included a criterion that stated "reacts to criticism with feelings of rage, shame, or humiliation (even if not expressed)." As we later describe the power pendulum, you will see the similarities between it and this criterion.

You also can see in this description many characteristics we have discussed in the previous pages such as self-importance, entitlement, specialness (center of universe), and so forth. When we consider the thinking tactics and thinking errors, you will become aware of additional similarities between this description and the errors and tactics used by criminals.

Again, the narcissistic personality describes who the criminal is. Now, we will move on to the antisocial personality description that defines not who criminals are, but what they do with whom they are.

The antisocial personality description in *The Diagnostic and Statistical Manual of Mental Disorders*, 301.7 (2000) states:

There is a pervasive pattern of disregard for and violation of the rights of others occurring since age 15 years, as indicated by three (or more) of the following:

(1) failure to conform to social norms with respect to lawful behaviors as indicated by repeatedly performing acts that are grounds for arrest
(2) deceitfulness, as indicated by repeated lying, use of aliases, or conning others for personal profit or pleasure
(3) implusivity or failure to plan ahead
(4) irritability and aggressiveness, as indicated by repeated physical fights or assaults
(5) reckless disregard for safety of self or others
(6) consistent irresponsibility, as indicated by repeated failure to sustain consistent work behavior or honor obligations
(7) lack of remorse, as indicated by being indifferent to or rationalizing having hurt, mistreated, or stolen from another (page 279)

Reprinted with permission from the *Diagnostic and Statistical Manual of Mental Disorders*, Copyright 2000, American Psychiatric Association.

Criminals' thoughts of or about themselves, as described in the narcissistic personality description, lead to their behavior that is described in the antisocial personality description. Again, we believe that you can begin to see some of these behaviors much before the age of fifteen. *The Diagnostic and Statistical Manual IV* (2000) describes these behaviors in a category called "conduct disorder" and lists fifteen criteria.

EMPATHY

Criminals lack empathy. They have an inability to recognize and experience how others feel. If people are very self-centered and think of themselves as the center of the universe and that everyone around them should have their best interest at heart, they are not going to develop skills of empathy toward others. They think they should not have to think about anyone else; everyone else should be thinking of them. "[They] display a general lack of empathy. They are indifferent to the rights and suffering of family members and strangers alike" (Hare, 1993). The world is here to serve them. Much like Calvin, everyone is here to serve their needs, and when they realize that fact, everything will be okay.

When we talk to criminals about their criminal activity, most of them do not want to think about their victims. There is no reason for them to consider their victims since they feel justified in all their actions. Individuals in our group have talked about burglarizing houses and not wanting to think about the people that they were ripping off. Some of them have even turned family portraits over to not have to look at these photos. Many of them express a strong dislike of having to face their victims in court because then it becomes more personalized, and criminals operate from the belief that much of what they do is not personal; it is their job. It is what they do. They do not have to think about the victim, the victim just happens to be in the way. If they do face the victim, it is often with scorn or ridicule; they had it coming. They may play the victim's role as we discussed earlier when talking about the good-guy image.

Another tactic the criminals use is to bait the victim so that the victim attacks them. Then, they can self-righteously defocus on the victim's outburst—away from their own actions.

A news writer describes an outburst against a child killer (Locke, 1996). This was the case of the 1993 kidnapping, sexual molestation, and murder of twelve-year-old Polly Klaas in Petaluma, California. Richard Allan Davis had been found guilty, and the sentencing portion of the trial was being concluded. Locke quoted Davis:

> The main reason I know I did not attempt any lewd act that night, was because of a statement the young girl made to me while walking up the embankment: "Just don't do me like my dad."
>
> The moment finally came for Mark Klaas (the father of the girl) when the rage he felt at his daughter's murderer swept instantly from his mouth down to his hands, feet and gut. Klaas shouted obscenities and lunged for . . . Davis . . . "I knew he would try to get at me in some way," Klass said after deputies hustled him out of the courthouse, where Davis was sentenced to death.

This illustrates not only the lack of empathy for the victims, but taunting, defocusing, and use of power to control issues. These topics will be discussed under tactics and thinking errors, later.

An article the next day illustrates how Davis' response was not understood by the public. Early on, we said that often the criminal justice system and the treatment programs that attempt to treat the criminal have failed because they do not understand the criminal mind.

In discussing Davis' outburst, Robert Pugsley of Southwestern University School of Law stated, " . . . it exceeds the bounds of decency that we expect even from people convicted of the kind of vicious crime for which he (Davis) was sentenced to death" (*Herald and News*, 1996).

When we begin to expect decency or empathy from the untreated criminal, we are attributing to them the very values and presence of mind they do not have. If Mr. Davis had the decency not to taunt Mr. Klaas, he would have had the decency not to have kidnapped, molested, and killed the child. As prosocial people, we do not understand that antisocial people do not have these values. They ridicule the prosocial value system as being for pigeons, fools, and victims—for being "Joe Lunch Buckets"— for you and me. Criminals discuss seeing other people as pawns or chess pieces that they can use to whatever advantage they feel is necessary.

It is very difficult for a person at any position on the thinking-pattern continuum to understand the thinking of a person one position before or after him or her on the continuum, let alone several positions removed. Thus, for a person at the prosocial-external thinking position, it is almost impossible to understand a person at the criminal-thinking position and vice versa.

A twenty-year-old murderer of a young cheerleader laughed and mocked her family when the jury gave him life instead of the death penalty. This is one more example of the difficulty criminals have in feeling any empathy. It also shows power to control. This criminal escaped and not surprisingly, within hours had killed again.

Prosocial people will say things to hurt other people, but they still have a certain amount of empathy toward people. Criminals have no concern for the people around them. As discussed earlier, this is not personal. The criminals are not out to be deliberately mean to anyone; it is just that others do not count in their world. The only person in their world who counts is himself or herself.

The most difficult assignment to ask criminals to do is to describe the feelings that their victims may have had while they victimized them. It is not guilt manifesting itself, but it is their inability to be able to identify what those feelings must have been or the thoughts that those people must have had. Again from Hare (1993), "One rapist . . . commented that he found it hard to empathize with his victims. 'They are frightened, right? But, you see, I don't really understand it. I've been scared myself, and it wasn't unpleasant.'" They are so disconnected that they are unable to identify what the victim is feeling. It is important that they not relive the crime and enjoy how the victim felt. They can get excited about reliving the incident and feeling the control and excitement over their victim. Mr. Davis, the killer of Polly Klaas, is an example of this.

The timing of when criminals do attempt to feel empathy is important. If a counselor senses excitement by the criminals as they describe the victimization, then it is not time for them to go to this exercise. Empathy is not the first order of business in treating criminals. It is far down the road after they have accomplished many other things and have made some commitments toward getting well, including admitting that they are criminals. Also, they need to have some sense of the thinking errors that they use most often. They first must develop an understanding of their thinking process and have gained an ability to rewrite their thoughts into positive affirmations, before they can develop empathy for others.

SEMANTICS

Problem of understanding that comes from word selection

Be alert to problems of semantics; that is, "a client may use a regular everyday English word and mean something totally different from your interpretation of it" (Samenow, no date). Be conscious of the terminology used by the criminal. When we believe we know what clients mean, we often will be mistaken. It is imperative to ask them what they mean by their use of words and even situations. This is another place where criminals display a great difference from prosocial people.

When talking to criminals about their family and how they see their wife, a male criminal often will say that she is a real support to him. What he means is that she will lie for him, she will manipulate, she will steal, she will con and cover for him. That is what a good piece of property would do for you, take care of you. She is doing exactly what he wants her to do for him. His meaning of support is dramatically different from a prosocial person's. It is important to clarify what criminals mean when they use words.

Words mean different things to different people, especially the criminal as will be seen in the thinking errors discussion. Words or phrases such as "kind of," "sort of," "need to," "because," "but," "probably," and so forth have special meaning to criminals. If a person says "I was 'on the streets' for five years," some people recognize that as living a life of crime, while others see it as homeless (Barbara Down, CADCC II, R.N., Consortium treatment center counselor). Elliott and Verdeyen (2002) suggest that to a correctional officer the term, "time on the street" often refers to being suspended.

A client was asked if he ever abused his children, and his response was "no." He was asked what abuse meant to him. He responded by saying, "You double up your fist and break a bone in your kid's face." He then was asked if he had ever struck his children, and he said "yes." When asked how he did that, he replied, "A couple of times I got so mad that I backhanded them. Once I knocked one of them through the screen door, but that is not abuse; they had it coming." He had a totally different perception of what the term "abuse" meant than would a prosocial person.

Another example came from a group that a new staff member was leading. A client was describing a past episode where a person had over-dosed on methamphetamine, convulsed, and died. Several group members were present when this had happened. The teller of the story and several others in the group were laughing about this scene. The staff member said that she did not understand how they could laugh about this incident. In debriefing this with her, the staff made several suggestions.

First, we pointed out how the focus had been redirected toward her and her understanding instead of keeping the focus on the client's behavior and thinking. Secondly, we explained that, probably, each of them was laughing for a different reason. A better intervention here would have been for her to have had each of them describe the source of their laughter. This, then, would have assumed nothing and gotten them to clarify their action and thinking. It also would have kept the focus on them.

"But there is something . . . about the speech of psychopaths that is equally puzzling, their frequent use of contradictory and logically incon-sistent statements that usually escape detection" Hare (1993). A story from Pilot Rock, Oregon illustrates this. A man was found guilty of attempted murder after freely admitting that he slit his five-year-old son's wrist. When asked by his attorney if he meant to kill his son, he responded, "No, I love my son more than anything in the world." The word "love" sure means something different for him than for a prosocial person. Later, when sentenced to fifteen years in prison, he claimed he did not get a fair trial because his lawyer should have been replaced and the judge was prejudiced against him. He was the victim here, not his five-year-old son (Brickey, 2004; White 2004).

"A man serving a term for armed robbery replied to the testimony of an eyewitness, 'He's lying. I wasn't there. I should have blown his fuck-ing head off" (Hare, 1993). He goes on to call these hollow words. They are words that do not have the same meaning for the criminal as they do for prosocial people. In fact, they may have no meaning whatsoever for the criminal himself, except to escape accountability and responsibility.

Barbara Down, a Consortium counselor, reminds us that not every person using these words is using them as criminal errors or tactics. We should look at who the person is, as well as the context in which the word is being used. Remember, these are all perfectly good words when they are used in the right way. We will look at several examples and place them on the thinking-pattern continuum.

The word "because" may alert others that here comes my excuse or justification. This is not always so; it depends on the person using it and what his or her motive is. When a prosocial external thinker says, "I am going to the store because we need milk," he will likely be back in ten minutes with the milk. The erroneous thinker may be back in twenty minutes with the milk and a six pack of beer. The problem thinker may not come home until tomorrow—hung over and smelling of cheap perfume. He probably will not have any milk. The criminal thinker may or may not come back at all. He most likely will call wanting to be bailed out of jail.

Prosocial	Prosocial	Erroneous	Problem	Criminal	Chronic
Internal	External	Thinking	Thinking	Thinking	Psychopathic
Thinking	Thinking				Thinking

The word "but" is a word that often separates a lie from the truth and may alert others to an excuse coming up. For instance, "I want to see my grandmother, BUT I don't have time." When a prosocial external thinker says, "I don't have time," most likely, if you look at his schedule, you will find he is working ten hours a day, going to the dentist on his lunch hour, and has a child's ball game to attend after work. If this guy says he is too busy, it is the truth. An erroneous thinker is probably one who is working eight hours, then going home to nap or watch a ballgame on television. The problem thinker may never even see his grandmother unless he needs money. And the criminal thinker may have done so many bad things to his grandmother that she will not even give him her address, and she now has an unlisted phone number so he cannot find her.

The phrase "I love you" has many different meanings. To the prosocial thinking person, it may indicate "That I leave you free to be yourself, to think your thoughts, to follow your inclinations, to indulge in your fantasies, to behave in ways that you decide are to your liking. You have that freedom and you have my love in the process" (De Mello, 1992). To the erroneous thinker, it may mean, "I love you when you love me. I expect a return on my love. Love means you need to cut me some slack." The problem thinker's "I love you" may mean, "I can still stay out with the guys whenever I want to. If I stop off after work and don't get in until after two in the morning, just stay off my back." To the criminal thinker, it means, "I own you. You are to do my bidding; you are to lie for me. You are to wait on me hand and foot and if I want a girlfriend on the side, that is nothing to you." In the previous account of the man who slashed his five-year-old son's wrist, we see how he used the word "love" when discussing a family member. It was his son, so he could do what he wanted. Why were people upset?

POWER PENDULUM

We distinguish power to control (Zukav, 1990) from authentic power. We discuss this more thoroughly in coming chapters. Authentic power for prosocial people is about honor and empowerment of self and others. It has nothing to do with controlling others. However, criminals are either gaining or losing power to control others and their situation. Generally, they are never static.

They operate mostly from extremes. Everyone is seen as good or bad, friend or enemy. There is no in between. You either win or lose. "A

CHART 2.1. THE POWER PENDULUM

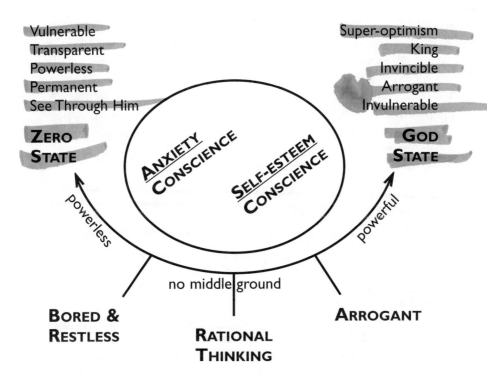

37

'win-lose' orientation dominates many inmates' interpersonal relationships. They are either using others or being used until they are all used up" (Outside Woman, 1989). It is about "human beings using other human beings" (Zukav, 1990). "To these inmates, the only way to really win is to force someone else to lose. The sense of triumph that results from this type of 'winning' is the only way such offenders have learned how to achieve personal satisfaction from their interpersonal relationships" (Elliott and Verdeyen, 2002).

Much of what you see is their perception of their loss of power to control everything in their world or their attempt to regain the power to control what they feel they have lost. They are on a constant pendulum called the "power pendulum," as illustrated in Chart 2.1. When they perceive that they have power and are in control, they are in a "God state." When they perceive that they have lost power to control, they are in a "zero state." Generally, there is no middle ground.

In the "God state," they are super optimistic. They feel that they are very powerful persons, invulnerable, often invincible. They respond arrogantly. They see themselves as king of the walk with people being afraid of them.

In the "zero state," they feel powerless. They are bored and restless. Criminals perceive themselves as transparent and vulnerable. They believe people can see right through them. All of their defenses are gone. The most overwhelming sense is that this will be permanent. They have a terror of not ever being in control of their safety and well being.

Again, this is different from a prosocial person's response to life. Most prosocial people maintain their lives someplace in the middle of those two extremes. They operate out of a sense of rational thinking. On occasion, they may feel that their life has gone in the toilet, wonder if life has much meaning, and feel quite worthless. Occasionally, they will be super optimistic; they have life by the tail. For the most part, most of us operate in the middle with only an occasional sojourn in either direction. By contrast, the criminal resides in one extreme or the other.

Another comparison between how prosocial people and criminals think is seen in the way criminals get into and out of the "God state" or "zero state." Prosocial persons generally have some rational reason or action that moves them toward one end or the other. A divorce, loss of a job or promotion, or a missed opportunity can contribute to a prosocial person moving in the direction of the "zero state." Success, promotion, hitting sixty home runs, or even scoring the game-winning hit in the game of life, publishing a book, and so forth may contribute to a feeling of being on top of the world. For the most part, there is some rational reason prosocial people move in one direction or the other.

This is not true for criminals. Most of the time, there is no rational reason they perceive a loss or gain of control. A criminal may walk down the street and see an acquaintance across the street. The acquaintance does not wave or acknowledge the criminal. Regardless of whether the acquaintance even sees him, the criminal generally will respond either with a great sense of power to control or a severe sense of a loss of power to control. On not getting a wave, he may feel very powerful. He might believe that the acquaintance is afraid of him and thus is afraid to acknowledge that he saw the criminal. "He is afraid of me because I am so powerful. He does not want to acknowledge me until I give him permission to do so." On the other hand, he may perceive that the acquaintance is ignoring him—is snubbing him; that the person can see right through him—he is transparent. The person sees him as no account. Thus, he feels very powerless. Neither perception has a basis in reality. The simple fact may be that the person just did not see him.

"James," who was in one of our groups, shared a story of how he was home working on his car one day and a buddy came over. As he was working on the car with the friend watching and talking with him, he apparently did something incorrectly to the carburetor. His friend commented that he had done something wrong. James turned around and hit him with a wrench, saying that the friend was putting him down and insulting him. He felt the friend was calling him stupid. He hit him with a wrench and felt that the guy had it coming. The client had moved to the "zero state" instantly.

This is another element of these two states. Not only do criminals move in and out of these states without rational reason, they can move from one extreme to the other very quickly. And then, they can move back in with the same speed. Keep in mind that this all happens in the criminals' mind—in their perception. And the thought is their reality. To change the reality they must change the thought.

When the criminals are in the "zero state," they will do anything and everything they can to get out of this state and regain control. This is important for counselors to remember when working with criminals. There are many instances when criminals will perceive that all of their power to control has been taken away from them. At those moments, one of two reactions will manifest itself. The least-frequent reaction will be one of suicidal ideation or threats of suicide. These need to be examined carefully; however, most often these threats are a form of manipulation to allow the criminals to regain their sense of loss of control. If staff is giving them special attention, is putting them on a suicide watch, or attempting to reason them out of a suicide attempt, they feel they have regained power to control. They are controlling the situation and have commandeered all of the staff's attention. Elliott and Verdeyen (2002) refer to this as "suicide as a means to an end type of manipulation."

The criminals' most frequent response is one of attack. They will attempt to take their control back and often attempt to get the best counselor. Later, we will discuss power thrusting. Realize that criminals will attempt to control the counselor in anyway that they can. They will push all the buttons, challenge, ridicule, shame, curse, and so forth to establish their return to the "God state." If they can frustrate the counselors, get the counselor to fight back, scare them, get them to give in, and so forth, then, they feel they have won and have their control power back.

A good example of this is the Davis and Klaas illustration used earlier. Mr. Davis was just about to lose all of his control power and be sentenced to death. He regained that control by attacking Mr. Klaas. Mr. Davis provoked Mr. Klaas to react to such a point that he had to be restrained and taken from the courtroom. Mr. Davis' perception would be one of complete control. He provoked Mr. Klaas to a violent reaction.

Other ways criminals attain or maintain the "God state" is to exaggerate. They present themselves in a grandiose way regarding their accomplishments and their crimes. An individual may have been busted for two ounces of cocaine and before he completes the story, he will explain that he has been busted for fifteen pounds of cocaine. He will relate how he was set up and betrayed; besides, it really was not his fault for getting busted. However, he was busted for a very heavy crime—not any of this petty stuff. We had one inmate telling other inmates about a murder he had committed. When we became aware of the story, we began to gather more information and check out his confession. Sure enough, a murder had been committed in the act of a robbery. It happened in his town. It even happened on the same date he was claiming to have committed the murder. This was getting to be a pretty serious situation. We began to have his background checked out. For instance, was he where he said he was when the murder was committed?

Surprise, surprise! Our inmate was in a different prison and locked up when the crime was committed. He had read about the case—had studied it—and used it to present himself in a "God state." As we discussed earlier in the "push pin caper," there was also a "spin the therapist" element here. He was controlling us—getting us to run around to check out this story. We spent much energy on investigating his story. He could not lose because he had not done the crime. The client had prestigious power with the other inmates as long as they believed he had committed this crime. When they found out he had not committed the crime, he still maintained his power to control the situation. This was accomplished by pointing out how he had gotten the staff to waste so much energy on chasing this wild goose tale.

POWER TO CONTROL

Another major focus for the criminal, which is actually self-evident in much of this, is the power to control. Under the topic of "power thrusting," we discuss the difference between power and force. The use of the word "power" in this chapter is probably better called "force" or "external power." Criminals use force or external power to control others. The criminal constantly is seeking to gain a controlling power over, and control of, others—children, spouse, therapist, friends, situations, and anyone else who is around. To him, it is all about who has the control and who does not (Zukav, 1990). Their perception even includes the change agents. If they perceive a staff person with little power, they can begin their manipulative games, either to gain favor with the staff person or to discount the person. This can be very direct or very subtle.

When spousal abuse is examined, the only real issue is power to have control over the spouse. As a side trip, if we are managing offender-abuse groups and are not considering the issue of power to control, we probably are not being effective. Most experts, especially women, have been saying for years that rape is not about sex. It is about power to control. It is about dominating the victim.

For the criminal, power to control always has the question of "can I get away with it?" The need for power to control overcomes fear and any values the criminal may have. I want—I need power over others—no matter the cost. We saw in the Klaas case how Davis gained control. Note the examples of subtle power to control issues in the following three council reports.

ORIENTATION DEPT. WEEKLY REPORT

COORDINATOR: Allen
DEPT HEAD: Larry

41

CREW CHIEF:　　　David
NUMBER OF CREW:　5

Comments

Mr. _____: Took over as Crew Chief on 6-1-94. Mr._____ has been having problems adjusting, and has received one Summons, one Problem Sheet and one Verbal Warning. I assigned Mr._____ and Mr._____ as Sponsors 6-1-94 to help show more support and direction!

There are three subtle references in this to power-to-control issues. The first, "I (the "I" is assumed) took over" displays power to control. Another way to say this that would avoid power to control would be to say "I was appointed crew chief," or "I became crew chief." In case you are thinking this is too petty or subtle, refer back to the discussion on "The Thought is the Deed." Remember, we pointed out the phrasing and use of words for prosocial individuals, which are different from consequences for criminals. If the thought is the deed, then this takes on a different slant for the criminal. This issue will continue to be addressed as we proceed. Again, we see power to control in "I assigned." Self-centeredness is also evident. An improved wording and thought pattern would be: "Mr._____ and Mr._____ were assigned as sponsors." This avoids centering on self and being in forceful control.

Continuing in this report, we find the following:

Mr._____: I'm back on Orientation Dept. as Dept. Head this week. My Crew Chief, Mr._____ is doing an excellent job organizing the Dept. making sure, the new Residents have Sponsors to help them out for their first month here.

The troublesome phrase here is "My Crew Chief." The first issue that jumps out is the ownership contained in the phrase. Whose crew chief? My crew chief. The second concern is the implied power to control. If it is my crew chief, and I own everything that is mine, then I have power to control him the same as "my dog" or "my car." A better way to phrase this would have been "The crew chief, Mr._____." No ownership or control is implied.

This report continues with the coordinator and illustrates a proper way to avoid these issues. He states:

> Mr._____: Mr._____ and Mr._____ are doing a good job. They are making sure that all the new Residents have Sponsors. Keep up the good work guys.

One can see there are no "I" statements, no "ownership" issues, and no "power to control" issues.

Another example from the same report comes from the recreation department. It states:

> Mr._____: I had a rec. Crew Meeting with everyone from the Rec. Department, and I believe that everyone will do a good job.

Again, we see the big "I" twice in this statement. In addition, there is the phrase "I had a rec. Crew Meeting." What we addressed with this resident was how to rephrase the statement to avoid both the "I" and the "control" issues. A more appropriate way to phrase this could have been "A rec. crew meeting was held with everyone . . . and it appears everyone is committed to doing a good job." These are subtle differences but very important issues to raise with the criminal in treatment.

Another example of this ultimate need for power to control comes from a murder case. It was in Seattle, Washington, where Wesley Dodd was the perpetrator of several cases of sodomy, rape, brutalization, and murder of young children. He was apprehended when a young boy screamed as Mr. Dodd hustled him away. Mr. Dodd was found guilty and sentenced to death.

During the appeal process, psychiatrists, his mother, and many others were trying to figure out how this man could commit such horrendous crimes. This is generally the response to crime; we look for a cause. A psychiatrist and his mother decided that this poor young man was not in control of himself. Regardless of what treatment attempts were tried, he just could not control himself. They trotted out how he had been molested, treated badly, and so forth. The articles in the paper made Mr. Dodd appear as a sick, helpless, victim of his environment. The picture painted of him was that he was not in control.

Often, the criminal will go along with this line of defense because it allows him to escape all accountability and responsibility for his behavior. However, in Mr. Dodd's case, it had the opposite affect. He appeared to enter the "zero state" as he was painted as this animal that was out of control. How could he regain the control taken away from him? The only avenue left open to him was to control his appeal process and how soon the death sentence would be carried out. He refused all but the mandatory appeal steps. He talked about how he needed to die, because if he were not stopped, he would continue to commit these crimes. He was executed quickly, when compared to most death-sentence executions.

Most people saw this as a great understanding on his part, as a sense of remorse, an acknowledgment and acceptance of his guilt and need for punishment. Yet, most people were reacting to this from their prosocial point of view and understanding. From a prosocial point of view, you could come to those conclusions.

However, we see something different in his refusal of appeals and desire to have the execution be carried out as swiftly as possible. The first is being in control. "You are saying all these bad things about me. I am being portrayed as an out of control, weak, untreatable person. How do I get back in control? I can control my own death." It is the ultimate example of having power to control. All the people and organizations that were trying to force the appeal process—going to court on his behalf without his permission, forming rally groups against the death penalty—had no control over his choice to have his sentence carried out as quickly as possible. He alone was in control. There is no more powerful sense of control then to have the power to control one's own death.

Joseph Wambaugh, the former policeman and best-selling author, who has dealt with criminals, comments, "The electric chair can be a sociopath's greatest triumph if he thinks he can manipulate his audience to the end. To die in control is to die in ecstasy" (*Echoes in the Darkness*, 1987).

A second ingredient in Mr. Dodd's rejecting the appeal process and in controlling the time of his death is the good-guy image, discussed previously. "See me—I know how bad I am. I do not want to do any more killings. Please stop me. I deserve to die. Put me to death to save other young children. I really am a good person and do not want to hurt anyone else." You might be thinking to yourself that this is a very harsh response to Mr. Dodd's choice to refuse to have the execution of his sentence delayed. However, remember, criminals see themselves as good persons despite the crimes they commit. How can a person such as Mr.

Dodd reconcile his crimes with his image of himself as a good person? He does this by doing the ultimate good act—dying. We did not see any confession, remorse, or self-enlightenment until he was caught, found guilty, and sentenced to death. He was confessing to impress.

The following story illustrates power-to-control in the same manner. It also illustrates a complete lack of empathy. A young drifter who had killed a young boy in a restroom smiled as the jury gave him the death penalty. He had previously asked them for death. His attorney was seen congratulating him for getting what he wanted. Again, this keeps him in control. He also had told the jury, much to the shock of the mother, that he would do it again in a minute if given the chance.

Elliott and Verdeyen (2002) suggest "other factors that enhance an inmate's sphere of influence (control) include a reputation as a violent predator, having a notorious criminal history, and having occupation of a leadership position in an organized crime 'family,' drug cartel, or notorious gang."

TACTIC—ANGER AND ATTACK

The tactic of Anger and Attack and the thinking error of Power Thrusting go hand and glove with Power to Control. Anger and Attack are both tactics and thinking errors. Being angry and attacking are used very effectively to keep the change agent off balance, defensive, and timid. Criminals can be very scary as they use their anger and attack the change agent. They often display a huge amount of verbal anger, posturing, and useing aggressive behavior. Criminals often will be hypercritical, sarcastic, and derogatory. If allowed, they will be abusive and even threaten violence. This usually is expressed as having done so and so to people who crossed them in the past. They will share horror stories about how they have lost control and put someone in the hospital. These are all calculated attempts to intimidate the change agent. Anger is a basic part of this criminal personality and response to life. Their anger often makes them vulnerable to the "zero state," discussed previously.

If and when the session becomes angry, inform clients that this behavior is not tolerated. If they persist, terminate the session. Address the subtle anger and sarcasm immediately to prevent the clients from escalating it. In a group session close to Halloween, clients were discussing going to a party. One female client said to another, "I suppose you are going as a prostitute." The other client responded, "It is better than going as a bitch." The counselors ignored this exchange. During break, the clients engaged in a hair-pulling and slugging match. By ignoring the original attack and sarcasm, the incident escalated into a fight.

Another example of attacking is shown in a senior coordinator's report.

> Early this morning I observed Mr. _____ calling Mr. _____ a "freak and a weak punk." Mr. _____ got up from his seat and approached Mr. _____ in a fighting stance, Mr. _____ also approached Mr. _____ in a fighting stance.

In this observation, note how criminals use anger and attack each other by name calling and posturing. This is also evidence of the power-to-control issues discussed previously and power thrusting, which will be discussed next. The report goes on to say:

> Myself and a couple of other residents told Mr. _____ to stand down, take a time out! I asked Mr. _____ to take a walk with me. Mr. _____ did so, he informed me that fighting wasn't worth losing his program! I went and informed staff of the situation! Staff informed me that they would handle the situation—that most likely Mr. _____ would be removed from the program!
>
> At 10:30, I noticed that Mr. _____ was still here and no apparent actions had been taken. (*When he says "no apparent actions had been taken," he is criticizing the staff for not moving and acting as he wants them to. This is a subtle attack on staff. If you were as smart as I am, you would . . .*) He goes on to say " . . . I am very concerned about Mr._____'s attitude and how he gets away with very antisocial behaviors with little or no consequences, it's not a very good example for the new residents to observe.

He continues his criticism of staff and does it in a power-thrusting manner, which is a form of attack. He is telling staff that they ought to be doing what I tell you. Why aren't you listening to me? Act now on my suggestions. This is an attack to discredit staff and build himself up.

THE POWER THRUST: BOTH A THINKING ERROR AND A TACTIC

We dealt with the concept of the power thrust earlier in the discussion on power to control and in the discussion on anger and attack. A power thrust is basically a spitting contest to see who can spit the furthest. It goes like this: "My daddy can beat up your daddy. Oh yeah, my mommy is better than your mommy." Each person tries to out spit the other. This argument continues to escalate, often times until violence occurs. One is referred back to the altercation between the two women in the previous section under "anger and attack." "In a power struggle [thrust], their desire to manipulate and control [others] conflicts with [other's] desire to manipulate and control [them]," (Zukav and Francis, 2001).

The authors call this external control versus internal control. In external control, one is striving to control others, the weather, the outcome of a contest, a marriage, and so forth. Zukav and Francis go on to say that in internal control there is a "striving to do your best for the joy of expressing all that you have to contribute as a satisfying experience that does not depend upon the outcome." They call this "authentic power." This definition greatly corresponds to the prosocial internal thinking on the thinking-pattern continuum, while the power thrust corresponds to the problem-thinking or criminal-thinking grids.

Hawkins (1995) refers to what Zukav and Francis are calling external power as "force" and to internal power as "true authentic power." In *Becoming a Model Warden, Bartollas* (2004) in talking about power versus force says the following:

> In the traditional prison, there are destructive feelings of hopelessness, fear, frustration, rigid positions, and divisiveness toward everything. This response is one of force. Force leads to explosive anger that bursts forth on others and resentment and revenge permeate everything. In contrast, the power of the warden in the proactive model is expressed through treating people with dignity and respect, creating a safe environment, being responsive to the needs of inmates

and staff, and encouraging staff and inmates to pursue self-growth experience.

Wayne Dyer has an eight-tape lecture called "It's Never Crowded Along the Extra Mile." These tapes are an expansion of his book, "10 Secrets for Success and Inner Peace." In the eighth tape, he discusses Hawkins' differences between "Power" and "Force." He comes up with what he calls his dirty dozen. Condensed and paraphrased, they are as follows:

1. Force creates counterforce; power creates grace.
2. Force is always loud and aggressive; power is silent.
3. Force is always moving against something; power does not move against anything.
4. Force is incomplete and always needs something to fulfill it; power is totally complete in and of itself.
5. Force makes demands; power has no needs.
6. Force is constantly consuming, demanding more; power is always content, makes no demands and consumes nothing.
7. Force takes energy away; power energizes and gives forth.
8. Force is always associated with judging and criticizing; power is associated with compassion, humility, and feels positive.
9. Force polarizes and creates conflict; power unifies.
10. Force has a high cost in that it needs enemies to fight; power is free and needs no enemies.
11. Force requires proof because it wants to argue—prove it to me; power needs no proof—it knows health is better then disease, honor is better then dishonor, truth is better then lies.
12. Force always is associated with sickness; power always is associated with health.

We will come back to this when we get to the chapter on the change-agent zones.

It is important that the change agent avoid getting into a power (force) thrusting situation with the criminal. Most often, the criminals will win this power thrusting because they have no boundaries or ethics that tell them to stop, whereas the change agent generally will only go so far and then their ethics and boundaries call a stop to the power thrusting.

Criminals need control over others. Their greatest excitement is in doing the forbidden and getting away with it. Their need for force, control, and dominance show in all areas of their lives. The occasions when criminals appear to show an interest in a responsible activity are generally opportunities for criminals to exercise control.

In their thrusts for control, arrested and nonarrested criminals view themselves as extraordinary and prestigious figures. We use the term "control" to signify management of another person. "Power" (force) refers to the triumph criminals experience from managing others and achieving what to them is a victory at the expense of others. For the criminal, it is always about winning or losing as seen in the previous power-pendulum discussion.

Power to control is based on fear and intimidation. The payoff is excitement. It is a big high for criminals. Some other tools are sex, drugs, anger, tattoos, and bizarre grooming.

THE CONVICT'S CODE

Another difference between the thinking of prosocial people and criminals is in protecting each other—covering up for one another. Some inmates say that there is an inmate code. Older convicts like to believe that they have a more pure code than the younger inmates; our code is okay, but your code is not. Their code is one of honor while the younger inmates only keep their code as long as it serves their purpose. The inmates will turn someone over whenever it suits their purpose. What the older convicts do not say is that the convict code also serves their purpose. The convict code is a protective code that allows convicts to commit crimes without fear of being turned in. It was created and is maintained to protect criminals from being held responsible and accountable for their behavior. "You protect me and I will protect you. You assist me in my criminal behavior and I will help you. You look the other way and I will look the other way." The code minimizes all consequences of criminal activity.

Mario Puzo, in *The Sicilian* (1985), uses the word *omerta* to describe the Sicilian Mafia code. This code was enforced not only on Mafia members but on all Sicilians. It became a crime to share any information with the police. Silence was strictly enforced on all Sicilians, even the children, and included any information given to any outsiders.

Similarly, centuries of tradition surround the convict code. We will discuss the sense of criminal community that exists and the networking that goes on in the criminal community later. In attempting to break down this code within a treatment program, you will meet resistance. Inmates will say, "I am not going to be a narc, a snitch, a stool pigeon." When you ask who the code is for, who set the code up, who does it serve, they respond with uncertainty, confusion, and disagreement. All the criminal knows is that it is there, as ambiguous as it is, and it must be followed. The convict code is in direct opposition to the therapeutic community idea, discussed later. In the one, we ask them to hold each other accountable. In the other, they are asked to cover up for each other. To break through this code is one of the most difficult areas of treatment we face in this model.

At the Consortium Center, a can of rat poison was left in the community room by a client to discourage clients from holding each other accountable. In the Consortium's newly implemented jail treatment program, the drawing of a rat (shown here) was placed on the cell door of the senior coordinator as a threat against violating the convict code.

The code is based on fear, force, control, irresponsibility, false pride, and sentimentality. It is enforced by individuals who will not accept responsibility for their own behavior. They seek power to control others and a desire to protect their own criminal lifestyle as predators. There are no written rules, and the rules change depending on the individuals' self-interest (what is most important to them at that time). The only rights allowed by the code are those of the strongest, most powerful. It does not allow freedom. If one expresses individual opinions or feelings regarding irresponsible behavior, they are put down and looked on as weak.

Convicts choose to continue to live by this code for several reasons. They believe this is the way to live. They also desire to protect their own criminality. Those who continue to live by this code eventually will commit new crimes and return to prison.

However, the code goes beyond just assisting the criminal to commit crimes without fear of being turned in. It has a strong element of getting one over on the "man." The man is society in general—programs and change agents specifically. The criminal gets no greater high than to commit some violation and not get caught, as we have discussed already.

The convict code helps the criminal in setting people up and controlling their behavior. Remember, from the first time criminals meet you, their whole intention is to set you up and get away with it. Their purpose not only is to get away with it, but to gain some force over you.

This is far different from the responsibility code with which pro-social people live their lives. The responsibility code includes looking out for others' welfare. It puts others first and is concerned for the community as opposed to the self. The responsibility code can be seen in the therapeutic community where clients are taught to hold each other accountable. With a responsibility code, one chooses to live with and in cooperation with others. Members of this community do not keep secrets or hide from the truth. It is not a game of winning or losing. Its members find authentic power and do not have to use force. A responsibility code holds to the truth, looking inside for the power to grow and build.

THINKING ERRORS, TACTICS, AND MASKS

The development of the thinking errors, tactics, and masks began with Yochelson and Samenow (1994). However, many others have modified and added to these ideas. It is interesting to see how others were developing similar ideas in other fields (Dyer, 1976). Elliott and Verdeyen (2002) discuss Walter's description of these and the different names he gave to them. Andrews and Bonta (1998) give different names to them, which can be seen in the section on causation. Later, we will share a clustering list developed by the Consortium program.

Thinking errors are how criminals order their cognitive world. It is how they think to make sense of their behavior. The tactics describe how they act—their behavior. Masks are how they present themselves to the world—the faces they put on. There is considerable crossover among thinking errors, tactics, and masks, especially the thinking errors and the tactics. Sometimes, it is difficult to distinguish between the thinking error and the tactic. Often, the same word or description is used to identify both a thinking error and a tactic. "The sheer number of interrelationships among the thinking errors overwhelm both inmates who are trying to learn them and treatment staff who are endeavoring to teach them" (Elliott and Verdeyen, 2002).This is why the Consortium program clustered them together.

When discussing errors, tactics, and masks, we are addressing criminals' entire belief system. It is how they make sense of the world. They have functioned using this belief system for many years. As Hyrum Smith says (Graham and Hyrum, 1999), "They have a faulty belief on their belief window." Criminals surround themselves with individuals who have the same belief system. They dissociate themselves from more prosocial or functional people and then make choices as time goes on to continue to associate with other felons or substance abusers. This thinking process becomes more and more concrete. The criminals find it hard to believe that prosocial people do not think in the same terms as they do. They think that everyone thinks the same way that they do. With the company they keep, it is understandable that they believe other people think the same way they do.

What follows are descriptions of some major errors and tactics that we have used in The Consortium program and in the Powder River program, though as has been said, the Consortium clustered these, and the Powder River program has since embraced the "Truthought Corrective Thinking Process." These are modified versions that come from many sources. This list is not exhaustive. Some of these errors and tactics have been addressed in previous sections of this book.

TACTICS

The tactics are the behaviors and responses criminals use to avoid responsibility and accountability for their behavior. They use these to defocus, to get the attention off themselves, and focus attention on to others. They use the tactics to throw therapists off track and avoid having to follow through. Most criminals will have a cluster of several tactics they use most often, though they can and often will use all of them in their attempt to defocus. It is important, as will be discussed in the chapter on thinking reports, to have clients identify the cluster or pattern of tactics they use.

Three tactics are used to deal directly with any change agent. A change agent is anyone who attempts to hold the criminals accountable and responsible for their behavior.

TACTIC—PUT DOWNS

Criminals build themselves up by putting the change agent down. This tactic can discount or discredit the change agent. The purpose is to make the change agents begin to doubt their ability and question whether they can work with these clients. The clients will ask such questions as "Have you ever been in prison?" and "Have you ever been an alcoholic/addict?" They are attempting to imply that you cannot truly understand them if you have not experienced what they have. If the Change Agent answers "no," then he can be discredited because he has no personal experience. If he answers "yes," his credibility is challenged for the opposite reason (Elliott and Verdeyen, 2002).They may challenge your education or degree or lack of one to discredit you.

When criminals try to discredit you, it is important to always turn it back on them. Always maintain the focus on them. Avoid responding or justifying your behavior, experience, or credentials. It is helpful to ask them what this has to do with their treatment process. Ask how this information will change their situation or have an impact on what is going on right now.

Often, they will attempt to inform you of the rules as though you did not know as much as they do. Yochelson and Samenow (1977) talk about criminals using sarcasm by suggesting you probably do not know something, and the criminals must tell you what is really going on. They intimate that the change agent is ignorant. One time, a client said, "You probably do not know much about my kind of mental illness." If the change agent is intense, the client may accuse him of being angry. The criminal may try to embarrass or humiliate the staff.

They will want to inform you of how bad the treatment program is and how it should be changed to help them. They portray themselves as experts, with the implication that if you only would ask them, they could set you straight. They suggest that you should let them redesign the program.

An example of putting the change agent down comes from a client's report in the jail treatment program:

> Last week during breaking barriers Lori (staff member) gave us clients an assignment of numbering lines on paper 1 to 100. Then told us to list all of the positive things about ourselves. One for each number. There was a time limit so speed was of the essence. I had 34 items written down before time was up. Lynn (staff member) looking over my shoulder said in a loud voice sarcasticly (sic) 34, you got 34? and then loudly told Lori well look he listed walk, talk, and so forth. I was thinking of how unprofessional she appeared to be behaving.

The client's counselor addressed this issue with this client and his next report contained the following put down.

> I think you people in the staff, especially Boyd Sharp, are so funny getting so adamant over a little constructive criticism. Until now I was impressed by what I was and am learning here at the Consortium. Darrell _____ would have eaten you up. This episode weakens you're (sic) credibility.

Again, it is important to remember that none of this has anything to do with the change agent. It is their attempt to avoid accountability and responsibility. We will address this in the section on counselor behavior.

TACTIC—TELLING WHAT STAFF WANTS TO HEAR

Criminals feed the change agents what the criminals think the change agents want to hear. Sometimes, the criminals appear to be model clients. They are always on time, participate fully in the group, offer to do extra assignments, and are compliant in all things. Whatever they think the therapist wants to hear and wants them to do, they will do and say. This is true even if and while they secretly are doing and saying the opposite. If the excitement of criminal behavior is not available, they can find some of this excitement by being a senior coordinator, an editor, or a crew chief. It is easy for a change agent to either accept this behavior as real change or to reject it as a facade. The best approach is to say that "time will tell if this behavior is honest." In Hyrum Smith's "Franklin Reality Model" his test is "Will results of my behavior meet my needs over time?" (Graham and Hyrum, 1999).

Criminals often will confess to impress. In a show of sincerity, criminals will confess their crimes, misdeeds, and program violations. By listening carefully, the change agent can detect if the confessions are only of things already known to the program, whether the confessions are issues that will become known to the agency, or if they are the confessions of issues that really will not have any consequences attached to them. Criminals may reveal small infractions to avoid dealing with larger issues. A therapist should look for change to go along with the confession.

Earlier, we recounted the story of a client confessing to something he did not do, a murder during a robbery. The client defocused attention from his treatment issues by having the staff research the accuracy of the confession. We discussed this as a power-to-control issue. He successfully spun the staff.

TACTIC—FEED THE CHANGE AGENT WHAT CRIMINALS THINK THE CHANGE AGENT OUGHT TO KNOW

Criminals have a grandiose idea that they know what is best for you to know about them. They will tell you only what you already know and then whatever else they think is important for you to know. They will share only those things that put them in a favorable light. Most of the time, what criminals think we ought to know and what we think we ought to know are quite different. They will give you enough information to keep you from knowing who they really are and will keep you from really being able to direct them in terms of any change.

In the film *The Outside Woman*, discussed earlier, the incarcerated criminal only told the visiting woman enough to get her to commandeer the helicopter. For one thing, he failed to tell her that he was married.

The criminal will tell you he cannot confide in you about some things because they are too personal and he does not want to break down. Often, in the prosocial treatment program, therapists will back off at this point because they will not want to push the client over the edge. With criminals, this is their manipulative way of getting the therapist to defocus. They will say such things as "let's let it drop." "I'd rather not go into that right now," and so forth. This is the time to continue to focus on the criminals and get them to accept their delaying tactic.

TACTIC—LYING

Lying is both a tactic and a thinking error. Lying is what the criminals do best. They often will lie when telling the truth would be better for them. There are three main ways criminals lie. They lie by commission. That is, they make things up as they go along. They flat out do not tell the truth. Secondly, they lie by omission. This is probably the most common. They tell part of the truth, but leave out part of the story. If you discover a lie of omission and ask criminals why they did not share that information with you, they will respond by saying that you did not ask for that information. It is your fault that they did not tell you. They certainly would have told you if you had asked. They claim that they did not know you wanted that information.

The third way criminals lie is by assent. The criminals pretend to agree with you or approve of your actions or ideas when they have no intention of going along. Criminals lie because lying is a way of life for them. It is habitual. They do not know how to live any other way. If they told the truth, they always would be in prison. If they honestly told their significant other what they were doing, they would not have a significant other. If they told the police what they were doing, they would be arrested—so they lie. They lie to build themselves up, discussing crimes they really never committed, talking about accomplishments they never had, and claiming successes they never achieved. If the criminals can get someone to believe them, they get a great rush. They have found a gullible person.

TACTIC—VAGUENESS

Being vague is a tactic criminals use very well and quite often. The whole idea is to never make a commitment. It is important in working with criminals to have them make a commitment both verbally and in writing. They will say "I will try," "I want to," "I need to," "you might say that," "I guess," "kinda," "I can" and on and on. In all of this, the criminal has not made a commitment and always can fall back to the position of never having said they would. You then get into focusing on whether they have made a commitment or not. Eliminate the vagueness up front.

The criminal thinker is unclear and nonspecific for a purpose—to avoid responsibility and accountability. An example of this comes from a community meeting the staff had with all of the clients. One client said that he wanted to apologize to a staff member. We acknowledged that we understood he wanted to apologize and asked him when he was going to apologize. He replied that he had apologized, and we informed him that he had only said he wanted to, but, in fact, he had not yet apologized. He then said, "I apologize to Mrs. _____ for what I said yesterday." Again, our response was that this was good, but still vague. We informed him that he needed to be specific about what he was apologizing for. He then said, "I apologize to Mrs. _____ for calling her a bitch yesterday."

If we had not continued to guide him in his apology, he could have denied in the future the specific event for which he had apologized. For instance, if he called her a bitch the next day and we reminded him that he had apologized for this, he could say that he, in actuality, was apologizing for something entirely different and that we had misunderstood him. In like manner, if we had not insisted that he go beyond wanting to apologize, he could and would deny making the apology by saying he had only said he wanted to apologize.

This exchange took approximately thirty minutes to accomplish. It took place before the entire community and was used as a learning tool for the whole community. As we have said, working with criminals will take time if we are to be successful with them.

It is important to get criminals to state their commitments in a proper form. Instead of saying "can," we know they can, or "will," which is in the future—get them to say "am." This present tense is immediate. When we discuss affirmation writing, we will list the five keys to affirmation writing.

TACTIC—MINIMIZING

Minimizing makes a situation or behavior seem smaller than it is or less significant. Some examples include the following: "I only stole a stereo. I could have ripped off the whole house." "I did not hand that paper in when it was due, but I have handed in everything else, so it's not a big deal." Criminals will tell you that it was just a prank, a joke, that they did not mean anything by it. A criminal will down play hitting his wife by saying he is not hitting her as often as he has in the past, only twice a week now instead of five times a week. He will claim that, yes, he did commit a robbery, but he did not carry a gun. He might admit to selling drugs, but he does not sell to kids. He will use phrases such as "not as bad as," and "just a little." The senior coordinator in our recently opened jail treatment program wrote "C pod was a little bit loud."

Other minimizations we have heard include "I only had six beers that night. I usually drink half a case." Of course, his parole orders state he is not to drink at all. "I only had half a mile to drive. It's not like I was going very far." However, his blood alcohol level was .18 and the legal level is .08. It is important not to accept this line of thinking because it comes across to the criminals as support for what they have done or are doing.

Examples of minimization of criminals abound. A recent newspaper article about a criminal sentenced to more than seventy-seven years stated:

> Rincker carried an assault rifle and other weapons into the KOIN Center last January. He wounded two men on a lower floor before taking hostages. . . . Rincker, whose attorney argued that he was insane, apologized in court to the shooting victims but said that, with the weapons he carried, he could have done much more harm (Herald and News, 1995).

This is a classic case of minimizing. I am really a good guy because I did not shoot as many people as I could have.

Another example comes from a client-accountability group, during the pull-up section of the group. This is where persons can cite themselves for misbehavior during the week. Here is one client's pull-up: "Mr. _____ for using the bathroom during the first two minutes of recreation."

The client makes the pull-up on himself; however, in the process he minimizes his actions by including "first two minutes." He would have been better off just saying "for using the bathroom during recreation."

TACTIC—SELECTIVE ATTENTION AND PERCEPTIONS

Someone has called this "minimal literalization." Criminals only hear what they want to hear and then interpret it literally. They ignore everything unrelated to their objectives. They hear what supports their prejudices and desires. For example, in the Hagar cartoon, Hilda says to Hagar: "Didn't I tell you last week not to spit on the floor?!" Hagar answers, "I'm sorry! I thought you meant just that one time!" (Hagar, 1994). Like the criminal, Hagar heard her message very literally and only minimally.

TACTIC—SILENCE

Silence is a powerful tactic the criminals use to defocus and avoid accountability and responsibility for their behavior. They use silence to get the change agent agitated. The purpose of silence is to maintain secrecy. The clients do not want the therapist to know what is going on in their mind. There are many ways to be silent. Of course, they can sit there and just not talk. They also can use such phrases as "I don't know," "I don't care," "Do what you want," "My mind's a blank," "No comment," "I forgot," "Nothing happened," "I can't explain it," and shrugging.

You might state to them, "If you did know, what it would be?" Or "If you did care, what would you care about?" Or "If you could explain, how would you explain the situation?"

If they chose not to talk during their session, then you should tell them that you are going to get some work done, and they may just sit there in silence. You can let them know that you are glad they are not talking because you have a ton of work to get done and this will allow you to do it. Also, inform them that they will be charged for the session whether they talk or not. Tell them that they will be scheduled back next week, and the same subject will be addressed. Let the criminals know it is their choice to sit in silence, and when they are ready to talk, you are available. What they want to do is have you become frustrated and send them home. They want out of the session. They want to control what is discussed and how much you are to know about them. What is important is for the therapist to control the situation without getting into a power-thrusting situation with them.

The criminals use other tactics discussed and outlined by other people, but these seem the major ones for us. Some, such as "zero state," "God-state," and "power to control" have been addressed previously. The next section discusses other thinking errors.

THINKING ERRORS

First, we will examine the thinking errors of blaming, excuse making, and using justification. Later, we will see how these are clustered together.

THINKING ERROR—EXCUSE MAKING

The responsibility-evader makes excuses for anything and everything. Whenever criminals are held accountable for their actions, they make excuses. Excuses are a way of finding a reason to justify problem behavior.

Excuses include: "I forgot," "Someone told me it was okay," "Nobody told me," "I forgot what time it was," "I was never loved," "My family was poor," "Someone cheated at cards," and one of this author's favorites, "I can't see good in the rain."

THINKING ERROR—BLAMING

Blaming is an excuse to not solve a problem. It is used by the responsibility-evaders to excuse their behavior and build up resentment toward someone else for "causing" whatever has happened—"I'm miserable and it's your fault."

In blaming, criminals point a finger at someone else and say they caused whatever was happening. This takes the focus off of them and often allows them to build themselves up by putting others down. "You make me angry" is another blaming statement, and if we accept that we make them angry, then it is not their fault.

Some blaming includes: "It's the cops' fault; they know my car," "The cops wait to get you on weekend nights," "You know the way the laws are now," "The trouble is you're being too critical," "I couldn't do it because he got in my way," "The staff didn't tell me it was time for my medication," "My group member is asking for a beating," "She doesn't care about me so why should I give a damn what I do," "My lawyer turned over on me," "I had a bad judge."

When a deputy from Seattle, Washington, was convicted of trying to hire a man to kill his family, he blamed his behavior on drugs and rationalized it by saying he was building a case against the hit man. Luckily, the judge did not buy his blaming or rationalizing and sentenced him to a long prison term.

THINKING ERROR—JUSTIFYING

Thinking errors are criminals' ways of explaining the reason for things they have done and for which they do not want to take responsibility. They find justifications for any and all issues for which they take no responsibility. It is their way of proving they are right and correct. Examples include: "I usually don't drive if I'm drinking, but my friend got too drunk that night;" "If you can, I can;" "I was so lonely I had to . . .;" "We had a fight, so that's why I went out and drank;" and "No one listens to me so that's why I can't do anything."

Excuse making, blaming, and justifying are all errors that closely resemble each other. One wants to be alert to the slight differences in working with a client. For instance, if a client is fifteen minutes late for group, he might say that the reason he was late was because he had a flat tire. That would be considered an excuse. He might say he was late because he had a flat tire and that his wife must have driven over a nail. She is always like that. That statement would be blaming. Again, he might say that he was late because he had a flat tire. He would continue by saying we should not hold him accountable because all people get flat tires and are late sometimes. That would be considered justifying.

THINKING ERROR—VICTIM PLAYING

Criminals act as if they are unable to think, to solve problems, or do anything for themselves. They often will whine, shuffle, look pathetic, and helpless, as if they are incapable of doing anything for themselves. The victims' wish is to get pity and be excused for their behavior. Even if they act aggressively, they may use a victim stance to justify their behavior. They believe that if they do not get what they want, they are a victim. Those playing the victim get people around them to either put them down or rescue them from their problems.

In the section on the good-guy image, we portrayed the rapist in Spokane, Washington. He saw himself as the victim instead of the victimizer for his rape of the young woman. Earlier, we discussed the Calvin and Hobbes cartoon about Calvin being the helpless victim of a pampered society.

We had a criminal in prison because he had sex with his thirteen-year-old niece. He felt he was the real victim. He said that night after night she would sit on the couch across from him and flash him, intimating that she was coming on to him. His comment was, "What was a person to do?" She wanted it and then he got in trouble. Others will play the victim role by saying they were abused, they were poor, or it was the neighborhood in which they grew up. Always in the end, they are victims of a cruel hoax perpetrated on them.

Another client was in prison for driving drunk across Burnside Bridge in Portland, Oregon, and hitting and killing five people. He maintained he was the victim because they were illegally walking across the bridge. The client was right in that they should not have been on the bridge. But, he totally ignored the fact that he was driving his car so drunk that he did not even realize he had hit the people. Yet, he saw himself as the victim. If they had not been on the bridge, he would not have hit them. If you had not left the keys in the car, I would not have stolen it.

In the James Rincker case, cited previously, he made a victimization comment. Mr. Rincker continued to address the court with these words. "It's hard to feel remorse in a society that pushes you into a corner." He plays the victim. He also is blaming society for his problems. They did it to me.

One last example comes from the cartoon "Berry's World." A criminal is standing before a judge. The criminal addresses the judge: "Hey, what's the story here? You're supposed to treat me like a VICTIM, not like a CRIMINAL."

It is counterproductive to allow criminals to go on about how they are the victims of society—how their behavior is due to the way they have been wronged by others. Criminals will use this to defocus attention off their behavior. This victim's role is used almost as often as the anger role. They have convinced even themselves that they are the victims and that is a reason they can convince us that they are the victim. However, in almost all cases, criminals are not the victims but the victimizers.

THINKING ERROR—REDEFINING

Redefining is the process criminals use to shift the meaning or focus off an issue to avoid having to take responsibility for their actions. It is a way of refocusing/defocusing the attention to something or someone else. It evades addressing the issues and behavior. When you ask them how many times they have been in prison, they may reply by redefining the situation to focus on whether you have been in prison. When asked how they got busted, they may reply "The cops surely have more important things to do then harass somebody just trying to get home."

Other examples from actual conversations with clients include the following:

Question: "How often have you driven intoxicated in the last five years?"

Answer: "Not as often as a guy I work with. Boy, he should be in here."

Question: "What was your BAC when you were arrested?"

Answer: "Those breathalysers aren't that accurate—they can be thrown off even by breath mints—they shouldn't use them."

Question: "Why are you running up and down the hall?"

Answer: "I'm not running. I am just practicing a new dance step."
Question: "Who put this paper here?"
Answer: "It wasn't there yesterday."
Question: "Where are the books that I borrowed from the library and left on this desk?"
Answer: "John was hanging around here this morning."
Question: "Tell me how you assaulted that storekeeper."
Answer: "When the incident happened, I was arrested."
Question: "I understand you repeatedly beat and molested your child."
Answer: "Sometimes an urge overtakes me. I guess I have a quirk"

Redefining is used as a power play to get the focus off the person in question.

THINKING ERROR—I AM UNIQUE

"I am unique" is a constant cry of the criminal. I am not like the rest of those people in here. Yes, they are criminals, but I am not. Let me explain the differences. Later in the chapter on thinking reports, we will illustrate a criminal who constantly attempted to get us to see how she and her case were unique and why she should not be treated the same as the others.

All criminals believe they are unique and special, that no one else is like them, so any information applied to other people simply does not affect these individuals. The beliefs going along with this are things such as "I know everything and I can handle things alone." "I don't need anyone. No one understands me anyway." This last belief is held to even if there are recovering addicts and/or criminals as counselors. The notion of not self-disclosing is covered in a section on self-disclosure. However, criminals discount the stories of recovering people because they believe they are unique and the stories of others do not hold true for them. It is common in an alcohol/drug treatment group with criminals for clients to see their own situation as unique. Rules and laws do not apply to them as they do to others. "I took a fifteen-minute shower (the rule is five minutes) because I work harder than the other clients in this place."

UNCENSORED THINKING REPORT

Here is an uncensored thinking report by a client, Joe. It illustrates many of the tactics and errors. Joe was a twenty-six-year-old, single, Caucasian male. He had three children who lived with his mother. He had twelve arrests: one for shoplifting, two assaults, one disorderly conduct, two driving while intoxicated, three driving while revoked, and three parole/probation violations. His primary drug of choice was alcohol with methamphetamine being his second drug of choice followed by marijuana. This was his third admission to our program. The first time, he remained in treatment for three days. The second time, he remained in treatment for three months before he absconded. In his third admission, he finally completed treatment and graduated from the program.

During his third treatment experience, he was given a thinking report for saying, "I don't give a shit" when asked to respond to another client's feedback. He wrote the thinking report and presented it in the next group. He was removed from the group after reading it. The team leader and director addressed this with him—pointing out thinking errors, tactics, and attitudes. He was assigned to find all his thinking errors and write how he used them in the paper. His rewrites are found under thinking reports.

The following, his original report, illustrates thinking errors and tactics.

WHY I DON'T GIVE A DAMN

Like I've said over and over I m In Recovery for me i m doing my best to do what I got to do for me. and I refuse to do it for your or anybody else. I really can't give a shit about anybody in order to get on with my own Recovery. I need to focus all my energy in my own Recovery I will not set here and feed you shit just cause thats what Oscar wants to hear I think this is out of line and just tryin to piss me off and push my buttons and its only making me not give a damn that much more for I m just being honest when I say I dont give a damn about Oscars group or Oscar also I feel Oscar has got a problem with me and just bein a fuckin Asshole by giving me this two page report and letting me to turn around and right it right know and that was wrong and I don't give a damn and Oscar or anybody else can make me give a Damn until I m ready to give a damn about anything or anybody that I choose not to give a damn about and until I m ready to give a damn about whatever it is that Ocar wants me to give a damn about I just wont give a damn. Knowing its all in my attitude toward treatment in a place I think really sucks or its just the way I ve always been yes and thats what got me here folks So I recognize I need to change my I dont give a shit attitude but until I m ready to do so and think about what I need to do in or order to do just that. I dont see it happening over night just like everything else its going to take time and thats one thing I ll alway have, so this is my Attitude and something I ll work on in order to have a better attitude and outlook on treatment or certain parts of it that I dont feel applys to me.

There are many thinking errors and tactics in this letter. Before we discuss them, try analyzing the letter and spotting the problems yourself. You should note the following: blaming, attacking, putting the change agent down, justifying, making his behavior okay because that is the way he has always been, and so forth. (See a rewrite of this report in the section on thinking reports.)

MASKS

Criminals wear some major masks or facades. Here are some.

Good Guy—These individuals tell you what you want to hear, have a confident attitude, are a cool breeze, but are back stabbers.

Nice Guy—These individuals try to please everybody and are very wishy washy, clinging persons who will not tell you like it is and will not confront people. They are heavy back stabbers.

Naive Ned—These individuals come off sweet, innocent, and naive and use this method to get their way. They really are vicious and cunning manipulators.

Illiterate Dummy—When confronted, these individuals come off like morons or dummies, and in this way try to manipulate people into excusing them. They want people to believe they are dumb, when just the opposite is true.

Con Man—These individuals are usually older persons who have been around a lot and think they can get whatever they want. They can use any mask, are heavy manipulators, and have no values.

The Pimp—These individuals are very materialistic. They have shiny cars, flashy clothes, diamonds, and so forth. They are big spenders and heavy players and use this mask for attention and recognition.

Tough Guy—These individuals manipulate people by intimidation, by being pushy, loud, and aggressive bullies. They are very paranoid and do not know how to act around other people. They project hostility to keep people away. Inside they are scared creampuffs.

The Preacher—These individuals focus on religion as a way of supporting their own image to others. They are concrete thinkers and use religion as a shield to justify behaviors and keep the focus off themselves.

Sam Sentimental—These individuals present an image of someone who loves and cares for puppy dogs, kittens, old people, family, and others. This is a criminal ploy to avoid being discovered. It also helps the individuals maintain the victims' role as they build themselves up.

Sarcastic Sam—These individuals are smart alecks and loud. They seek sick attention, and try to be the life of the party. However, inside, they are very lonely persons, resentful, and angry.

These are some masks. The biggest problem with criminal masks is that by living with and projecting this false image, persons lose touch with their true selves in time. They become the criminal mask and no longer a real person experiencing and expressing true thoughts, feelings, and emotions. In the process, they also become lonely persons without real relationships with other people. "He is unaware that he is wearing a mask, or what the mask hides. The mask conceals his fears from himself. He becomes the mask, and the mask controls his perceptions, thoughts, and actions" (Zukav and Francis, 2001).

In 2001, the Consortium staff bundled the errors and tactics into fourteen closely linked clusters that seemed to be closely linked. It gave us another way of viewing them. The following is a look at the clusters. For complete description of each cluster, contact the Consortium.

1. POWER TO CONTROL
   Power Thrusting
   Anger
   Putting Change Agent Down
   Attack
   Sexuality
   Ownership

2. VICTIM
   Excuse Making
   Blaming
   Justifying
   Rationalizing

3. SILENCE
   I Can't
   Corrosion and Cut Off
   Concrete Thinking
   The Loner
   Feeding the Change Agent What the Criminal Thinks the Agent
     Ought to Know
   Closed Channel
   Total Inattention

4. ZERO STATE
    Fear of Fear
    Fear

5. GOD STATE
    Pride
    Perfectionism
    Superoptimism
    Pretentiousness
    Center of Universe

6. GOOD PERSON
    Sentimentality
    Uniqueness
    Religion
    Minimization

7. SELECTIVE ATTENTION
    Postponement
    Vagueness
    Deferment
    Minimization

8. LYING
    Commission
    Assent
    Omission
    Feeding the Change Agent What the Criminal Thinks the Agent Ought to Know

9. VAGUENESS
    Attempt to Confuse
    Misunderstanding
    Selective Attention

10. DIVERSION
    Defocusing
    Generalizing to the Point of Absurdity
    Redefining

11. ENERGY
    Excitement
    Fragmentation
    Rule Breaking
    Suggestibility

12. CONVICT (CRIMINAL) CODE
    Failure to Assume Obligation
    Failure to Assume Responsibility

13. LACK OF EMPATHY
    Failure to Put Oneself in Another's Position
    Failure to Consider Injury to Others

14. LACK OF TIME PERSPECTIVE
    The Thought Is the Deed

chapter 3

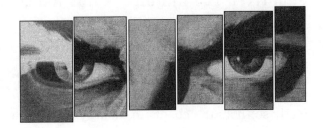

THE TREATMENT APPROACH IS DIFFERENT

If we agree and accept the idea that criminal thinking is far more hurtful, destructive, and counterproductive than prosocial thinking, then it makes sense that treatment must be different. As previously stated, it is not enough to superimpose a prosocial model on an antisocial population who thinks differently from prosocial clients.

This chapter addresses the two major themes of the book: (1) Criminals commit crimes without remorse and guilt because of the way they think. Their crimes make perfect sense to them, and when they are arrested, they feel grieved and victimized. (2) To change criminal behavior, it is necessary to get the criminals to change their way of thinking. The belief, supported by overwhelming documentation, says that thinking leads to feelings, which lead to behavior, and the behavior reinforces the thinking. We offer specific exercises to help criminals change their thinking and then discuss the societal background that reinforces criminal thinking and suggest ways counselors and other correctional workers can help their clients understand these pressures and overcome them.

COGNITIVE TECHNIQUES—NOT AFFECTIVE TECHNIQUES

We depart from traditional treatment by initially addressing thinking rather than feelings. We use a cognitive-restructuring position in the first several months. Feelings are not addressed (with some exceptions) until criminals can approach their feelings with the ability to think correctly. Most prosocial traditional alcohol/drug treatment programs (and correctly so) help the clients to identify and express the feelings they have bottled up for so long. They attempt to deal with the client's inner child. They heal the inner child so that it may respond appropriately to the outside world. With prosocial individuals, helping them identify their emotions can have therapeutic value because their thinking allows them to take responsibility for their thinking and feelings. For the most part, they do not blame others or circumstances for their situations.

A criminal's thinking does not allow this exploration; therefore, we avoid this issue initially, much like we avoid the disease idea of alcoholism. We believe criminals use their feelings to avoid accountability and responsibility for their behavior. They use feelings to get their own way and manipulate those around them, including the change agent, whoever that might be—counselor, parole officer, family, and so forth. Criminals are well aware of the value prosocial people put on identifying and expressing true feelings. Criminals use their feelings to exploit people. Often criminals in group will say that anyone who expresses pain, love, empathy, or any type of real emotion is a weak person. For them, there are two types of people in the world, *the weak* and the *strong*. They see prosocial people as vulnerable, weak people who can be exploited.

Many times, criminals try to feed the therapist feelings instead of what they actually are thinking. They hope this will get the counselor off target about what is really going on in their mind. They are very skilled in telling the change agent what they think this individual wants to hear. So, when they want to avoid the issue at hand, they begin to defocus off the issue and talk about their hurt, angry, fearful, sad, and other feelings. "The outstanding feature of modern criminal psychiatry is 'the recognition of the emotional rather than the intellectual genesis of crime.' This triumph of recognition is particularly offensive because it removes the criminal from responsibility for his crimes" (Rhodes, 1999). Criminals successfully detour the call for accountability and responsibility if the therapist allows them to defocus on their emotion.

Our philosophy is that criminals' thinking (self-talk/thinking errors) leads to their feelings. The thoughts and beliefs criminals have about the world, themselves, and the way things are, lead to how they feel and see themselves. The feelings (self-image) lead to their behaviors, and the behaviors lead back and reinforce their thinking. It is a self-fulfilling prophecy.

"It is part of our job as a criminal justice worker to help offenders to recognize their self-destructive behavior, to challenge their self-consistency motives, and to change their patterns of self-talk that contribute to their negative self-esteem" (Walsh, 2005). "Different thoughts create different emotions (and behaviors). Thoughts of vengeance, violence, and greed, or thoughts of using others create emotions such as anger, hatred, jealousy, and fear" (Zukav, 1990). These emotions lead to being abusive, stealing, robbing, and killing.

The opposite is also true. Thoughts of forgiveness, peace, generosity, and cooperation lead to emotions of love, serenity, happiness, and oneness. These lead to behaviors of giving, forming harmonious relationships, accepting others, and engaging in helping actions.

Criminals may believe or think people are ignoring them because they do not think much of them. They feel discounted and vulnerable and enter a "zero state." Criminals decide to gain back their power and return to the "God state," so they hit someone. The person who was hit avoids the criminal as much as possible because of the assault, thus reinforcing the criminal's belief that the person was ignoring him or her. It is the criminals' thinking, that creates their self-image—either of being God-like or being a zero.

Graham (1993) tells a story about a man who believed he was dead. He went to a counselor who asked him to go home and several times a day for the next thirty days tell himself that dead men do not bleed. At the end of thirty days, he was to return to the office. At the end of thirty days, he returned to the counselor and shared that he did what the counselor had instructed him. The counselor then took a pin and pricked his finger so that it bled. He asked the man to observe that he was bleeding. The man remarked, "I'll be damned—dead men do bleed."

Dyer (1976) states "By using a simple syllogism (a formulation in logic, in which you have a major premise, a minor premise, and a conclusion based upon the agreement between the two premises), you can begin the process of being in charge of yourself, both thinkingly, and emotionally."

Logic-Syllogism

MAJOR PREMISE: Aristotle is a man.

MINOR PREMISE: All men have facial hair.

CONCLUSION: Aristotle has facial hair.

MAJOR PREMISE: I can control my thoughts.

MINOR PREMISE: My feelings come from my thoughts.

CONCLUSION: I can control my feelings.

Your major premise is clear. You have the power to think whatever you choose to allow into your head.

Now, someone might say that is not true, that others control how I think, but this is not true. A simple exercise can demonstrate that each person has the power to think what he or she wants. Close your eyes for a moment and picture a beautiful sunset. Notice how you feel about the sunset. Now, with your eyes still closed, think about driving your car and a police car, with its sirens blowing and its light flashing, pulls you over. Notice how you feel now. Then, ask yourself the question: How did the thought about the sunset get into your head? How did you change the thought of the sunset to one of a police car? Did someone else do that, or did you do that? Of course, the answer is clear—you had the first thought and then changed it to the second thought. You did it.

Another exercise might illustrate this further. Relax in your chair with your eyes closed. Imagine a tranquil and peaceful place. Now, try to clench your fist and frown. Change the scene. Imagine a hostile angry environment. Now, try to clench your fist. "Thoughts have concrete consequences; they shape the way we see life, which in turn affect our health, our behavior, our choice of work and friends—in short, everything we do," according to *The Bhagavad-Gita* (Easwaran, 1985).

Dyer says, "Becoming a free and healthy person involves learning to think differently." In his book, *10 Secrets for Success and Inner Peace* (2001), his sixth secret is "You cannot solve a problem with the same mind that created it." He credits this saying to Albert Einstein. He tells a story about a man driving on an old country road late at night who runs out of gas. He remembers passing a farmhouse a mile or so back. He begins to walk back to the farmhouse to see if he can get some gas. As he walks along, he begins to think that the farmer will not be happy to be awakened this late at night. As he continues walking, his thinking progresses to the point of thinking the farmer will be angry when he is awakened from his sleep. As the man knocks on the door and the farmer answers it, the man shouts at him, "Take your gas and shove it," as he hurries away. His thinking led to his feelings—which dictated his behavior and he received no gas.

Remember, it is criminals' thinking that makes it okay for them to commit crimes and hurt people. We believe that changing the thinking changes the self-image and, therefore, changes the behavior. It is important to change criminals' thinking to change their feelings and their behavior. You can start changing or putting the brakes on the criminals' thoughts.

THINKING REPORTS

Thinking reports are central to the antisocial model. However, different people use them in several different ways. We present various ways thinking reports can be used. One method of having clients complete thinking reports is to have them write a narrative of their thinking about a particular behavior. Another method is to have clients write about their thinking on a particular subject, such as anger. We have them do this at the same time each day for several days. Another method is to have clients write down their present thinking about anything that comes to mind as they are writing. Predesignated times throughout the day are set, generally three times a day.

Staff review these reports with the clients and point out the thinking errors. The clients are asked to rewrite the report, eliminating the thinking errors. The clients may need to rewrite the report several times before they begin to be able to eliminate the thinking errors. We saw this in the discussion of the clients' weekly therapeutic community reports on the departments in which they worked.

An example of how the writing can improve is displayed with the client's rewritten report on "Why I Don't Give A Damn," the thinking report of the previous section. This is his final report on the behavior we had asked him to document. Remember, he wrote this final report after several rewrites and counseling sessions. We pointed out some thinking errors, but also encouraged him to find others. We helped him get in touch with his attitude. We pointed out the bash trip and used the idea of the video of his life. A bash trip is where a person sees his blood on the wall from previously bashing his head on the same wall, time and time again.

I recognize and take responsibility for the way I presented my thinking error Report. In the future I will intervene on my thinking and not let it go out of control. I was wrong by Attacking Oscar [remember Oscar is the group counselor] also putting the Blame on everybody and everything else when its my actions and the way I think that gets me into the situations I get myself into. I will be more open minded and just accept the things I can't change. In my thinking error Report I used. Energy from getting angry to let my pencil flow and be a self centered guy Blaming Everyone else. Also Anger and alot of it to justify and make the way I felt ok. Pride by thinking everything Im doing is right Concrete thinking my not listening to what is being gave to me knowing this place is hear only to help me not hurt me. Uniqueness by thinking Im different and dont have to care about other peoples recovery when. Playing dumb by saying I dont care I dont understand Closed Channel not taking nothing thats said to me focusing on my Anger by presenting a Bad Attitude total self-centered and being Rude I Can't by saying I refuse to do anything for anyone total self-centered.

The victim by thinking Oscar had something against me and was just trying to piss me off and just out to see me fail When I know hes just doing his job trying to teach me the right things Failure to put oneself in anothers position By sayin I dont care about anyone but myself realizing we are all in this thing together treatment alse that we all need each other to help us through. Failure to assume obligation. By expressing my anger when asked to do my thinking error report in class. Lack of interest in Responsible Performance. By not being interested in what was going on in group thinking I could just breeze through. Poor decision making for Responsible Living. By not wanting to talk and sayn I dont care cause I felt it didn't apply to me thinking I was being put down and reacting erashionally. Corrosion cuttoff. Not listening to anyone just shaking my head agreeing with everything just to get along. Building up the opinion of my self as a good person. thinking I dont need to hear this cause it dont apply to me . Pretensionness

Ranting and Ragin just carrying on with I dont give a damn about this place or I dont a damn about that and so forth Parania thinking Oscar was out to see me fail by getting on me everyday but I know hes just trying to help Who Cares By just saying I don't give a damn about anything but myself. Not so Bad, By thinking I could present that thinking error the way it was and everything be ok. I would like to add that I apoligize to the group for having a Attitude that I dont care cause I do also I am going to change my Attitude and behavior and work my program thank you

Note the amazing difference between the first thinking report and this last one. There continue to be several thinking errors, but this report is a vast improvement. Only time will tell if he was feeding the change agent.

Here is another example of leading a client through a writing process. The client wanted a day off. The first letter is as follows.

I'm writing this letter to request a day off per week I am currently in level II working on my thinking errors and step 3 and my request is to spend time with my 3 children and myself and due to my work and treatment schedule I haven't been able to do that and this would allow me to do just that.

This first request is vague and has the thinking error of: blaming"—due to my work and treatment . . ." He wants to blame work and treatment for his not spending time with his children. Here is his second letter.

I'm writing this letter to request 1 day off per week. I'm currently in Level II attending Church and AA twice a week. I've been clean for 5 months also working on my thinking errors in criminality and step 3 (the paper work) knowing I need to work especially on Pride and Closed Channel by being more open minded and open my ears and shut my mouth My Request for a day off is to spend more time with my children and due to my work and treatment schedule I have not been able to do that and if this day off is granted it would allow me to spend time with my children in addition to working on myself.

The second version has more specificity, including greater detail and commitment. However, there continues to be vagueness. He continues to blame, and he uses the phrase "I need" instead of I choose to. The last letter, which follows, eliminates most of these problems. However, he still has the "I need" statement and other subtle statements that require work. Besides that, the letter is acceptable.

> I'm writing this letter to request 1 day off per week to spend quality time with my children I'm currently working full time and in treatment. I'm in level II attending church and AA or NA twice a week also working on my thinking Errors in criminality and my 3rd step (the paper work) knowing I need to focus especially on the Pride and closed channel by being more open minded and open my ears and keep my mouth shut. I've been clean for 5 months also have a sponsor I talk to weekly about my problems or if things are going good.

There are several items to continue to address with this client. The use of "quality time" remains vague. We would encourage him to define it. He could eliminate the term "more." The best writing of this would be "by being open minded." Each of these requests was presented in group for feedback from his peers before it was presented to staff. Peer feedback is another good tool to use when working with the criminal.

Here is one last example that illustrates how to use inmates' writing and reports to address their thinking errors. This comes from a thirty-one-year-old divorced female, a poly-drug user with fifteen arrests. During her first admission, which lasted six months, she did not move out of denial about her criminal behavior. She continued to deny that she was a criminal. She repeatedly used drugs and committed crimes. Eventually, she was discharged from treatment with a recommendation for jail time and subsequent referral to a residential care facility. She did serve time in jail and completed treatment at a residential care facility.

Upon returning to the community, it was decided that she would complete her aftercare in a less-restrictive environment than the Consortium. She subsequently was discharged from that facility as non-compliant. The judge gave her the option of trying to get back into the Consortium or go to prison. The next three letters are her requests to enter treatment at the Consortium. She wrote these letters after we had met with her and a community support person. In that meeting, she was not honest, wanted to instruct us on how to treat people such as herself, and did not make any commitments.

January 30, 1997

The Consortium

Dear _____

I am writing you to ask to be readmitted into the Consortium program.

_____ has turned me down to reenter the KAT. Why? Because instead of giving me just the one chance, he gave me two and I blew both of them.

After talking to you, _____ and _____ the other day, I know what you are saying is true, but just getting that fixed in my mind is hard.

_____, I want more from life than drugs. I want more from life than jail or prison. I want more from life than the creeps that have been in my life. I'm better than that I know, but I can't do it alone. I feel washed out and used up. Yes, I tried manipulation over and over — I don't know why — I do it not even realizing I'm doing it — somehow I think I convinced myself that the manipulations worked — I guess all of you could see through me like I was glass — how stupid can I get? I fought the Consortium program from the day I entered it last year — _____ kept telling me I had the wrong attitude—I didn't listen to any-one. The Consortium is my last chance —_____ has given me one last chance. Because she has told me I have one last chance, the courts have given me exactly thirty days to be in a program, be drug free continuously, be meeting with [my probation offi-cer] everyday at 8:30 a.m., taking a drug test daily, getting mental health therapy and following up on all parts of the work plan once it is developed or I will be sentenced to jail, period.

I need help. May I please be reentered into the program?

Sincerely,

Note the vagueness in the letter. She does not make any commitments to change. She tells us what we know already. She talks about what she wants out of life, but not what she is willing to do to get the good things. She talks about how she is better than that—a reference to being a good person although she uses and commits crimes. Her manipulation is excused by her saying she does not even know she is doing it—thus, it is not her fault. She tells us that we have told her thus and thus, but she does not admit that she knows these things to be true. We met with her and pointed out her continued use of tactics and thinking errors. She was asked to write another letter, being honest, accepting responsibility, and making commitments. The following is her second letter.

February 4, 1997

The Consortium

Dear Mr. _____

I am writing this letter to you in hopes that I can re-enter your program with some real honesty this time. I was asked to write down exactly what it is I wanted out of the program and what it is I was willing to change to get there. I am tired of my life as I know it today. I want to be free of all drugs to include of course alcohol. I want more than anything to become a functional human being, free of the system, free self-bondage, and free of any and all critical thinking errors. I realize that I must keep my mouth shut in order to learn something, and I realize that my mouth is probably my biggest enemy. I am more than willing at this point to change these behaviors. I am willing to do whatever it takes to make these changes without arguing or fighting with those who have my best interest and success at heart. I have taken this opportunity to write down what I know without a doubt these are, and what I have realized about myself. They are as follows:

1. I am a criminal. If I weren't, I would not have been arrested as many times as I have been. I may fight the concept, but, I am a criminal. Using and possessing illegal drugs is against the law

— therefore I have been involved in criminal activity and that makes me a criminal. I have developed criminal thinking in that I obviously think I can get away with my activities.

2. I am an addict. I have a long history of using drugs since I was 11 years old. The last five years have escalated my addiction and my addictive behaviors.

3. I have developed addictive and criminal behaviors. I make poor choices, I try consciously and unconsciously to manipulate just about every situation I get involved in. My behavior has had tremendous consequences for me aside from the criminality and addiction.

4. I also have come to realize that I am not a chronic victim, and that the world is not picking on me as I have seen it in the past. I have many areas I need help in and am willing to go to any length to be successful, realizing of course that this is not going to be an easy or a painless task. Bottom line is that, I'm willing to do whatever it takes. My way doesn't work.

I need to overcome the criminality, the addiction (including the ritual that goes with drug usage), the behaviors of criminality and addiction, and the response of trying to manipulate situations to my advantage. I also understand that I have some real trust issues, and in order to be helped I need to start trusting somewhere with positive influences and not the negative ones I have chosen in the past. Thank you for your consideration in this matter.

Sincerely,

This letter shows improvement. She admits that she is a criminal and an addict with criminal behavior. However, in the first paragraph she does not come out and ask to be readmitted. She is vague. She talks about "some real honesty," but makes no commitment to being honest. She talks about "wanting to be free of drugs," and again makes no commitment to quitting.

She says "I realize that I must keep my mouth shut," but does not say she will keep her mouth shut. She talks about being "willing to do whatever it takes," but does not say she will do whatever it takes.

In the first three paragraphs, she admits it would have been better if she had then said "I will quit." In the fourth paragraph she is again willing, but does not go the next step and say that she will. As she finishes her letter, she talks about needing to overcome. The need is outside of herself. If she had started the paragraph with "I choose," then it would have been a commitment and would have come from within her. She would have taken responsibility for herself and her behavior.

We pointed all of these observations out to her. We then asked her to rewrite the letter a third time. The following is her third letter.

February 10, 1997

The Consortium

Dear Mr. _____,

I am writing this letter to re-enter "The Consortium" program. It is clear to me, "my way" does not work. This program will give me the tools to live a life that works. I will use these tools. I will be drug free. I will be a functional human being, free of criminally wrong thinking errors and addictive behaviors. I will do what it takes to make the changes outlined by this program, without being argumentative and manipulative! I have written down four pertinent things I know about myself without doubt, they are as follows:

1. I am a criminal.

2. I am an addict.

3. I have addictive and criminal behaviors.

4. I manipulate the system and others around me to get my way and to protect my disease.

I have many areas in which help and guidance. I will have the humility this time to listen and learn. I will overcome my behaviors of criminality and addiction.

Thank you for your time and consideration.

Sincerely,

The letter continues to be vague. However, she does make commitments and take ownership. She met with the treatment team after this third letter. We helped her to be specific and we developed a treatment plan with her. Only time will tell if her commitment is more than words. However, in keeping with our belief that the thinking or words lead to the behavior, we have gotten her to change the words. Over time, this could change the thinking and the behavior.

A postscript to this story is that this client made good progress for approximately four months. Then, her boyfriend threatened to leave her. She reverted to her manipulation and victim stance. She created a scene in group and got into an argument with a male client. She became hostile and aggressive. When the group leaders attempted to walk her through the situation, she refused. She left the group and went home and told her boyfriend that a male client had threatened her. The boyfriend came down to the clinic and threatened the client staff. He had to be escorted off the premises.

The next day, she informed the staff that she was going to see her mental health worker—that she was too traumatized to come into treatment. She was informed that she had to come in so we could talk with her. Her boyfriend called up and said she was not coming in and that was it. She saw the mental health worker the next day and he cosigned her victim stance. He attempted to excuse her from our treatment.

Her situation went downhill from there, even after several meetings with her and all change agents. Currently, she is on abscond status and probably will go to prison when or if she comes back to this county. By reverting to some tactics seen in her first letters, this client was able to manipulate staff and her boyfriend. The client escaped being held responsible and accountable for her behavior.

Ray Ferns teaches a thirty-two-hour cognitive-change training course to train staff in helping clients to change their thinking (Bush and Bilidoeau, nd). This same course is delivered to clients to help them understand their thinking process and provide them with tools to change it. The course includes many other elements, but we want to address the thinking-report portion of the training. With their permission, we took that portion and adapted it to meet our philosophy and needs.

Clients are told to take a situation that has gotten them into trouble and to write up a description of the specific event in a brief and objective way. They are instructed then to list all of their uncensored and unedited thoughts surrounding this situation. After they have listed all of their thoughts, they are asked to list all the thinking errors in each thought. The next task is to look for a pattern of thinking errors.

Then, the clients are instructed to list a disputing thought or to put a brake on each thought they have listed. This process is called "disputing" or "brakes" and is a cognitive intervention. After the clients have developed this material, they list everything on a flipchart or blackboard and present it to the group. The group assists clients in flushing out all of their thoughts and all of the thinking errors. By doing this, the clients begin to see how their thought pattern leads to their behavior. They also begin to see how to replace these thoughts with positive thoughts that will lead to self-correcting behavior. A client may write a hundred of these thinking reports. All of them are not addressed in group, but will be given to the individual therapist or case manager. The therapist reviews them for progress toward changing the thought pattern and will discuss this with the client.

Ferns and others also include other areas in the report. They include the feelings that went along with the thoughts, beliefs/attitudes, physical responses, and patterns observed. We just stick with the thinking portion. We do not want to dilute the thinking report by beginning to address the feelings at this juncture of their treatment. As we discussed, we believe that criminals use feelings as a way to avoid accountability and responsibility for their behavior.

Here is an example of a thinking report using this technique.

Situation: I had suggested that we get divorced. When she agreed, I changed my mind, but she is going through with it.

Thoughts:
1. You screwed my life up, but I always showed you love. (victim stance, lying, zero state)

2. She made a commitment. She has a duty to stay with me no matter what. (lying, concrete thinking, perfectionism)
3. I hate you. I want to kill you. (anger, power thrust, failure to consider injury)
4. You'll see who has the last laugh. (anger, power thrust, corrosion, and cutoff)

Patterns: The major thought pattern is one of anger, power thrusting, and lying.

Interventions:
1. She put up with me for a long time.
2. She gave me thirteen years of her life.
3. She's trying to keep me in touch with the kids.
4. I put them through hell.
5. I put myself here. She didn't have anything to do with it.

BRAKES

The following self-talk brakes were adapted from the work of Samenow and Yochelson by Volunteers of America of Oregon and the Multnomah County Department of Community Corrections. We have adapted them from these sources.

HARMFUL THINKING PATTERNS

HARMFUL THINKING	SELF-TALK BRAKE	HEALTHY ALTERNATIVE
1. I can't (you say "I can't" to escape accountability).	A. "I will." B. "I can and will begin and consistently continue to work for positive change in my life."	a. Do what you don't want to do. b. Call yourself on and allow others to call you on your resistance to change.
2. Suggestibility (you are very suggestible with respect to any behavior that leads to what you want and very resistant to suggestions involving responsible thinking and behaviors).	A. "Want healthy people to influence me." B. "I will be open to positive influences and closed to negative ones." C. "I will become more and more willing to change."	a. Seek and be willing to follow advice from healthy people. b. Break criminal ties. c. Admit to your support system when you are being drawn back to negative influences. d. Learn and use recovery tools.
3. Closed channel (you are secretive, close-minded, and defensive).	A. "I can't trust some of my own thinking, it gets me in trouble." B. "I will share my secrets."	a. Keep no secrets. b. Report all thinking and acting-out behaviors. c. Share more and more about yourself each week.
4. Fearful of fear (you deny fear in self and attack fear in others).	A. "Fear is my friend—it's my number 1 brake." B. "I will learn to listen to my fears and let them help me change my behaviors."	a. Talk to others about your fears. b. Stop attacking others when they voice or show their fears.
5. Lack of empathy (you rarely stop to think about what other people think, feel, and expect).	A. "Other people have feelings and problems too." B. "I will consider other people before I act." C. "I will stop hurting others."	a. Go out of your way to help others just to be helpful. b. Practice identifying with what others might be thinking, feeling and expecting. c. Express gratitude to others for their support.
6. Victim stance ("poor me"; you blame others for your circumstances).	A. "How am I responsible for my circumstances?" B. "Others are not responsible for my actions."	a. Write down and discuss the choices you made that led to your present circumstances. b. Take responsibility for your choices.
7. Superoptimism (you believe you can do anything without getting caught; you have an unrealistic belief that progress and success come easier than they do).	A. "Like everyone else, I have to work for what I get." B. "I will become responsible." C. "It will take more than a little progress to turn my life around."	a. Engage in realistic activities that will bring about positive change. b. Work for what you need. c. Continue such efforts even when bored.

HARMFUL THINKING PATTERNS *(CONTINUED)*

8. Uniqueness (you believe you should get everything you want—others exist to meet your needs and desires).	A. "I am a responsible member of the community." B. "Other people's rights are just as important as mine." C. "I will stop using and abusing others to get my wants and needs met."	a. Stop trying to get special privileges from staff. b. Don't allow yourself to use others. c. Learn how to deal with the boredom involved in certain responsibilities.
9. Power and control (conquest and getting over provide you self-esteem, excitement, and an emotional high; you believe that without criminal excitement you are nothing).	A. "I have no right to control others or to take what I want." B. "I can feel good about myself and feel satisfaction in life without the excitement of being in control."	a. Stop trying to get over on staff and peers. b. Avoid seeking power positions. c. Be open to positive changes and growth. d. Be helpful to others.
10. Lack of time perspective (instancy—you want it all now).	A. "Everything takes time." B. "Today I'm building a healthy future step by step."	a. Write down and discuss your future goals. b. Meet your goals one by one. c. Wait for results.
11. Fragmented thinking (you think one way one minute and the opposite way the next minute).	A. "Will the thoughts I currently have help me to become who I want to be?" B. "I will be consistent in my thoughts and actions."	a. Have consistent effort; follow through on all tasks and projects. b. Write out your goals and make decisions based on those goals.
12. Failure to think about injury to others (the resulting injury to others does not stop you from committing harmful acts).	A. "I've hurt many people, even people I care for." B. "I do not want to continue injuring others and I will stop."	a. Take personal inventory regarding past injuries you have caused. b. Become willing to make amends for those injuries.
13. Criminal pride (you tell yourself that: "no one can mess with me." "I'm better than others and they had better treat me that way." "I'm right and others are wrong.")	A. "I don't have to get my way in order to be valuable." B. "Thinking that I am or will be the best is not the same as working to do my best." C. "It is not a sign of weakness to have to ask questions if I don't know something or to receive support from others."	a. Cooperate instead of compete. b. Make a list of what others can reasonably expect of you. c. Stop trying to appear more knowledgeable than others by trying to set them straight. d. Begin admitting when you are wrong and admitting when you don't know something.
14. Lying (you lie as a way of life in order to avoid accountability and/or to get what you want).	A. "I do not have to lie." B. "I can and will stop lying." C. "I will become willing to accept the consequences for my actions."	a. Stop trying to control your life by lying. b. Learn the benefits of telling the truth and of being an honest person. c. Strive for personal growth. d. If you do lie, admit it.

continued

87

HARMFUL THINKING PATTERNS *(CONTINUED)*

15. Loner and refusal to be dependent (you lead a private, secretive life; you fail to believe that a certain amount of interdependence is a necessary part of existence; you view dependence on others as a sign of weakness).	A. "I am part of a larger community in which I can care for others and be cared for." B. "It does not mean that I am weak if I rely on others for assistance and support." C. "I will create mutually supportive relationships that are conducive to my recovery."	a. Look for similarities rather than differences in others. b. Become willing to give and receive support. c. Create situations where you have to ask for assistance. d. Stop isolating. e. Become a healthy contributor to the treatment community.
16. Criminal sexual patterns (you get excitement from the conquest, ownership, power, and deception rather than from intimacy and sensuality).	A. "I don't have to view people as sexual objects." B. "I do not have to have sexual conquests in order to have self-esteem."	a. Have no sexual contact that breaks the law or breaks any treatment rule. b. Strive for intimacy rather than for conquest.
17. Anger as a manipulation (you use expressions of anger to get what you want).	A. "Anger is not a weapon to be used to get what I want." B. "I can learn to get my needs and wants met without having to use manipulative anger."	a. Identify and admit when you are using anger to manipulate. b. Learn and practice healthy ways to get your needs and wants met.
18. Failure to assume obligations (you view responsibilities and obligations with irritation and resentment; you expend little effort in doing things that are contrary to what you prefer to be doing; you feel that it is a sign of weakness if you assume obligations).	A. "Having responsibilities and obligations does not make me vulnerable to other's control." B. "I will stop being resentful about having responsibilities." C. "I will assume obligations." D. "I will create healthy priorities and goals in my life."	a. Assume obligations without resentment and anger. b. Fulfill your obligations in order to build self-esteem. c. Learn how to deal with the boredom involved in certain responsibilities. d. Set and keep goals for yourself that will further your recovery growth.
19. Denial and criminal scheming (a mental process that you use to eliminate deterrents to commit a crime; the deterrents are eliminated to the point where the desire to commit a crime outweighs the deterrent factors; the excitement connected to the anticipation of the crime clouds realistic thinking).	A. "I can and will face reality." B. "I can and will interrupt the scheming process before it gets to the end result of committing a crime." C. "I can find sources of satisfaction other than the excitement that is connected to scheming."	a. Identify and talk about the rationalizations and justifications you have for engaging in criminal activity. b. Let others know when you are scheming. c. Work a first step on your scheming—even if you have a strong compulsion to commit a crime; you do not have to do it.
20. Lack of trust (you do not trust others, but you demand that others trust you).	A. "I will begin to trust others." B. "I will demonstrate through my actions that I can be trustworthy."	a. Work at being open, honest, and vulnerable with others. b. Through your actions show that others can trust you.

continued

88

HARMFUL THINKING PATTERNS *(CONTINUED)*

21. Negative thinking (having a negative outlook on things/events in you life the majority of the time; automatically viewing things negatively before you even know the truth about the situation, known in AA as "contempt prior to investigation").

A. "I do not have to view everything negatively."

B. "I can and will change my negative thoughts to more positive ones."

C. "I will stop automatically having disdain and contempt for new situations/events and so forth."

a. Stop having "contempt prior to investigation."

b. Create a gratitude list (a list of people, things, events, situations, and so forth that you are grateful for having in your life).

c. When you find yourself having negative thoughts, change them to more positive ones.

22. Sense of entitlement (you strongly believe that you are entitled to getting your own way—that the world owes you; this often leads you to steal because you believe that you are entitled to take what you want).

A. "I am not automatically entitled to my way all the time."

B. "I will work for positive growth and changes in my life."

C. "I will stop taking things that are not rightfully mine."

a. Admit it when you are feeling inflated, unrealistic or have an unwarranted sense of entitlement.

b. Make responsible decisions, rather than decisions based on a sense of entitlement.

c. Stop stealing.

d. When you are having obsessions and/or compulsions to steal, talk about it in treatment or in a 12-Step meeting.

Adapted from *Brakes to Errors,* by Greg Stone, LCSW, Volunteers of America Oregon, and Tichenor McBride, MSW, Multnomah County Oregon, Department of Community Justice.

AFFIRMATIONS

Having clients rewrite their thoughts is a good idea. One area of concern is in the use of the phrases "I will" and "I can." These, as stated earlier, denote future and ability, not action. "I am" is a better phrasing. In Gordon Graham's training videos (1991, 1993, and 1999), clients are taught affirmation writing so they can start having positive and dynamic thoughts about themselves and others. "Left to itself, the mind goes on repeating the same old habitual patterns of personality" (Easwaran, 1985). However, each time the client repeats the affirmation, it is as though it happened one time. So, the more often they repeat the affirmation, the faster it becomes a reality in their life. Here are five of Graham's seven guidelines for affirmation writing.

1. Affirmations need to be personal. You cannot affirm for someone else. This is an inside job. As will be discussed later, "If it's to be, it's up to me."
2. Affirmations need to be positive. We are always affirming. The problem is that our affirmations are often negative and life-defeating.
3. Affirmations need to be in the present tense. Not "I will" but "I am." For example, "I am controlling my self-talk, because I am aware that I move toward that which I think or self-talk about." Too say, "I am not as bad as I used to be" concentrates on what I used to be, not on what I am today.
4. Affirmations need to have words that describe how they are today. This includes words such as proud, warm, happy, trusting, and successful. For example, "I enjoy taking responsibility for myself and being accountable for my actions." Also, clients are taught to change phrases such as "I'm not as bad a parent, drinker, and so forth as I used to be." We want them to focus on today. When they say "as I used to be," they are focusing on what they used to be—not on what they are affirming for themselves today. They are affirming what they used to be. "Not as bad as I used to be" is also a minimization. I am okay because I don't steal as much as I used to. We want the thinking and action to be "I am honest and trustworthy." Or when they say or write "I don't steal anymore," we have them change it to "I am enjoying a criminal-free life."

5. They need to be realistic. To affirm that, "I am out of jail or off probation" when that is not so, is not realistic. But to affirm "I am a responsible individual who is eagerly working toward freedom" is realistic.

The idea is to get clients to picture in their mind what they want and then write affirmations that confirm this and to repeat these affirmations several times a day. You might have clients write their affirmation on a 3 x 5 card and place it where they will see it several times a day. The idea is that each time they say the affirmation, their brain records it as though it were true. Also, positive affirmations replace the negative affirmations they have been saying to themselves.

Dyer (1992) says it this way:

Begin a process of affirmations reflecting a consciousness of confidence and strength by talking about your unlimited capacity to learn any new intellectual skill and appreciating the fears you have overcome. Stress how capable you are both in conversations with others and to yourself. Remember, what you think and talk about expands into action. If you are talking about your weaknesses and defending them, then you must be thinking about them as well. Keep in mind that what you are saying to others, even in what seem to be insignificant ways, are reflections of that inner mental equivalent. If you want confidence to expand in your life, you must speak of your confidence, and mention examples of that confidence. If you want fearfulness to expand, then tell others about those fears and all of the gory details that will keep convincing you of your weaknesses. It may seem oversimplified, but it is the way to create a magical transformation in your personality. Keep that zone of self-assuredness in your mind and practice letting those new miraculous thoughts develops their material equivalent in your daily world.

In 2004, Dyer discussed the self-talk cycle. We mentioned the self-talk cycle in previous sections when we discussed how our thinking leads to our feeling, which leads to our behavior, which reenforces our thinking. Athens (the criminologist who Rhodes is writing about) says, "We think by seeing ourselves talking to themselves in one or more of the languages we have learned" (Rhodes, 1999). He goes on to say, "We talk to ourselves . . . even when some one else is telling us something, we must simultaneously tell ourselves what they are telling us in order to comprehend the meaning of what they are saying" Rhodes (1999).

Graham says that we talk to ourselves four times as fast as someone else is talking to us (1999). So, in changing the criminal's self-talk cycle, we have them change from negative self-talk to positive self-talk affirmations. They constantly are making affirmations; we want them to make positive ones. We want them to shift their thinking from "what I find missing in my life, what I do not like about my life, how things used to be for me," to "what I absolutely intend to attract into my life" (Dyer, 2004).

Dyer discussed how, when we place our attention on what it is we do not want, that very attention will guarantee that we just get more of what we do not want. The alcoholic places his thinking on not wanting to drink and winds up drinking more. The angry person thinks about not being angry and becomes angrier. The more we think about what we do not want, the more we get it. So, the trick is to think of what we do want—not what we do not want. Here are some changes in affirmations. We illustrated some of these when we discussed the thinking-pattern continuum.

- From "My partner is grouchy and boring" to "I am focusing my thoughts on what I love about my partner."
- From "I cannot get a job with my record" to "I am employable and will be successful in finding work."
- From "I hate being in prison" to "I am working to be free."
- From "I dislike the work I am doing and the fact that I am not appreciated" to "I am creating the work or job of my dreams."
- From "My background was abusive and I cannot get above it" to "I am creating a present that is empowering and crime free."

Stewart and Gabora-Roth (2003) say this about cognitive-restructuring techniques:

The basic principle is to have the offender identify an antecedent event that led to a violent incident: identify the "irrational beliefs," "self-talk," or "risky thinking" at the time of the event; identify the consequences or the emotions or behaviors that are the outcome of the thinking; and dispute the thinking and replace it with more prosocial or less "risky" beliefs or thoughts. This process repeated many times in the course of a program with practice through role play, allows the participant to take control of his life and behaviors by changing the way he thinks about a given situation.

Hyrum Smith calls this "running it through your belief window" (Graham and Smith, 1999). Again, "If you change the way you look at things; then, the things you look at will change" (Dyer, 2004).

BEYOND CAUSATION

This idea is a major focus in restructuring the thought process of the criminal. "I am not at fault, someone or something else is at fault" is a major theme of criminals in their denial of accountability. This chapter flows from the previous one on changing the individual's thinking process and leads into the next section on denial.

The treatment for criminals is different from prosocial treatment in the area of causation of criminal behavior. We are not denying that many conditions contribute to a person choosing to commit crimes. Conditions such as childhood abuse, poverty, unemployment, homelessness, parental drug use, sexism, racism, and living in a ghetto must be addressed and eliminated, however, not when treating the criminal.

They do not cause crime, and the place to deal with them is not in the counseling sessions with the criminal. "Important, personal and environmental conditions are not considered causative factors in criminality" (Elliott and Verdeyen, 2002). It is not that we cannot and should not change society nor change situations; it is not that we should not help dysfunctional families or abused children. Of course, we should work to eliminate poverty. This is not the issue at all. We believe that as a society and as human beings, these things should be addressed. We should do everything in our power to help people obtain a good life.

However, in treating criminals, we cannot get sidetracked by these issues, because then we will not be able to help them change their thinking and behavior. It is important to abandon all of our previously held beliefs and only work with criminals to allow them to become functional human beings. "Poverty, race, subculture, mental illness, child abuse, and gender are all disqualified, singly and collectively, as explanations for criminal violence by the sheer number of exceptions within every category that even a causal investigation reveals" (Rhodes, 1999).

Stewart and Gabora-Roth (2003) look at many theories of violent family behavior and conclude the following:

> At different levels of explanation, each of these theories could account for aspects of men's abusive behaviors toward women. While there is evidence of brain damage among some individual male perpetrators and a history of being a child witness to violence in the home and disruption in early attachment patterns that are associated with elevated rates of adult violence, these theories cannot account for the abusive and nonabusive behavior of the majority of men who have experienced violent childhoods but establish nonviolent adult intimate relationships. Evolutionary theory has provided intriguing analysis for the deep-seated motivation of men's violence, but it has provided no convincing empirical evidence and cannot provide guidance for practitioners on what we should be doing to address violence toward women.

As mentioned in the preface, until recently, there have been two schools of thought concerning the causes of crime-nature versus nurture. Richard Rhodes, in *Why They Kill* (1999), suggested that there are many "theories invoking moral, supernatural, behavioral, social, neurological or genetic causes. None of these well-known theories credibly and authoritatively explain the violent crimes you and I follow in the news every day."

According to Andrews and Bonta (1998), the nurture theory "focuses not on the individuals as the targets of service, but on the development and strengthening of welfare agencies, neighborhood organizations and inborn leadership. . . . Those programs that were explored systematically were found to have either no impact on delinquency or to increase delinquency."

This is debunking the idea that nurture is the cause, so if you eliminated troublesome areas, the delinquency would stop. But this is not true.

Another thought looks for biological malfunctioning. They point to the XYY chromosome theory (Andrews and Bonta, 1998), theories on this enzyme or that neurotransmitter being missing or altered. Even Hare (1993), when discussing the lack of empathy in criminals, suggests there might be a bilateral brain problem. We continually seek out a medical cure or drug therapy. "Many, if not all, of the biological correlates of crime could have a nongenetic basis. . . . Some of the biological correlates of crime may be indisputable, but their origins are not" (Andrews and Bonta, 1998).

We are suggesting a third school of thought, and that is choice—free will. The criminal chooses to commit crimes. Hare (1993) says "their behavior is the result of choice, freely exercised." Rhodes (1999) says "violent criminals describe in detail what they thought . . . when they committed murders, rapes or vicious assaults. . . . Thus . . . the data reveal that violent people consciously construct violent plans of action before they commit violent criminal acts." He goes on to say, "The debate, deep and basic—ultimately a debate about whether human behavior is predetermined or freely willed—continues to this day." However, he comes down on the side of free will. We all make choices. Sometimes the choices are very basic, but we still choose (Graham, 1991, 1993). Even to choose not to choose, means that we have chosen.

As we previously discussed, when we believe something or someone has caused criminals to commit their crime, we then are excusing the criminals. We are not holding them accountable and responsible for their behavior and we contribute to their denial system in that it is not their fault.

Again, Calvin of Calvin and Hobbes says, "I've concluded that nothing bad I do is my fault . . . Being young and impressionable, I'm the helpless victim of countless bad influences! An unwholesome culture panders to my undeveloped values and pushes me to malfeasance. I take no responsibility for my behavior! I am an innocent pawn! It's society's fault."

A recent cartoon provides a further example of this. A judge tells the defendant, "These are serious charges, young man! If you weren't abused as a child, you're going to be in a lot of trouble!"

It was society's fault, according to the *Herald and News* (1996) in the article "Portland Shooter Off to Prison for Crimes."

The man who stormed into a downtown office tower, shooting two people and taking others hostage, has been sentenced to 300 years in prison for crimes including attempted murder and kidnapping. . . . Rincker, whose attorney argued that he was insane, said, "It's hard to feel remorse in a society that pushes you into a corner . . . I have no problem with doing the rest of my life in prison. Let's get it over with."

An article by Susan Estrich (1993) summarizes this thinking:

There is no double standard of justice in America. If it proved nothing else last week, the much-criticized jury in the Reginald Denny beating case proved that.

The two black men who were videotaped beating innocent whites at the corner of Florence and Normandie got the same sort of leniency that allowed the white police officers video-taped beating Rodney King to win acquittals in their first trial and reduced sentences in their second.

Don't blame us, said the police—it's a jungle out there, and we're just trying to protect you. Don't blame us, said the Denny defendants—we were angry; we were just part of a mob. The sympathy defense is the hot growth stock in American criminal law.

Don't blame us, we were abused, say Lyle and Erik Menendez, the Beverly Hills brothers who confessed to murdering their parents. Don't blame me, I'm a mother and this man was suspected of child abuse, says Ellie Nesler, who was charged with murder in Jamestown, Calif. Don't blame me, I suffer from battered woman's syndrome and my husband was an abuser, even if he was asleep at the time, is the increasingly successful defense when women are charged with murdering their partners.

Other common "don't blame me" excuses include the following: Don't blame me because I am a minority; I am from the ghetto; I am poor; I am unemployed; the school system did not teach me, and on and on.

Andrews and Bonta (1998) offer these don't-blame-me rationalizations:

1. Moral justification: "It is all right to fight/lie/steal in order to protect your friends/to take revenge for your family."
2. Euphemistic language: "It is all right to fight/steal/take drugs when you are just joking/giving someone a lesson//just borrowing property/doing it once in a while."
3. Advantageous comparison: "It is all right to fight/lie/steal when others are doing worse/other acts are worse."
4. Displacement of responsibility: "You can't blame me if I live under bad conditions."
5. Diffusion of responsibility: "You can't blame me when the whole gang was involved/friends asked me to do it."
6. Distorting consequence: "No one was really hurt."
7. Attribution of blame: "If I misbehave, it is the fault of my teacher/parent."
8. Dehumanization: "It is all right to hurt those who deserve it."

A well-known family had two sons who went very different ways. One boy is in his fifties now and in the Oregon State Prison. He has been in prison most of his adult life. He was out for just a few months then came right back into prison. The other boy ran the family's trucking firm.

The boy's mother died when they were quite young, about five-to-seven years old. That was a difficult time for them and for their father. Their father began to drink. He eventually became very strict with the boys. He sent them to military school to provide them a strong discipline.

Eventually, he remarried. The youngest boy accepted the step-mother, but the older one absolutely refused. He kept rebelling, getting into more and more trouble. The father became increasingly harsh with him. Eventually, this boy wound up in MacLaren, an Oregon facility for youth who break the law. As he left MacLaren, he said to himself, "I am going to be the best burglar in the State of Oregon." This son spent the rest of his life in and out prison in his attempt.

If the circumstances of the mother's death, the father's discipline, his drinking, or the stepmother were the cause of the boy's criminality, then both boys would be criminals. Both boys made a choice. One boy chose to adjust and work this out. The other boy chose to misbehave and be a criminal. Society, bad mothers, bad fathers, and other conditions help influence that choice, but the ultimate choice belongs to the criminals themselves. "Not every shy young woman becomes a charismatic humanitarian, and not every frightened child becomes a violent criminal" (Rhodes, 1999).

Criminals choose their way of life and knowing the values of prosocial counselors, they manipulate them to get their own way and avoid accountability and responsibility for their behavior. "Most of us are accustomed to the idea that we are responsible for some of our actions, but not all of them. We consider ourselves responsible, for example, for the good deed that brings our neighbor and us together, or for responding to it positively, but we do not consider ourselves responsible for the argument between us and our neighbor, or for responding to it negatively. If we feed and clothe ourselves through our successful business, we credit ourselves. If we feed and clothe ourselves by burglarizing apartments, we blame our difficult childhood" (Zukav, 1990).

An individual in our program made significant efforts to change his lifestyle and seemed sincere (though only time will tell) about wanting to overcome his problems and difficulties. He was a heroin addict and an alcoholic. He told a story about being arrested in Portland, Oregon and being placed in the Justice Center. While he was in the Justice Center being held for trial, he decided that he wanted to be the very first individual to escape from there. He knew he was going to be returned to the state prison. Before returning, he wanted to go out on one last big weekend fling before he entered the state system again. The client went through a very elaborate and deliberate process to escape. In his escape plan, he relied on the bureaucracy to do several things. One was not to talk with each other. Another was society's belief in looking for causes.

He said he knew that when he got back into the system that he was not going to have to do any additional time for his escape. He was going to blame it all on his drug addiction. He said he had this planned weeks before he escaped. His plan was to come back and turn himself in after his big weekend fling. He was going to turn himself in to an alcohol/drug counselor. He planned on telling the therapist that he had escaped, and the reason he escaped was that he needed heroin. He said that while he was a drug addict, that was not his real reason for escaping.

He knew that this therapist would accept that excuse. He wanted to manipulate the therapist into telling the judge and the district attorney that this was the reason he escaped. And, it worked.

He was successful in going before the judge with the support of his therapist and the district attorney's office saying that he was an identified heroin addict and that was the reason he escaped. Because of this collaboration, he did not receive any additional time for the escape. Knowing the system's need to find causes allowed this individual to accomplish what he set out to do by placing responsibility for his criminal act on alcohol/drugs.

Stanton Samenow (1991) said there are myths about the causes of why people commit crimes. It is time we abandoned our search for causes of crime. Poor people do commit crimes, but so do rich people, and not all poor people commit crimes. Criminals use the excuse of childhood abuse as justification for committing crimes. It is important to remember that criminals lie about how much abuse they have been subject to. They know what prosocial counselors want to hear and will accept. Even if they were abused, not all abused children commit crimes. Criminals cause crimes!

A good example of the fact that criminals cause crime comes from *Clear and Present Danger*, by Tom Clancy, copyright © 1989 by Jack Ryan Enterprises Ltd., used by permission of G. P. Putnam's Sons, a division of Penguin Group (USA) Inc.

Henry and Harvey Patterson were twin brothers, twenty-seven years of age, and were proof of whatever social theory a criminologist might hold. Their father had been a professional, if not especially proficient, criminal for all of his abbreviated life—which had ended at age thirty-two when a liquor store owner had shot him with a 12-gauge double at the range of eleven feet. That was important to adherents of the behavioral school, generally populated by political conservatives. They were also products of a one-parent household, poor schooling, adverse peer-group pressure, and an economically depressed neighborhood. Those factors were important to the environmental school of behavior, whose adherents are generally political liberals.

Whatever the reason for their behavior, *they were career criminals who enjoyed their lifestyle* and didn't give much of a damn whether their brains were preprogrammed into it or they had actually learned it in childhood [emphasis ours] (Clancy, 1990, pp. 435-436).

Our stance is that we do not deal with causation. We focus on the clients' freedom of choice and their need to accept the responsibility for their behavior.

The idea of responsibility is foreign to criminals. Most of their past treatment experiences have dealt with looking at the reason they commit crime. What is the cause that forces them to criminal activity? Criminals are schooled at denying responsibility and accountability for their crimes. We have to overcome Calvin's cry of "I take no responsibility."

"It is better for you to take responsibility for your life as it is, instead of blaming others, or circumstance, for your predicament. As your eyes open you'll see that your state of health, happiness, and every circumstance of your life has been, in large part, arranged by you—consciously or unconsciously" (Millman's teacher to him, 1984).

Millman's teacher tells him a story about a construction worker who would open his lunchbox at noontime and complain about having peanut butter and jelly sandwiches. This went on for days, until one day one of the other workers said, "For crissakes, Sam, if you don't like peanut butter and jelly sandwiches, why don't you tell your ol' lady to make you something different?" "What do you mean my ol'lady? I'm not married. I make my own sandwiches."

Focusing someplace else rather than on the criminal is a reminder of the early days of alcohol/drug treatment. Most professional counselors working with alcoholics and addicts were looking for the symptoms—the reasons why the person drank or used. Not until we quit looking for the symptom or cause and began focusing on the fact that alcoholics drank because they were alcoholic did we begin to be able to assist alcoholics into recovery. We believe the same is now true of the criminal. We must stop looking for causes and address the idea that criminals commit crimes because they are criminals. It is not because they are poor, mistreated, abused, alcoholics, addicts, and so forth. They commit crimes because they are criminals! Dyer (1976) says, "I do not believe in fancy formulas or historical excursions into your past to discover that you were 'harshly toilet trained' and that someone else is responsible for your unhappiness."

The first decision that we have to make when working with the criminal population is to examine the idea we hold about the causes of crime. If we believe that there are causes for criminals' crime, then we are going to address the causes in society and not address the criminals' irresponsibility and unaccountability. We, then, will address the symptom and not the problem, and the criminal will continue to commit crimes. If criminals do not change their thinking, they never will get into recovery. Hawkins (1995) says it this way, "By taking responsibility for the consequences of his own perceptions, the observer can transcend the role of victim to an understanding that 'nothing out there has power over you.' It isn't life's events, but how one reacts to them and the attitude that one has as about them, that determines whether such events have a positive or negative effect on one's life, whether they're experienced as opportunity or as stress."

Most programs treating offenders have the offender complete an alcohol/drug autobiography. Some treatment programs even have the offender complete a criminal autobiography. Those biographies must go clear back to their earliest memories and include all crimes—whether or not they were arrested for them. Often, in reviewing these biographies, we find that the criminality began before the alcohol and drug use. They were pulling wings off flies before they took their first drink. Many criminals say that it was the power, excitement, and control that turned them on before the alcohol and drugs. The alcohol and drugs just heightened the sensations. Alcoholics do not commit crimes for the fun of it, but the criminal does, and that is the difference between prosocial and antisocial behavior. The Patterson brothers in Tom Clancy's novel loved what they were doing.

If we get bogged down in causation and do not address the criminal thinking and behavior of criminals, all the well meaning alcohol/drug therapy will not be successful in getting criminals to cease committing crimes. We have to move them out of their criminal behavior, past the manipulation, past the exploitation, and past the lying about how much they were or were not abused. We need to get them to see who the real victim is. Most of the time, we find that these individuals were not so much the victims as they were the victimizers. They were the predators.

We must get them to give up the blame game. "Removing blame means never assigning responsibility to anyone for what you're experiencing. It means that you're willing to say, 'I may not understand why I feel this way, why I have this illness, why I've been victimized, or why I had this accident, but I'm willing to say . . . that I own it. I live with, and I am responsible for having it in my life.' Why do this? If you take responsibility for it, then at least you have a chance to also take responsibility for removing it or learning from it" (Dyer, 2001). At this stage, it is time for the criminals to give up their personal history, Dyer's fifth principle. He goes on to state that one's personal history is like the wake of a boat. The wake does not drive the boat. It just comes along behind. The motor drives the boat forward. So it is with personal history. It does not drive behavior. The thought process drives the behavior. He says "It's my experience that most people live their life in the wake by hanging on to personal histories to justify their self-defeating behaviors."

Carlos Castaneda said, "One day I finally realized that I no longer needed a personal history and just like drinking I gave it up. That and only that has made all the difference in my life" (from *Journey to Ixtlan* by Carlos Castaneda, copyright 1972 by Carlos Castaneda. Reprinted by permission of Simon & Schuster Adult Publishing Group).

Thus, if we do not get them beyond this stage of denial, then we have found that treatment seldom is successful. Graham (1999) and Millman (1984) both tell a story about two monks who are traveling from one monastery to another monastery. They had been traveling for several hours and came to a stream. A young woman was standing on their side of the stream and could not get across, so the older monk picked her up and carried her across the stream. He set her down, and the two monks traveled on for several more hours. Finally, the young monk turned to the old monk and said, "We took a vow never to touch or look at a woman. You carried that woman across the stream." The older monk replied, "Yes I did, but I set her down. You are still carrying her." It is imperative that we get criminals to give up their past. They must set it down as they continue their journey on the road of recovery. The criminal is stuck in his position on the continuum until he can look beyond causes.

BEYOND DENIAL SYSTEM

We confront the denial system. As we address the thinking process of criminals and remove all excuses and causation for their behavior, we begin to get the criminals to take full responsibility for their behavior, past, present, and future. Our task is summed up in the following poem by Portia Nelson (1993).

Autobiography in Five Chapters

1) I walk down the street.
   There is a deep hole in the sidewalk.
   I fall in.
   I am lost . . . I am helpless.
   It isn't my fault.
   It takes forever to find a way out.

2) I walk down the same street.
   There is a deep hole in the sidewalk.
   I pretend I don't see it.
   I fall in again.
   I can't believe I'm in the same place.
   But it isn't my fault.
   It still takes a long time to get out

3) I walk down the same street.
   There is a deep hole in the sidewalk.
   I see it is there
   I still fall in . . . it's a habit.
   My eyes are open.
   I know where I am.
   It is my fault.
   I get out immediately.

4) I walk down the same street.
   There is a deep hole in the sidewalk.
   I walk around it.

5) I walk down another street.

What we are attempting to do is to get the criminals beyond their denial system. A comparison is in alcohol/drug treatment, where it is important for alcoholics or addicts to accept that they are alcoholics or addicted before they can begin recovery. Since they remain in denial about their addiction, they will not take the first step to become clean and sober. They will continue to use and drink. It is the same with criminals. As long as criminals remain in denial about their criminal behavior, they will continue to commit crimes. Therefore, a first order of business is to get the criminals to accept the idea that they are criminals. If we cannot move them through this denial about being criminals, they cannot get into recovery from committing crimes.

We use the word "criminal" the same way that we use the word alcoholic. We do not use the term as a derogatory remark—it is simply a term used to describe a particular behavior and activity that individuals have been engaged in for many years. The word "criminal" is offensive to some people. They say, or at least feel, that you do not call my brother, sister, mother, father, or me a criminal. This is much the same way the word "alcoholic" is offensive to some. Again, do not call me or a loved one an alcoholic. Sure, I drink a little too much, but I am not an alcoholic. Father Martin's video, "Chalk Talk," (1972) asks when is too much too much? You wait until he dies and then conclude he drank too much. Most alcoholics and drug addicts initially come into treatment denying their addictions until they have moved through their treatment process long enough and have developed some insights around their using patterns.

In alcohol/drug treatment, the words "addict" and "alcoholic" finally are accepted as terms used by recovering people to introduce themselves and signify, for the most part, that they have acknowledged and accepted their alcoholism and addiction. We believe it is much the same with criminals. When are they criminals? Sure, they do petty offenses; they are just lightweights. They only do small petty crimes, only property crimes. Do we wait until they rape, beat, or kill someone before we conclude that they are criminals? "Criminal" is used as a term that allows individuals to acknowledge and accept their criminality so that they may move into recovery. We believe that, like alcoholics, they will be criminals the rest of their lives. They simply will not be committing any more crimes. However, the minute their thinking returns unchecked to their former thought process, they will commit another crime. There are no ex-offenders—there are only recovering offenders who constantly must be alert to any thinking that allows them to avoid accountability and responsibility for their behavior. As has been said, they cannot even entertain these thoughts because the thought is the deed.

We have met very few criminals, in any criminal justice or treatment setting, who felt that they were, much less admitted that they were, guilty of their crimes. Our experience in the programs has been that the denials of many of these individuals around their criminality are as strong as or stronger than their denials around their alcoholism or drug addiction. "Although criminal behavior, in all of its forms, is not a disease, it is maintained by keeping it secret, calling it something else, rationalizing the effects, or simply pretending it does not exist" (Walsh, 2005).

When asked why he was in prison, one man in the Powder River program said that he was in prison because another person cheated at cards. We responded by saying that this was a new one on us. We had never heard of someone coming to prison because of someone else's behavior. He went on to say that he was playing poker with some people and one of them was cheating, so he stabbed him with his knife. We responded with, "Oh, so you are in prison because you cut someone with a knife." He came back with "No, I am in prison because he cheated. If he had not cheated, I would not have cut him." All of the other criminals around him were agreeing with him that he was not at fault—he was perfectly justified in stabbing the person. If this man were allowed to continue to believe that he was in prison because someone else had cheated at cards, then he is the victim. He will remain in denial, believing he was right in what he did. He will leave prison, and the next time someone cheats in a card game he is in, he will cut him also. If we do not move them beyond their denial about their crimes and being criminal, they will continue to commit crime after crime.

Remember the resident who felt he owned his ex-wife? He had gone in and beat his wife's boyfriend and felt justified in doing this because she was his wife. As long as he would not accept his crime and the fact that he was a criminal for committing the act, he would leave prison and assault someone else who he felt violated his rights.

Gordon Graham (1991) describes himself as a consumer of correctional services for seventeen years in Washington State. He talks about being in prison one time for five years. For all of those years, he told everybody that he was in prison because his partner could not drive a stick shift. They used his stick shift car to get to the place they were to rob. As they entered the place, the waiting police confronted them. As they fled from the scene, Gordon was shot. He yelled to his partner that he was shot and for his partner to drive them from the area. They jumped in the car, and as his partner started the car and put it in gear, he killed the motor. He restarted the car and they went leapfrogging down the hill with his partner not able to get the car going, as he had never driven a stick shift before. They got caught before getting off the hill. Thus, Graham claimed he was in prison because his partner could not drive a stick shift. It never occurred to him that he was in prison because he attempted to rob the dwelling.

We modified the Consortium program to include this antisocial model. One of our clients was a man who had been in treatment for approximately six months for raping his estranged wife. He had gone over to her house because he wanted to have sex with her. He proceeded to tie her spread eagle to the bed and sexually assaulted her. Although he had confessed to rape, he denied that he actually had raped her. He said that he only confessed to rape to get a lighter sentence, but he had not really raped her. She really liked to have sex this way and although she turned him in, this was really the way they usually had sex.

As could be expected, he was not doing well in treatment. He would not follow the rules, was aggressive in the program, and threatening to people outside the program. We began to confront him heavily about his denial concerning his crime. He steadfastly claimed he had not raped her and, no matter what, would not admit to it. We discharged him as untreatable. This client committed new crimes, absconded several times, always winding up back in jail. Each time he came to jail, he would call and ask to come back to treatment. Our conditions were always the same—"Are you willing to admit your crime of rape?" We told him that was the only way we could help him. Each time he would not make that admission, so we did not admit him to treatment.

After several additional arrests, he was willing to admit to his crime and was admitted back into treatment. After a short time in treatment and not getting his own way, he again began to deny the rape. As we confronted him frequently on this, he again absconded. Although he admitted his crime, he did not accept the truth that he had raped. We knew that he would continue to commit crimes until he was willing to move beyond denial. And he had one additional crime spree which included first-degree kidnapping, first-degree rape, first-degree sodomy, first-degree theft, theft by receiving, parole violation, assaulting a public safety officer, and resisting arrest.

Tim Allen of the television show *Home Improvement* spent some time in prison. He describes his prison experience and the denial of criminals in prison.

Prison is filled with guys in whom their lunatic is free. The lunatic is finally where he wants to be. He's in a place where lunacy works. The more of a lunatic you are, the better you get along with the other lunatics. Prison is a wonderful place for the lunatic to be since it's the lunatic in you that gets you there. The difference between the lunatic living in the outside world and killing time in prison is that inside the lunatic actually speaks. He goes, "I didn't do it." Or "if I had a chance to do it again I certainly wouldn't get caught." The lunatic is always in denial because he never admits the slightest responsibility.

"It was the other guy."

"If you'd trusted me to begin with, I would have shot them both, no reservations. Then I would have burnt down the bank."

One guy I met actually denied that he'd robbed the bank even though he was caught at the teller's window with a ski mask on and a shotgun in his hand. I said, "So why were you in the bank?"

"That part I don't know. I don't know why I walked in there."

"But you had a ski mask on!"

"It was cold!"

"You were holding a pump shotgun and wearing a ski mask; what did you think the response was going to be when you walked inside that bank?"

"Well, I didn't think they were all going to go nuts on me!"

Like I said, prison's a great place for the lunatic. As for me, let's be honest. I didn't do anything. I wasn't even there when the cops busted me. I was at my house, watching *Home Improvement*. I was framed! I didn't do it! And I was among guys who actually believed me.

From *Don't Stand Too Close to a Naked Man* by Tim Allen (1994) Hyperion, New York: Boxing Cat Production, Inc. Reprinted with permission.

"Prison is full of bullshit artists who get off on lying to you" (Rhodes, 1999).

INNOCENT UNTIL PROVEN GUILTY

Society provides many opportunities for criminals and even change agents to invoke the denial system. Some are built into our system and others play to our sense of being for the underdog. We may romanticize criminal behavior and often cheer when criminals get off. *Ocean's Eleven* and now *Ocean's Twelve* with Brad Pitt, George Cooney, Julia Roberts and others, are good examples of this. In these films, the good guys rob the bad guys and that is okay. *Thelma and Louise* (1991) is about two women out for a good time, and they end up killing one man, robbing a store, locking a policeman in the trunk of his car, and blowing up a trucker's truck. With the police on their tail, they commit suicide by driving off the Grand Canyon. And we cheer all the way. *Going in Style* (1979) starring George Burns, Art Carney, Lee Strasburg, and others is also a good example of the public romanticizing crime. Three old guys, bored with life, decide to put some spice into their life by robbing a bank.

Rhodes (1999) says, "I . . . believe that readers needed to be confronted with the full, ugly reality of violent crime not only to enlarge their understanding of these offenses but *to prevent them from romanticizing their perpetrators.*" Emphasis ours.

Our judicial system of innocent until proven guilty contributes to the denial system. There probably is not a better system, but it does promote denial. Lawyers often counsel people arrested for crimes to plead innocent. They do this in the face of overwhelming evidence to the contrary. Criminals plead innocent; yet, they know they are guilty. Their lawyers know they are guilty, and everyone else knows they are guilty, but we all pretend they are innocent. We go to such extremes as to have evidence dismissed, kept from the jury, or have only part of it introduced.

In the State of Washington, a woman secretly listened to a telephone conversation between her fourteen-year-old daughter and a young male friend. The mother overheard the young man telling her daughter that he had knocked an elderly woman to the pavement, breaking her arm, and snatched her purse. The young man was convicted using the woman's testimony that she had overheard. In 2004, the Washington Supreme Court overturned the verdict, saying Washington State's privacy law protected this young man's right to talk with the woman's daughter without being overheard. Even though the young man was guilty by his own admission, he cannot be convicted with the testimony of the mother. The case was thrown out.

The integrity of our society calls for the insurance that we do not send innocent people to jail. We would rather let ten criminals go free rather than send one innocent person to prison. (Though it is good to remember most criminals have committed ten crimes for every one for which they are arrested). And deep down we often wonder if innocent people are going to jail and prison. So often, high-profile murder cases raise the suspicion that the police have misbehaved. Films such as *The Shawshank Redemption* (1994) play to our sense of innocent people being wrongly sentenced. In this movie, an innocent man is sent to prison for the murder of his wife. We suffer with him as he is raped by other inmates. We continue to suffer with him as he is brutalized and abused by prison guards and the warden. We then applaud him as he becomes a hero of the inmates and cheer him as he escapes and gets even with the warden. Criminals are aware of our feelings and appeal to our value of not sending innocent people to jail and our occasional wondering if we do. They claim to be innocent and are often very convincing, and we doubt. In addition to portraying an innocent man sent to prison, *The Shawshank Redemption* romanticizes the criminal and incarceration.

The integrity of our system requires us to give each arrested person the best defense we can. Even if the persons are found guilty, lawyers continue to counsel them to maintain their innocent plea and denial of the crime. There could be, and most times will be, many appeals. So, the criminals continue the facade of innocence. Then, we get the criminals into treatment and they continue in their denial as they have been coached. They often tell us that their lawyers have instructed them not to admit anything. The lawyers even might promise that they can get the sentence reduced if not reversed—so they instruct the criminals to deny their crimes. This denial of their crimes is the major reason criminals are so very difficult to treat. If they have not committed a crime, then they are victims of the system, and it is the system that has to change—not the criminals.

Scott Peterson was convicted of murdering his wife and unborn baby on Christmas Eve, 2002. The jury recommended the death penalty. Within hours of the verdict, appeal possibilities were put forth (*Tri-City Herald*, December 14, 2004):

Stan Goldman, a law professor at Loyola University in Los Angeles, said the Peterson case "is an appellate lawyer's Petri dish;" offering a variety of issues on which to build future appeals. Among them, he said, are the circumstances that led two jurors to be dismissed during deliberations and the judge's refusal to instruct the jury to consider a manslaughter charge. The defense attorney requested a new jury and location for the penalty phase after jurors were exposed to the crowds that cheered Peterson's conviction. The denial of that request could provide another route to appeal, Goldman said.

America's self-imposed morality and ethics insure protection of citizens even in the face of letting a criminal go free. However right this may be, it does contribute to the denial system. There is an elephant in the living room, and we pretend it is not there.

PLEA BARGAINING

Another area that contributes to the criminals' denial system is the plea-bargaining system. We know that plea bargaining helps in clearing the court docket by providing for a lesser conviction when the original conviction is in doubt. But, it promotes denial.

A member of one of our groups had broken into a woman's house and raped her. The district attorney did not believe she had enough evidence to convict the man. However, she did feel she had enough evidence to convict him of burglary. The criminal was very willing to plead guilty to burglary, as opposed to rape.

When he came into prison and was asked the standard question of why he was in prison, his answer was, "Because I burglarized a home." Our response to him was that his actual crime was that of rape. He denied he had raped anyone. He referred us to his rap sheet that listed his crime of record as burglary. We told him that he knew and we knew that he had committed rape and plea bargained it down. His task was to get honest and own up to his original crime and not hide behind the reduced sentence. If he would not move beyond the denial, he would leave prison to rape again because in his mind, he is not a rapist.

An article in the *Herald and News Newspaper* illustrates this idea:

> The house of a convicted child molester accused in the slaying of two girls was set afire Saturday, possibly by neighbors angry about the killings, police said. . . . Howard Steven Ault was arrested Wednesday and jailed without bond on charges he killed half-sisters Alicia Sybilla Jones, 7, and DeAnn Emerald Mu'min, 11. . . . Police said he sexually molested one of the girls, strangled both and stuffed their bodies into his attic. . . .
>
> At the time of the slayings, Ault was under house arrest for molesting a 6-year-old in 1994 and was under investigation for molesting another girl last New Year's Eve. . . . Prosecutors in the 1994 case didn't feel they had a strong enough case to prosecute Ault and agreed to reduce the charges (Nov. 1966).

As you read the paper, review criminal histories, and watch court proceedings, you will become aware—repeatedly—of this denial phenomenon.

THE COMMUNITY'S NONACCOUNTABILITY

A further example of society's contribution to the denial system comes from the "Judge Lets Shoplifter off the Hook, Chastises Store for Selling Cigarettes" article:

> Leroy Kelley walked into a Lynnwood Safeway store last spring and walked out with two stolen packs of Marlboros in his coat pockets. On Aug. 20, Kelley walked into a courtroom to plead guilty to shoplifting and probably walked out with a smile on his face.
>
> South District Court Judge Robert Schillberg fined Kelley $1, then paid the fine himself to make a point about the hazards of smoking and limited law-enforcement resources. *"I think the store's more culpable than he is* [emphasis ours] for selling cigarettes," he told the attorneys during Kelley's

sentencing August 20. "Let's get it off your record. It's a waste of time, next case."

. . . Kelley, 27, has prior convictions for shoplifting, third-degree rape, malicious mischief, assault and resisting arrest. He also is a registered sex offender.

. . . "Four hundred thousand people get killed every year from cigarettes," he said. "Kelley is doing a foolish thing to begin with by smoking, and he's doing an illegal thing by stealing," he said. "But it's a much, much better utilization of resources than going out and trying to protect the sale of cigarettes. . . . To spend a lot of law-enforcement resources to go after one or two packs of cigarettes . . . Is that the most important allocation of resources?" he asked.

But Snohomish County Sheriff's Deputy Matt Onderbeke, who arrested Kelley, said the message being sent to other would-be shoplifters is "it's open season." "Why should this guy not go back to Safeway and steal again? And for that matter, why should I arrest him again?" Onderbeke asked.

He wondered how far Schillberg's reasoning could be carried. "Do we let people off for stealing steak because it causes cholesterol problems?" (Houtz, Jolyanne, 1993. "Judge Lets Shoplifter Off the Hook, Chasties Store for Selling Cigarettes." *Oregonian.* Reprinted from *Seattle Times.*)

Most of the many inherent messages to the criminal touch on denial. The judge minimized Kelley's behavior thus denying the seriousness of his criminal activity. Kelley was not a first-time teenage offender. He was a person who had hurt many other people by assault and rape. He allowed Kelley to deny his crime by blaming Safeway. Kelley now will say it is not his fault—it is Safeway's fault for having cigarettes for sale. Criminals receive the wrong messages from this approach.

In Portland, Oregon, in 1998, three young high school boys who were model citizens by day were robbers by night. They were led by an honor student who was liked by the other students. They came from good homes and excelled in most activities. They robbed for the thrill of it. When one boy was caught and gave up the other two, the ringleader fled to Mexico, where he was visited by his classmates on senior break. They protected him and cheered his escape and bravado. The school authorities and the parents were shocked that these boys were leading double lives. The police were outraged that their fellow students protected the ringleader while he eluded authorities for three months in Mexico. He was cheered by fellow students as he was brought back to Portland in handcuffs. The cheering of fellow students illustrates an attitude of glamorizing crime.

ALCOHOL/DRUG PROBLEM VERSUS CRIMINALITY

Another departure from traditional prosocial treatment philosophy for us is in the question, "Which came first, the criminality or the alcohol/drug problems?" We believe these clients are dual diagnosed when they get to us. When they present themselves to our programs, they are both alcoholics and/or drug addicts and they are criminals.

In debating this issue, we return to the great debate of yesteryear between mental health and alcohol/drug treatment professionals. Mental health professionals wanted to diagnose a mental illness as the primary diagnosis. Alcohol/drug professionals wanted to diagnose addiction as the primary diagnosis. Both admitted that besides the primary diagnosis, there were secondary diagnoses and were magnanimous in their assignment of the secondary diagnosis. However, the mental health field was prone to say, "Let us treat the mental health issues and then the alcohol/drug problems will diminish if not disappear." The alcohol/drug field cried, "Get the drugs and alcohol out of their system and then see if there is any mental health issue." They would go on to say that 90 percent of the time there was no need for further counseling. The field finally came to understand that it was a dual diagnosis and that a new treatment model was needed for this population.

For some clients, criminality came first. For others, addiction came first. Both diseases developed together for others. It is time to quit debating the issue of the chicken or the egg. It is time to stop asking, "Are they first alcoholics/drug addicts who commit crimes or are they first criminals who abuse alcohol and drugs?" We will never know which came first, nor does it matter. We have discussed the need for good diagnostic tests to assist us in evaluating the severity of a client's criminal mentality previously. We hope the thinking-pattern continuum will be helpful in this area. However, when is a criminal a criminal? When is an alcoholic an alcoholic? When is a cucumber a pickle? When is that exact moment when a cucumber turns to a pickle in the canning process? What we do know is that when we open the jar of pickles, they are pickles. Also, we know that when we get our clientele, they are criminals.

The disease concept is another area within the theme of criminality versus alcohol/drug addiction. We do believe in this concept; however, we do not emphasize it much in the first few months of treatment. Again, criminals will attempt to use their alcoholism as an excuse for their criminality. "It is not my fault I have a disease, the same as diabetes—and diabetes is not my fault." Therefore, we minimize the disease concept until criminals begin to understand their thinking and have found the ability to put brakes on their irrational thinking.

TRUST VERSUS EXPECTATION

In the area of trust versus expectation the antisocial model differs from the prosocial model. Most therapists, nurses, doctors, and others have been taught to establish a therapeutic bond of trust with clients/patients. As this bond strengthens, the clients become more willing to share their inner self. As they gain trust in the helping agent, they increasingly are able to reveal what is the matter. We have been taught that to really assist the client, it is important that the client trust us. This is important in working with prosocial people. Working to build that therapeutic bond between helping agent and client is beneficial.

Criminals are aware of our training and belief around this issue. They use our own values to avoid the therapeutic relationship, to escape accountability and responsibility for their behavior. They use trust issues much as they use feelings—to control others and to manipulate the situation. They will say things such as "I do not trust you enough to tell you that." They know that most often they will put the therapist on the defense—oh my goodness, why doesn't he or she trust me? What have I done wrong?

Criminals use this same line in dealing with the significant others in their life. They can control their response to them. They will say, "You never did trust me, no wonder I constantly screw up. If you would only trust me . . ." Trust for them means allowing them to do what they want without question. It means to believe them even when they lie. Their behavior is never to be questioned or challenged.

In an antisocial program, we are clear that trust is not an issue. We do not expect them to trust us. In their eyes, we are the man to be tricked, used, and manipulated. "The traditional therapeutic approaches can quickly lead staff into the psychological traps set by those who only desire to manipulate and deceive them"(Elliott and Verdeyen, 2002). They are constantly in a power struggle with us. Elliott and Verdeyen suggest that there is an imbalance of power in the correctional setting, especially in prisons, so the criminal is always trying to gain some power to control the staff by "engaging in deception and manipulative behavior intended to undermine the authority and influence of the staff."

They see us as their enemy. We are up front with them in that we do not trust them. We keep our office doors locked; many areas are off limits to clients. We have closely monitored treatment systems. If they call in sick, they either must come in for us to observe signs of illness or they must bring us a doctor's verification that they were sick. We also require them to give a urinalysis before excusing them to go home. If they claim to have an employment interview, a mental health appointment, or any other excuse for missing treatment, they are required to provide verification. There are many rules (expectations) and immediate consequences or what we call "learning experiences" for not meeting treatment expectations.

So, how do we establish any kind of therapeutic bond with criminals? Our relationship with criminals is built on expectation, accountability, and responsibility. They can expect us to do what we say we will do. We are consistent in the application and response to violation of program rules. We are immediate in our response. They do not have to wonder when we will respond. We do not manipulate them. We are up front in all areas of our dealings with them. We do not lie to them. We treat them with respect and dignity.

"You must have integrity in everything you do. You have to be up front, you have to be honest, you have to be fair" (Bartollas, 2004). We are firm, fair, and friendly—not friends—friendly. And we expect them to be and do the same. We are clear about our expectations and consequences. We expect them to be on time; we expect them not to use. We expect them to be respectful. We expect them not to escape or abscond, and to be in treatment.

They are always clear about where we stand. Out of this consistent behavior on our part, a bond begins to grow between clients and staff. We have seen that at the end of treatment, the clients really do not want to leave the program because of the strength of the therapeutic bond. Of course, when this method is used to build a therapeutic bond, the therapist has some very heavy responsibility and accountability to uphold. If we require this of the criminal, then, we must be willing to give it back in turn.

In the section on standing tall, we discuss the skills and attitudes needed by staff to be effective in working with criminals. In brief, it is very easy to see criminals with a tunnel vision when we constantly are confronted with their gross misbehaving, both in the crimes they commit and in their response to staff. It is hard to maintain a civil attitude toward them when they are manipulating staff to the point of ruining a career or throwing feces on them as they walk by. To see them as scum and treat them accordingly can become easy. But, we must resist this response. Staff is not asked to "hug a thug," but they are asked to "help the clients walk down another street."

The goal of treatment is to assist clients to live from their higher self or their authentic self. In *The Legend of Bagger Vance*, a caddy, Bagger Vance, comes out of nowhere to help Junah regain his golf swing. Junah had lost not only his golf swing in war, but his will to live also. In regaining his inner self-respect and integrity, he found his swing. Bagger Vance represents Krishna, an ancient Hindu god and Junah represents an ancient Hindu warrior about to go into war, but not wanting to (Pressfield, 1995). So, our job, much like Krishna's (and even if some people would scoff that it is impossible), is to help the criminal to regain his swing. We are to help him find an inner ethnical and intrinsic solution to his life instead of the criminal or alcohol/drug solution he has been using.

"Our goal is to treat inmates the way we would like to be treated, and the way we would like our father, brother, son, daughter, or close friend treated if they were in prison. We are not soft touches, we are not bleeding hearts; but we are individuals who hold to some basic truths about faith and morals" (Bartollas, 2004). It is appropriate to hold criminals accountable and responsible for their behavior. However, "it is not appropriate that we allow our actions to be motivated by feelings of indignation, righteousness or victimization" (Zukav, 1990).

SELF-DISCLOSURE

Another point of departure for staff from traditional alcohol and drug treatment is avoiding much self-disclosing about ourselves. "Self-disclosure means to communicate personal information to another who normally would not have that information" (Walsh, 2005). In traditional

116

counseling—following the lead of Alcoholics Anonymous—many programs encourage recovering counselors to share their stories. This is to help clients to become aware that they are not alone, to give clients hope that they too can attain a sober lifestyle. Most programs ensure that there is a good mix of recovering and nonrecovering staff to achieve this state and a balance.

This has limitations when working with criminals. First, criminals constantly are fishing for information to sidetrack the therapist and/or to invalidate or use the therapist. The more they know about the therapist, the more they can manipulate the therapist. "Correction employees should be mindful that their behavior is under continuous surveillance by inmates. Any hint of interpersonal relationships or conflicts involving staff members is especially popular subjects" (Elliott and Verdeyen, 2002). Therefore, we discourage much self-disclosure from staff. We encourage them not to self-disclose in group or individual sessions. We instruct staff to be very careful not to self-disclose to other staff in the presence of clients. Clients are always listening to pick up any tidbits they can. If staff is discussing the night before or any trouble they have had, the client stores that away for future use. We encourage staff not to decorate their office with pictures of the family or personal information.

A staff member was proud of how he dressed. Generally, he wore a sports suit and a tie. One morning at work, a new resident complimented him on his attire. The staff member thanked him and kept on walking through the dorms. The next morning, the resident was in the same spot again and made further compliments about his attire. The staff member again thanked him and continued down the room. The third morning, the resident was again on post to compliment the staff member. He said something to the effect that the staff member must really own many good clothes, must be really proud of the way he dressed, and so forth. This time the staff member stopped. He told the resident that this was the third consecutive morning the resident had made a point of complimenting him on his attire.

The staff member informed the resident that he knew that the resident was fishing to learn how proud he was about his attire. This could be used to sidetrack this staff member. It might be used to attack him someday if he were not as well dressed one day and was confronting the resident. Could he somehow defocus onto the staff member's attire to avoid having to address the real issues? He continued to inform the resident that he had thanked the resident for his compliments on two

117

previous mornings; however, he did not need or want the resident's approval and informed the resident to refrain from any further comments about his attire. Of course, the resident immediately went into the victim stance—after all he was just being nice, and perhaps he was, but most likely he was not. Only time would tell.

An example of being cautious in revealing anything to clients, even in discussing personal things with other staff, comes from the Consortium. A staff member was excited about working in the program and living in the community. He was enthusiastic about getting a home, a boat, and going fishing. The staff member shared his enthusiasm with other staff and was not too particular about whether clients were around or not.

He lived about thirty miles from town on his favorite fishing river. One morning, a female client showed up at his house. She implied that her most recent urinalysis was going to be positive, and she wanted to persuade him to cover it up. She intimated that she was willing to do most anything to cover up the results of her urinalysis. He refused and reported it to his supervisors. The client was confronted on her behavior. However, by listening to conversations of this individual, she believed she could compromise him. One of the ways in which staff can unwittingly permit boundaries to be violated by inmates is by disclosing personal information (Elliott and Verdeyen, 2002).

Another area, beyond self-disclosure, involves having recovering criminals on staff. Following the philosophy of hiring recovering addicts and alcoholics, we wanted to make sure that we hired ex-offenders at Powder River. We found that here was another place that the criminal thought differently then we did. If you tell criminals that you are like them and know exactly what they are going through and how they feel, then in their mind, you have lost accountability with them. They know what they are like and if you are like them, then you lie, manipulate, are conniving, and hurt people for your own benefit. It you are like them, then, they will discount you immediately.

However, not all authors agree with the premise of not disclosing. Walsh (2005) supports the Alcoholic Anonymous' concept of self-disclosure as important. He states "one of the most important qualities that criminal justice workers should possess is the willingness to share themselves with others, including offenders, through self-disclosure." He believes that self-disclosure is a good form of modeling; it gives the offender a new perspective and the change agent's self-concept is enhanced. And the self-concept, through self-disclosure, may be improved, but this self-disclosure probably is best done in one's own therapy sessions. Also, it is important to understand that self-help groups, including Alcoholics Anonymous, are peer-to-peer relationships where self-disclosure is beneficial. However, the correctional change agent is never in a peer-to-peer relationship with the correctional client.

If individuals working with criminals are recovering criminals or recovering alcoholics/addicts, then they must use that fact very carefully. This fact is not to be used until they are sure that criminals have begun to manage their own thinking correctly. When the self-disclosure is made, it is best to present it in terms that you used to be like the criminal. You used to think like the criminal, but that your thinking has changed and results in the changes being demonstrated today. This is a very delicate balance both for recovering alcoholics/addicts and criminals. Gordon Graham (1999) says, "Me too, but I don't do that any more." He makes it clear that his behavior today is much different than when he was using criminal thinking and behavior.

Walsh (2005) also offers some cautions concerning self-disclosure. He states "the offenders' problems must be the focus of any . . . counseling session. . . . Therefore, the worker's self-disclosure should be infrequent, relevant, and focused." It should be added that any self-disclosure always needs to be for the benefit of the client. Often we have seen, both in alcohol/drug treatment, mental health settings, and in criminal justice arenas, that change agents' self-disclose is an unconscious attempt to continue to work out their own problem. Any self-disclosure that benefits the change agent may be suspect even if it does enhance the change agent's self-concept. It is evident that self disclosure in Alcoholics Anonymous meetings is a vehicle not only to assist the new member but to assist the teller in keeping alcohol free.

Not only should we assess the client's ability to process the change agent's self-disclosure with the proper thinking process, but we should assess the change agent's ability to respond to any manipulation of this information by the client. A seasoned change agent, who is very secure in his or her self-identity, may self-disclose and be able to reflect back to clients any attempts to use this information to escape accountability and responsibility for his or her actions. However, newer staff may find this much more difficult and thus should avoid it.

"Employees must constantly ask themselves if and when it is appropriate to disclose personal information . . . to inmates. The staff members must be certain that he or she is not revealing something that can be misused. This is a tall order, because even seemingly innocuous self-disclosures can backfire" (Elliot and Verdeyen, 2002).

It is very important to be cautious about what we disclose and when. We will return to this topic when we discuss counselor's ethics when working with criminals. Later in this book is an example of a "Set-Up" of how personal information shared in an Alcoholic's Anonymous meeting came back to haunt a staff member.

In summarizing the topics of trust versus expectation, self-disclosure, thinking versus feeling, alcohol/drug treatment versus treatment for criminality and causation, Gendreau (1994) notes:

> Principles of ineffective interventions are grounded in therapeutic approaches that have little in common or are antagonistic to behavioral methods. . . . Offender treatment programs that have been based on these approaches have emphasized the following processes: a) "Talking" cures; b) Fostering positive self-regard . . . e) Self-actualization through self-discovery; f) Externalizing blame to parents, society; g) Ventilating anger . . . h) Change in diet; i) Plastic surgery; j) Pharmacological, e.g., testosterone suppressants, and k) Subcultural and labeling approaches.

PRAISE

As we continue to review the dynamics of an effective treatment program for working with criminals, another area of difference is when to give praise or rewards. An old saying seems to fit here: "one 'aw shit' wipes out a 100 'atta boys.'" In other words, one criticism wipes out all the praise we may give to someone. Thus, change agents have been taught to use as much praise as possible to reinforce a client's progress. When they reduce unwanted behavior, the therapist is to tell them "well done." When they have begun a new positive behavior, the counselor is encouraged to stroke them for their beginning success. Much is written about the need to provide a "four to one" ratio (Andrews and Bonta, 1998) in giving rewards over criticism.

For criminals, this has just the opposite effect. One "atta boy" reward wipes out all the criticism of their life. When they are given praise, they accept that praise as excusing them for all past misdeeds, all present misdeeds, and all future misdeeds. When you say to criminals that they are doing well, then everything else in the past that they have done wrong has been wiped out by the praise. Everything in the future that they do is also wiped out by the praise.

After having praised them for something or other, if the next day you point out a rule violation, they will respond by reminding you about how you had praised them the day before. When someone attempts to hold criminals accountable for any behavior, they will throw up the fact that they were complimented the day before by another staff member. On their own, they are unable to distinguish one from the other. They only see what they want to see. It is much like the previous discussion of criminals seeing themselves as good guys. Criminals see their occasional act of kindness, sensitivity, or caring as completely negating their acts of violence and criminal behavior.

When you praise criminals, it is really important that you do it very literally. You want to tell them that they have done a good job right now, but this has nothing to do with what they have done in the past. It has nothing to do with what they will do in the future. You say that what you want to do is praise them for what they did just at this moment. For reinforcement to be taken in the right attitude, it is important to "elaborate the reason why the approval is being offered (in other words, exactly what it is you agree with or approve of)" (Andrews and Bonta, 1998). You continue by telling them that you do not want them to apply the praise to the past or to the future but just to understand that it is for this deed right at this moment and nothing else. Thus, when praising criminals, you have to do it so they understand that your praise is just for the moment.

However, with these two premises in mind-criminals use praise to justify their misbehaving and the need to give out rewards—the Consortium Day Treatment Program began a "Recognition Token System." This is called "Contingency Management" in the literature. "Developing an incentive system, similar to a sanctions schedule, provides an opportunity to formalize recognition for good behavior so that restraints on the offender are reduced as progress occurs. An incentive system should be swift, certain, and progressive in the same fashion as a sanction system" (Montague, 2001).

We already had instituted the learning experiences or consequences for misbehaving. This is discussed in the section on rules and in the appendix. But, we wanted to develop a system that also could give immediate reinforcement for good behavior and yet not give the criminals an opportunity to use the reinforcement to excuse misbehaving. Similar to the intensity of misbehaving in the section on treatment intensity, reinforcement also needs to "stress the density of the rewards and costs. 'Density of reinforcement' refers to the number, variety, quality, and magnitude of rewards as well as the immediacy, frequency, and regularity with which they are delivered" (Andrews and Bonta, 1998).

"Contingency management, the systematic reinforcement of desired behaviors and the withholding of reinforcement or punishment of undesired behaviors, is an effective strategy in the treatment of alcohol and other drug use disorders" (Higgins and Petry, 1999).

Because Consortium-evaluation funding ran out in 2000, no research data is available. However, our empirical evidence suggests a marked improvement in desired treatment behavior of clients when we used contingency management.

Next, we will describe what the Consortium system entailed and explain our belief that it improved client retention and progress. We also describe what others say about contingency management. An old adage is that you cannot help them until they are willing to help themselves, and clients should be in treatment for treatment's sake. So, any monetary rewards to encourage treatment engagement or retention have been suspect. However, in the last few years, there has been a move to evaluate contingency management as a component in alcohol and drug treatment. (See the literature on Motivational Interviewing.) Whether it is effective with criminals is still open for discussion.

The Consortium's policy statement to clients states: "It is the Consortium's goal to assist clients to become productive members of our community and to lead a healthy lifestyle. We believe clients must remain crime free, abstinent from mind-altering chemicals, and develop a clean and sober support system. To accomplish this, clients must be held accountable and responsible for their behavior." Our experience and research show that it is equally important to emphasize the growth and positive accomplishment of each client.

We developed a reward system as an indication to the client and to their peers of the positive change taking place. Our reward system was not intended to alleviate past wrongs or excuse future behavior, but to acknowledge current desirable behavior. It is necessary to show accomplishment for a specific time and action. The following guideline is intended to give clients an opportunity to earn points toward a goal to reinforce desirable behavior.

The clients earned one point for each of the following behaviors:

- having punctual attendance at group
- submitting to an urinalysis as scheduled
- having a clean urinalysis
- turning in outside support-group meeting attendance slips
- completing and presenting homework in group

They could earn two points for the following: paying their bill on time and two additional points for paying their bill ahead of time. When the client accumulated fifteen points, he was awarded a token. This token could be turned in immediately for a reward or could be saved and combined with subsequent tokens for a larger reward. Once a point was earned, it could not be lost for other misbehavior. The misbehavior was handled according to the learning-experience grid—separate from this reward system. This is in keeping with other contingency-management protocols. "Incentives cannot be lost once earned" (Stranger, 2003).

In keeping with the philosophy of the program, the therapeutic community has no secrets. We place a community board in the client's common room listing each client's name. We note the points the clients earn on the board where all clients can monitor and keep track of points they and others earned. Empirical evidence that the program is working is the cluster of clients who gather around the posted token board at the beginning of each treatment day or evening to see where they or their peers are on the board. Retention has increased along with an increase in all rewarded behavior.

Patients assigned to the contingency management group remained in treatment significantly longer and reduced cocaine use relative to patients in the 12-step group. . . . Three-quarters of the patients in the voucher condition completed treatment, compared with 40 percent of patients who received the same behavioral therapy without the vouchers. . . . In one study at an HIV drop-in center, we found that providing reinforcement increased attendance at groups from an average of less than one patient per week to over seven per week and that reinforcing compliance with goal-related activities increased compliance rates from less than 30 percent to over 65 percent (Petry, Copyright © 2002 by CMP

Media LLC, 2801 McGaw Avenue, CA 92614, USA; Reprinted from *Psychiatric Times* with permission).

A research program that employed a contingency-management regime very similar to the Consortium program's was "Contingence Management and Treatment Engagement in a Sample of Cocaine-using Methadone Patients," presented by Grace A. Rowan-Szal, Ph.D. and D. Dwayne Simpson, Ph. D., who said (2002):

> Patients earned stars for target behaviors and these were placed on an incentive chart. Target behaviors included: individual and group session attendance, cocaine-free urinalysis, and progress toward treatment goals. Stars were traded for rewards, such as restaurants, groceries, gas, video rental, phone cards, or movie coupons. One star was given for individual sessions and group sessions. Two stars were given for clean urinanalysis and goal completion (per task). Eight stars were given for bonus weekly attendance. A maximum of 50 stars could be earned.

	Reward group	No reward group
Sessions attended first six months:	2.6	2.3
Times methadone dose "held"	0.4	0.84
Cocaine use during treatment	29%	54%
Cocaine use posttreatment	37%	52%

In summary, contingency-management patients attended more individual sessions, were less likely to have their methadone dose "held," and had fewer cocaine-positive urines.

SECRETS

Because of the convict code, it is important to teach the clients that there are no secrets in the programs. Everything is posted on Front Street. What is said in group can be used outside of group to benefit a resident or help a client be responsible and make appropriate changes.

The saying, "what is said in group stays in group," is not applied in the programs. This approach is embraced to eliminate the keeping of secrets, which is the criminal's most sacred behavior. Among the first areas to address in treatment with criminals is to ensure that no secrets are kept. When criminals are given permission to keep any kind of secret, they discount the therapist; they think they control these sessions, situations, and the counseling. They believe they are in a conspiracy with their counselor. In the past, this is what has diluted the counselor's ability to be effective with the criminal population.

Hare (1993) described his first experience in a maximum-security prison after receiving his master's degree in psychology. Immediately, the inmates began to test him. His first client violated a rule and then waited to see whether Hare would report the rule violation. For a variety of reasons, Hare did not report him and commented, "Ray had caught me in his trap. From that first meeting on, Ray managed to make my eight-month stint at the prison miserable." He relates how this inmate showed up in his life on his first job after receiving his Ph.D. This account shows what can happen when we agree to keep secrets with the correctional client.

"Staff members who have been conned need to discuss the situation with other employees and make sure that the inmates know that such a discussion has taken place" (Elliott and Verdeyen, 2002). Remember the previously described woman who showed up at the staff member's home to entice him to cover up her dirty urinalysis? He immediately shared that information with the other staff members and she was confronted in group, both to correct her, but also so all clients knew that we kept no secrets.

As we will discuss in the section on networking, counselors would keep secrets from the probation officer. An example is the information that the client had used drugs over the weekend. The thinking went something like this: "You (the client) have been doing well in treatment. We know that if this is reported to your parole officer, he will violate your probation. Since this is your first dirty urinalysis and you have been doing well in treatment, we will not share this information with the parole officer."

Our approach is that there will be no secrets from anyone who is involved in the client's treatment. "If the counselor will keep these secrets, then why can't I?" asks the client. Therefore, there are no secrets from staff, other residents, or parole officers. Everything is open.

When clients use drugs and bring it to our attention or come up positive on a urinalysis, they are instructed to share this information immediately with their parole officer. We also follow-up and share the information.

In one group session, a woman told the group that she was cheating on welfare. She said that she had not told welfare officials that she was in a residential treatment facility. So, welfare was still giving her child support checks each month. We asked her what she wanted us to do with this information. Her reply was that she did not want us to do anything with this information. She just wanted us to know about it. The counselor replied by stating that she wanted us to share a secret with her and that we were unwilling to do this. We would not be a part of her antisocial behavior.

She had several choices. With our support she could inform welfare of her fraud; we could inform welfare of her fraud, or she could drop out of treatment. After considerable counseling, she agreed to share the information with welfare.

Our program often made recommendations to the Motor Vehicle Department so that a client could secure an occupational driver's license after having lost that privilege because of a drunken driving conviction. In our recommendation, we had to attest to the fact that we did not think the client would drink and drive. Most often the client was required to be completely abstinent from alcohol. If we had evidence that the client was drinking, we were to notify the department of this. One of our staff frequented a local bar (off-duty behavior is discussed later). One evening while there, he observed a client who had an occupational license drinking. The next day, staff discussed this and although the staff member was reluctant to report the incident, we felt we could not keep this secret and maintain our integrity with either the clientele or with our partner, the Motor Vehicle Department. The next time the staff member visited the bar, he was asked to leave and not return. There is a price to pay for not keeping secrets, but there is a far greater ethical commitment to good treatment.

In using this book to teach cognitive-restructuring classes in the applied psychology program at the Oregon Institute of Technology, we had students attend group meetings at our program and other treatment facilities to learn firsthand the ideas we were teaching in the class. We emphasized that they had to report all contact with clients they encountered in the community. This included personal relationships, business dealing, and recreational contacts. Two women students were partying at a local attraction and observed a client drinking. The client saw them and knew they had seen him. In fact, he even asked one of them to dance with him. When they reported this in class, they were upset and unsure what to do. We insisted that they report this in group the next time they were in group with this client. Of course, this raised all manner of concerns. What would the client do? Would he harass them? Would he deny it? However, if this was not reported, then the client would believe that he and the students had a secret from the staff. The students and the program would lose credibility. The students could be blackmailed by the parolee because they had not reported the incident. Therefore, the students did bring this up in group and even though the client would never admit being in the bar, let alone drinking, we took appropriate action with the client. In fact, he did harass them and even threatened them. The program and the probation office dealt with this.

In the Powder River therapeutic community, a board in the common's room listed all of the learning experiences assigned to clients for misbehavior. Everything was out in the open. All clients were listed, and we held them accountable for their behavior (see the next section). Earlier in a discussion of an incentive program, we described a board in the common's room listing clients' rewards. There can be no secrets. Secrets undermine the program's integrity and set staff up for intense manipulation and exploitation by clients. This even can lead to the discharge of staff for violating program rules.

Where does confidentiality fit into all of this? It is our contention that with criminals, some confidentiality promotes their secrets and criminal lifestyle. Because of this, there is a requirement to sign releases of information to the community corrections department, the releasing authority, and the courts. Clients are not forced to sign! They may choose not to sign. However, we will not admit them to our program if they do not sign.

Also, staff cannot keep silent about fellow staff behavior that crosses the line or is in violation of our code of ethics and behavior. This is called "The Code of Silence" (Bartollas, 2004) and is discussed in the chapter on Standing Tall.

chapter 4

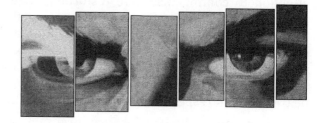

The Therapeutic Community

A therapeutic community is vital to the success of a program that attempts to work with criminals. Lipton (1996) says:

> . . . evaluative studies of therapeutic community programs in several states, targeted to diverse populations and including offenders with histories of violent offending, substantiate major accomplishments with incarcerated drug-abusing felons. The studies show remarkably consistent reductions in recidivism for offenders who complete the programs. . . . The evaluations show that therapeutic communities can produce significant reductions in recidivism among chronic drug-abusing felons and consistency of such results over time.

There are two types of therapeutic communities. One is what is normally called the Mental Health Therapeutic Community where everybody is equal, both the residents/clients and the staff. All decisions are made by team consensus. Everybody has equal weight. The other therapeutic community is the Synanon model. Each new client is reduced to his or her lowest level. Clients cannot speak unless spoken to. They may be made to wear diapers. Their hair is cut off. In other words, they are broken clear down and then built back up.

Programs that concentrate on the relationship principle without attention to contingencies are disturbing. Equally disturbing are programs that take the contingency principle to the extreme and focus on confrontation with name calling, humiliation and abuse. Yelling at and otherwise abusing people contingent upon expressions of procriminal sentiments or behavior is not consistent with the relationship or structuring principles of effective interaction. In human service, people should be treated with respect, concern and care (Andrews and Bonta, 1998).

In developing the Powder River program, we reviewed the literature made available by Stay'n Out, the New York State prison-based therapeutic community program, and we visited the Oregon State Hospital's Cornerstone program. We also reviewed program material from the New Outlook Therapeutic Community and the St. Clair Correctional Facility managed by the Alabama Department of Corrections.

We took the middle ground between both programs where the staff was the rational authority but residents/clients had a say in the program. We developed the programs, we set the rules, we set the parameters, and then, we said to the residents/clients, "You run the program under our supervision." We invited the residents'/clients' input and we invited their suggestions. We established a way for them to give us formal input, but we were the final deciding factor. Staff does the therapy, leads the groups, and handles the individual counseling. Everything else is done primarily by the residents under staff supervision and staff direction with many rules to follow. Later, we discuss the importance of following rules as part of inmate discipline.

Because of the hierarchy, we have a stratified community in a therapeutic community. When residents/clients first come into the program, they get the menial tasks and chores. They are called "crew members." Then, as they progress in the program, they can become crew chiefs, department heads, and eventually serve on the council. The council is like the board of directors for the community. This therapeutic community provides a variety of opportunities for practicing personal growth and change, in both individual and group settings.

The therapeutic community can be distinguished from other major drug treatment settings in two basic ways. First, the primary "therapist" and "teacher" in the therapeutic community is the group of people in treatment itself. This includes peers and staff (mainly peers) who are role models of successful personal change and serve as guides in the recovery process. Second, unlike other programs, the therapeutic community offers a more systematic approach to achieve its main objectives. For the

Consortium, this objective is to help clients stop using alcohol and drugs, and to stop committing crimes and hurting people.

A therapeutic community is a positive environment where people who have similar problems, such as criminality and alcohol and drug abuse, work together to better their lives. Participants strive to earn better privileges, jobs, and status within the community and its level system. They work to show growth and change. Residents work to move up the ladder or chain of command. They accomplish this by complying with the rules, attending functions regularly, participating in all program activities, and doing all current jobs well. Peers and staff work together to help all clients achieve these objectives. This includes clients addressing issues with other clients in groups and in additional sessions. They learn responsible thinking and truthful ways to act; then in the therapeutic community, they practice what they have learned.

When they make a mistake, they are confronted and then practice some more. They continue this routine until they go out into the regular community. This provides practice in living a responsible and truthful life. They hold one another accountable for these goals in the community and on an individual basis. "When both staff and clients support expressions of anticriminal efforts, a therapeutic community of some criminological potency has been created" (Andrews and Bonta, 1998).

We learned one important truth at Powder River and at the Consortium. The criminal clients know what is happening with each other far before and much better then we in the system (corrections and treatment) do. At Powder River, the community of clients knew when an escape was coming off, when some clients were bringing in contraband, or when a gambling ring was operational. In the community, at least in small rural communities, such as Klamath Falls, there already is a community of criminals in the community at large who know when crimes are being committed, and so forth. Both in Powder River and in Klamath Falls, they protect each other, cover for each other, and keep secrets and work to get one over on the community. Thus, in the therapeutic community, we require them to hold each other responsible, to confront each other on what they know about what each is doing, not only in the program but in the community.

We attempt to build a responsible community within the larger criminal community. Instead of covering up for each other, we teach and require them to reveal and confront each other. Two thoughts inherent in this confrontation are a breaking of the convict code that criminals hold and another core element of the antisocial model requiring absolute accountability and responsibility for all of the criminals' action and behaviors. Again, the therapeutic community is directly opposite the convict code.

Each week, the group of residents develops written reports for staff. This report is generally a single-spaced twenty-page typewritten report about what is happening in the departments and community. The supervisors of the programs sit down with the coordinating council and discuss what is happening based in part on these reports.

In the Consortium, the program was structured in an attempt to develop a therapeutic community in a day reporting/day treatment program. There were fewer departments, client roles, and formal, written reports

A therapeutic community is much more difficult to achieve in an outpatient setting, if it can be accomplished at all in that setting. Appendix C describes the therapeutic community developed in the Klamath County Jail Alcohol and Drug Treatment program and is reflective of the therapeutic community at Powder River and, to a lesser degree, the Consortium Day Treatment Program. The Jail Treatment program is discussed in much more detail in the last section on programs and development.

RULES

As we have said, one of the criminal's greatest means of excitement comes from breaking the rules and getting away with it. If he cannot get away with it, he wants to at least spin the change agent. In an earlier section, we discussed the "pushpin" caper of one of our clients. We also talked about the person who became a counselor. He had shared how what he missed was the excitement of setting up the drug buy, getting into the alley, making the buy, and getting out without getting caught.

This is very different from prosocial thinking. Criminals enjoy breaking the rules; prosocial people, for the most part, feel guilty when they break rules, especially when they are caught. If we jaywalk and receive a ticket, we probably will not jaywalk for a while. Criminals are going to try to figure a way to jaywalk without getting caught, or they will try to blame the system for their getting caught.

In "The Family Circus," cartoon, the oldest child asks, "Mommy, what does Y-E-S spell?" She replies, "Yes." Then, the child goes to his father and says, "May we have a Popsicle, Daddy? Mommy said yes!" The father gives them the Popsicle. While eating it, the oldest says, "Doesn't taste as good as usual, does it?" The youngest boy remarks, "Nope." For criminals, the response would have been just the opposite. For them, it would have tasted much better than if they had gotten it honestly.

Thus, we establish rules (expectations) for every phase of treatment and even rules for their home life. We leave nothing to chance. In Powder River, we went so far as to have expectations for how their shoes were to be lined up under their bunks and how the corners of their beds were to be made. We have rules for how they dress, how they make telephone calls, and how they eat. We attempt to have an expectation for every situation in which they find themselves. We even have rules for the sake of rules. If they cannot follow these simple program rules, such as how they place their shoes, they will not be able to follow more important rules of society, such as do not rob, do not beat, do not rape, and so forth.

It is vital that they follow these rules even if they seem trivial, such as putting shoes one certain way under the bed. Staff need to make sure that the clients do not violate any of these rules without a response from staff, no matter how trivial. What staff is doing if they see clients break a rule and do not bring it to their attention is giving them permission to not only break that rule but every other rule. Even if you do not see or are not aware that they broke a rule and the criminals think you are aware or did see it, they claim permission to ignore all rules. "An important role for the . . . worker is to serve as an anti-criminal model for clients. . . . Pro-criminal expressions include . . . tolerance for rule violations" (Andrews and Bonta, 1998). Clients need to see "that rules are actually enforced, for both staff and inmates" (Bartollas, 2004). A side observation by Elliott and Verdeyen (2002) is that they "have noted that staffs that tend to overlook minor rule infractions by inmates are at an even higher risk for manipulation."

We made room inspections at Powder River. One day, one resident was written up for not having his clothes hung correctly. His defense was that they had been hanging that way for a week and no one else had said anything. He did not feel it was right that he now was going to be written up for it. It did not matter to him that he knew what the rule was and had decided to ignore it. Because he had been doing it that way and no one had challenged him on it, that made it okay to do it that way any time.

Again, this illustrates the need to be consistent in addressing the expectation of violation. Later, we will discuss how easy it is to get in what we call "white zones" and miss some of these details. For the criminal, excusing or ignoring violations is a green light to break rules.

In walking through the dorm one day, a staff member noticed a resident with his shirt sleeve unbuttoned, a violation of a dorm rule. He was reminded of the rule and instructed to button his sleeve. He complied. About half an hour later in walking through the dorm, a staff member noticed that he had the same button unbuttoned. Again, the staff member stopped and instructed him to button the sleeve. Again, he complied. Yes—you guessed it—half an hour later, the button was unbuttoned. This resident was just testing the staff and having fun doing it. Criminals very often set up situations to see if we will notice that they have broken a rule and they wait to see what our response will be. "She told us before the group that she was going to throw you some bait and see if you'd bite" (Elliott and Verdeyen, 2002). Of course, the manner and attitude in which you confront this behavior is very important.

Remember, our silence is permission to break rules—no matter whether big rules or small rules. Whether concerning behavior or thinking, criminals will interpret the therapist's or other staff members' silence as agreement with what the criminal has just said or done. So, it is important to challenge their thinking and not remain silent. To remain silent reinforces criminals' thinking. Many drug dealers will admit that they sold drugs, but will qualify this by saying that they did not sell to children. If the counselors remain silent and do not challenge that comment, then they are telling the clients that they are not really bad at all since they did not sell to children.

Of course, if you have rules, the clients are entitled to know what consequences or learning experiences will result if they do not follow the rules or expectations. We must be clear, both in articulating the rules, and in clarifying the results of not following the expectations. "In other words, staff and inmates don't have to guess what's expected or required; they know because it's been communicated" (Bartollas, 2004). Appendix A outlines the program rules and consequences for violating the rules in the Consortium Center program. These are similar to the rules and consequence most programs have that are working effectively with the criminal population.

One psychologist notes, "Children obey mandatory rules not because they necessarily want to, but because they have no choice. The rules are stated clearly to avoid, or at least to minimize, misinterpretation and misunderstanding. Parents not only follow through to see that the rule is obeyed, but to the best of their ability to make sure that it is consistently obeyed" (Brodenhamer, 1983). If you substitute the word "criminal" for the word "children" and "counselor" for the word "parent," this quotation has the same wisdom for working in an antisocial program.

All program rules must be agreed on by all staff. All too often, management makes the rules and passes them down to line staff. This most often will not work. "The days are over and done where line staff is relegated to playing subservient roles; officers just being guards and food service people just putting a ladel of food on a tray. It goes well beyond that" (Bartollas, 2004). Bartollas notes, "If the staff is not involved in the establishment of the rules, they often will not insist on the clients following them and the staff themselves will not follow them." So, from the beginning, all staff (janitor, secretary, teacher, assistant, volunteer, clinician, supervisor, and management) must be involved with the creation of the rules and the consequences.

How the staff reach agreement is open to discussion. The most effective is by consensus. This is time consuming, but elicits the greater adherence. A vote by the majority can work; however, it does leave a few people disgruntled. In the final analysis, regardless of the method used, once the rules have been established, they must be followed by all. If a staff member does not agree with the rules, the individual has three options. One option is to enforce the rules, but continue to lead the discussion to change the rule. The second is to support the rule to the fullest. This can be combined with option number one, or it can stand alone. The third option is to resign. A staff member who will not or cannot hold clients to the rules established by the program creates a danger to the unit as well as undermines the success of the unit. Rules always can be open to suggested change by staff and even clients, but until they are, they must be followed. All staff must be on the same page or there will be staff splitting.

Staff splitting can be quite troublesome. The clients in group accused a female staff of saying "fuck you" to a client. The staff person denied this accusation and became angry when her male supervisor investigated the complaint. She felt he should just take her word for it. Of course, all of the clients stuck together. Elliott and Verdeyen (2002) call this "solidarity" on the part of the inmates. Because there was no other evidence, the staff member was not disciplined. However, she filed a sexual discrimination charge against her male supervisor.

NETWORKING

Using a whole-community approach is vital in being effective in treating criminals (Sharp, Clarke, and Pohl, 1996). As stated earlier, often criminal treatment is a second thought or a token effort for both the treatment community and the correctional community, which do not trust each other. The two communities often fight over scarce resources and barely tolerate each other. Often they keep information from each other on the pretext of confidentiality or need to know. What was true was that the criminal could split agencies and thus slip through the cracks. As has been mentioned in the rule's section on secrets and will be in the chapter on Standing Tall, criminals network very well. Their methods are generally self-centered and self-serving, but they often do this better then we do. "Ironically, members of these 'criminal subcultures' may have a greater sense of belonging and connection than members of mainstream society" (McCold and Wachtel, 2002).

However, if we are to succeed, we must take to heart an old Native American saying, "No tree has branches so foolish as to fight among themselves." And thus, we as a treatment community must work together to treat the criminal. "Local coalition building and planning have to become part of the fabric of a community" (Sharp, Clarke, and Pohl, 1996). "Could it be that the, 'what works,' literature is telling us that it takes a whole community to reintegrate an offender?" (Gadsden, 2003). John Perry (2002) says "When a crime is committed, it is more than just a violation of the law or an assault against a person or property—it affects the whole community." While Perry uses the term "community" more inclusively than we do here, his book provides many important statements about community that apply in networking.

The criminal is a community client. No longer can the judge say: this is my client and I will decide where he goes for treatment. No longer can the community correction agency or the state prison system say, not so, once you send him to us he is our client. (He will get out of prison and come back to our communities). And no longer can the treatment provider say, once you send him to us he now is our client—we will decide what is to happen to him. No one entity has ownership of a criminal client.

"The science of effective interventions also tells us that the treatment of offenders is a task beyond the scope of the correctional professional alone" (Gadsden, 2003). And more and more, the victim is being brought into the picture to assist in determining the sentencing or the plea bargain agreement (see examples under plea bargaining and in restorative justice). So, the client belongs to the whole community and it does take a whole community to habilitate a criminal. We all must be working together to accomplish this. And we must be on the same page, just as in the development of program rules. "The policy goal is a community response to a person's wrongdoing at its earliest onset, and a type and intensity of sanctions tailored to each instance of wrongdoing" (Perry, 2002).

Networking has to happen in each community where treatment for criminals is attempted. Probation officers, parole officers, jail staff, judges, police, and treatment people have to sit down and discuss mutual issues and concerns; otherwise, the criminal is going to win. Criminals are excellent at setting staff up. They play one against the other to avoid accountability and responsibility. It is necessary for all staff involved with the criminal's rehabilitation to follow and enforce the same rules. This is comparable to a family. If you have a rule that both parents do not enforce, you do not have a rule. It is the same with criminals. If you have a rule one group of people will not enforce, then you do not have a rule. The criminal is very good at finding out who does not agree with the rules. Many of them, as they progressed through treatment, openly would admit that they relied on separation between traditional alcohol and drug counselors, therapists, correctional officers, or parole and probation officers to manipulate the system and get out of being responsible or accountable. They openly admit that they rely on the system to be able to circumvent the system.

We noted earlier the story of a female client, who was admitted to the Consortium, did not like the regimen, and convinced her probation officer to admit her into a less restrictive treatment modality. She failed there, and to stay out of prison, was instructed to reapply to the Consortium. She eventually absconded when a mental health worker unilaterally decided that she was too fragile to continue the Consortium program. This client lost, though she thought she won, because not all the change agents were on the same page.

The Consortium program was, from the first, a community effort that had over a year of planning and development. After implementation, the effort continued to be a community project. "If we perceive a connection between each other and a common interest in the activities and well-being of the group . . . then we are, by definition, part of a community" (McCold and Wachtel, 2002).

All elements of the community made up the Board of Directors of this newly created nonprofit. It included directors of three substance abuse programs (one was the Native American program), the mental health director, the community correction manager, the jail commander, an adult and family service manager, a district attorney, a public health worker, two recovering people (eventually successful clients served on the board), and a representative from the police department. Thus, it was a community effort.

It is great to have a parole/probation officer assigned to the program full time. The officer can be dedicated to the clients when the clients are initially admitted into the program. The officer tracks the clients, makes home visits, administers sanctions, and so forth. The initial few weeks of treatment are critical to engaging and retaining the correctional client. The officer's assistance enhances these first weeks and the delivery of service by the project.

With the parole officer and a solid relationship with the parole and probation department, client participation and accountability rise dramatically. Having the parole officer as part of the staff allows quicker enforcement of sanctions against clients for noncompliance. Clients receive the message that they will be held accountable for their actions. Without the immediate sanctions, an outpatient or day treatment program for chronic nonincarcerated repeat offenders is impractical.

One reason the Powder River program was so successful was because the program has been a team effort. It was not correctional staff and contract alcohol and drug staff. It was a team effort, and all the management staff worked hard to make it happen. When the program first started, many of the alcohol and drug staff did not have very good opinions about the correctional officers. Coincidentally, the correctional officers' opinions of alcohol and drug staff were not very high either. It took considerable time to break this down. A team approach is needed to make the program work.

We achieved success in getting the team to work based on our contention that, both inside an institution (prison, jail, work release) and in the community, a network between the corrections and treatment staff is the place to start if there is to be any success in working with the criminal. A network has to be developed where everyone is on the same page with the criminal.

One thing that makes programs successful is that treatment staff and the correctional staff are equal partners—both inside and outside. Inside the facility, alcohol and drug staff have their own set of keys and access to the facility as correctional staff. They did not have to be let in or out. If they wanted to write department of correction misconduct reports on anyone in the facility, they had the right to do so. There were fifty residents in alcohol and drug treatment and 100 inmates in the general population. If any staff saw any inmate or resident misbehaving, they could and did correct that person.

Treatment staff responded to emergencies and came to the officers' assistance. All treatment and correctional staff attended a monthly staff meeting. Correctional staff sat in on treatment staff and clinical meetings. Treatment and correctional staff attended retreats together. They jointly celebrated Christmas, Halloween and other get-togethers. On occasion, the treatment staff filled in so that correctional officers could attend a certain function together and correctional officers covered the treatment facility so treatment staff could go to training together. Over time, this developed into a solid treatment approach. The program would have been diluted without this team approach.

Treatment staff received correctional-orientation training before going to work and yearly updates. Treatment staff also gave presentations about the program to all correctional staff and traveled to every county in the state to discuss the program and develop linkages with each county's correction and treatment community. The institution's management council included the executive director and clinical supervisor. Treatment staff also served on the training and safety teams.

Part of the networking that makes a successful program is client aftercare. This also is a team effort, not only inside the institution but within the community where the resident will be residing. If the aftercare does not work, then the success rate will be much lower.

Before clients left the Powder River facility, we set up a one-year aftercare program for them. Two months prior to them getting out, they moved into a transitional group and began completing an aftercare plan. Before the residents left or were discharged from the program, at least one, if not two, conference calls were made to the community in which they were going to reside. Staff talked to and had the residents make appointments with a counselor or a treatment provider and their parole officer. The conference call included the treatment provider, the parole officer, the resident, and a Powder River staff member. Staff detailed their planning for the resident over the next year that he was to be in the community. After discussion among all these players, the plan was finalized with their input. This networking is vital.

Family members are included in the networking. "Prior to release, family members or significant others are contacted and, if possible, included in the aftercare planning phase. It is critical to the resident's continued recovery from the disease of substance addiction and criminality that he does not return to the same negative environment that led to his criminal behavior and incarceration" (Sharp and Beam, 1995). "This is a transition that involves the offender, family, and community and necessitates the consent and will of all three to set and negotiate their roles, expectations and behavioral parameters" (Gadsden, 2003).

Two weeks after the resident leaves the program, the community treatment provider is called to find out whether the resident has shown up. If he has not, then staff immediately call the parole officer and let the parole officer know that the resident did not show up for his or her treatment. The parole officer is encouraged to follow-up on the parolee. A subsequent call is made again at four weeks with the parole officer being notified of a no-show. If there have been no shows, negotiations are begun on what needs to be done. Every month after that, a written follow-up report is requested from the treatment provider. We also send out a printed follow-up form to the parole officer every three months and ask for an update. Each discharged resident is followed for a year. If the resident drops out of treatment or is in relapse, staff attempts to renegotiate the aftercare plan with all the involved players.

COUNSELING THE INMATE

The following dialog illustrates some of the perils of counseling the criminal client.

INMATE: "I don't really have a problem. I made a few mistakes, but I'm not going to do that again."

COUNSELOR: "Your file says that you made threatening phone calls to your probation officer. Will you tell me about that?"

INMATE: "That was three years ago. I can't remember."

COUNSELOR: "It's situations like that one that will tell you if you have a problem or not. It may not be easy, but it would be really helpful if you could remember what you were thinking and feeling when you threatened the parole officer."

INMATE: "Look. You don't have any right to ask me that. You weren't there. I was angry but I didn't threaten anybody. That's in the past. It's gone. I'm not like that anymore."

COUNSELOR: "Do you really believe that you have your life completely in control? I suspect that if you look at things carefully, you will find that you have some problems left to solve."

INMATE: "Do you think you're a psychiatrist or something? You don't know what you're talking about. Just stick to your counseling. If you've got anything to tell me about alcohol that I don't already know, okay. I'll listen to that. But my past is my business. You're in way over your head."

COUNSELOR: "I don't appreciate your telling me how to do my job."

INMATE: "Now you're getting mad. You're the one with the anger problem, not me" (Bush, 1993).

The counselor had some needs and eventually got hooked by the inmate. And, that was exactly what the inmate was aiming to do. He is going to do whatever it takes to get the attention off him so that he cannot be held accountable and responsible for his behavior. "The criminal tries to manage others, whether in individual or in group session, and makes efforts to revise the format to suit himself" (Yochelson and Samenow, 1976).

Previously, we discussed the tactics that criminals use to avoid accountability. This example illustrates these tactics. He was successful in refocusing off his behavior onto the counselor's behavior, "Now you're getting mad . . ." The inmate also was able to put the counselor down by challenging his ability and competence, "Do you think you're a psychiatrist . . . Just stick to your counseling. . . ." The inmate also attacked the counselor's authority. "You don't have any right . . ." The inmate was setting the boundaries and dictating what was open for discussion and what was not open. Again, the criminal only was willing to tell the change agent what he thought the change agent ought to know. Finally, the change agent got into a power struggle with the inmate. "I don't appreciate . . ."

SPONGES AND DEFLECTORS

One effective approach is being a sponge or deflector (Brodenhamer, 1983). When the criminal is going off on a tirade about something, the counselor simply makes comments such as "uh huh," "I heard you," or "Anything else you want to say about that?" This gives the criminal an opportunity to say what he wants, then, the counselor responds with, "Regardless of . . . I want you to answer the question." Or "Nevertheless . . . please tell me your thinking regarding your anger." Or "In spite of all of that . . ."

You may have to spend the entire session just going back and forth between these scenarios. The important thing is not to get frustrated, angry, or discouraged. Keep repeating the same question until the criminal finally gives an answer.

Let us see if we can rework this session using sponges and deflectors.

INMATE: "I don't really have a problem. I made a few mistakes, but I'm not going to do that again."

COUNSELOR: "Regardless of whether you are going to make any more mistakes, tell me how your anger has gotten you in trouble in the past."

INMATE: "That was three years ago. I can't remember."

COUNSELOR: "If you could remember, what do you think your thinking would be?"

INMATE: "I told you I can't remember, now let's move on to something else."

COUNSELOR: "Uh huh, anything else you want to say about that?"

INMATE: "No"

COUNSELOR: "Regardless of whether or not you are like that any more, tell me how your anger gets out of control."

INMATE: "Do you think you're a psychiatrist or something? You don't know what you're talking about. Just stick to your counseling. If you've got anything to tell me about alcohol that I don't already know, okay. I'll listen to that. But my past is my business. You're in way over your head."

COUNSELOR: "Anything more you want to say about my abilities or skills?"

INMATE: "Just stick to what you know and don't go off into areas you aren't qualified for."

COUNSELOR: "Uh huh. Anything else you want to say about that?"

INMATE: "No!"

COUNSELOR: "Regardless of whether you think I am qualified to ask you about your anger, tell me how your anger gets out of control."

This could go on forever. The important idea here is to not get hooked into the traps the criminal is setting. (Of course, when you can be both the inmate and counselor, it is easier to avoid the traps). Remember, criminals are attempting to set you up from the first moment they meet you.

Comments like "uh huh" or "I heard you" are helpful to avoid the set up. This allows them to be heard, but does not give them power to control the process. This is one way to avoid a power struggle. When criminals attack your credentials or your ability to work with them, it has nothing to do with you. Realize that the criminal is trying to break you down. Do not take what the criminals say to you personally. This is just a tool they use to hurt you, and most likely, they do not even mean it. They use these tactics with every change agent who comes into their life.

Another technique we have found effective is to share with them the idea that we believe a videotape of their lives since the beginning of time would show them where and how they had used these tactics every time they were being held responsible. We point out that the video would show a pattern of behavior that continually gets them into trouble, including being sent to jail and prison. They can see their blood on the wall from the many previous times they have bashed their heads against the same wall. Someone has called this a "bash trip."

We then ask if they have any interest in changing the outcome of their behavior. We generally do not ask if they want to change the behavior. Most often, they do not want to change the behavior, but they do want to change the consequences of the behavior. Of course, if they are not concerned with the consequences, then, we tell them we cannot help them. We only can help the criminals if they are invested in changing the consequences. Now, we sometimes can help them want to avoid the consequences. As a wise sage once said: "I know you can lead a horse to water and not make him drink, but you can lead him to water and make him thirsty."

The major thrust of our approach is to teach criminals all of what we have discussed in this book. We want criminals to be fully aware of the thinking and behavior that has allowed them to escape accountability and responsibility for their behavior. We want to assist them in becoming aware of how their behavior has led to their arrest, incarceration, and probation. Once we have taught these principles, we then can begin to teach them how to change their thinking, which leads to changed behavior. We also teach them how to hold those around them in treatment accountable. The clients, under the guidance of staff, are more successful than counselors in helping each other to be accountable in a therapeutic community.

TREATMENT INTENSITY

Treatment intensity is an important concern. Too little treatment will not change hard-core criminals. Too much is not effective with criminals just beginning their career. It is important to be able to diagnose how far along the thinking-pattern continuum (discussed in Chapter 1) a client is. Describing and administering treatment depends on where criminals fall on the continuum. Criminal thinking follows the same pattern along this continuum from erroneous thinking, through problem thinking, and on into criminal and psychopathic thinking. However, it becomes more intense and all encompassing (as seen from the continuum description) as a person proceeds along the continuum. Thus, the intensity of treatment needs to become more intense depending on what position the criminal is on in the continuum.

Intensity refers to three elements. The first element of intensity is the dosage (hours) of treatment per week as seen in Figure 4.1. For clients just beginning their criminal career (erroneous thinkers—clients who have received their first drunk driving charge, or drug court clients who have received their first arrest), the dosage per week would start out with only several hours maybe once or twice a week. Clients who are on the criminal-thinking position would require up to fifteen hours a week, coming in five days a week or full time inside the institution.

The second intensity (see Figure 4.2-Treatment Length) refers to how long individuals remain in treatment. Again, as clients move along the thinking-pattern continuum, the length of treatment will increase as seen in Figure 4.2. Stewart and Gabora-Roth (2003) say that "Programs are more likely to be successful and more cost-effective if the level of service is congruent with the risk the offender poses to reoffend. Low-risk offenders should receive little or no intervention while more intensive treatment should be reserved for the higher-risk offenders." Though we agree with the idea of low-risk offenders receiving small amounts of treatment, we would disagree that they should not receive any treatment. As Figure 4.2 shows, the length of treatment is graduated depending on the client's entrenched place on the thinking-pattern continuum.

The Consortium Treatment program provided evidence that clients who were at the low end of the continuum and were placed in a twenty-hour-a-week, one-year program, usually did not complete treatment. While the clients on the high end of the continuum, with the same treatment regimen, were quite successful. Other research supports this finding (Ross et al., 1988; Fogg, 1992). In their "Evaluation of the

FIGURE 4.1
DOSAGE = HOURS OF TREATMENT PER WEEK

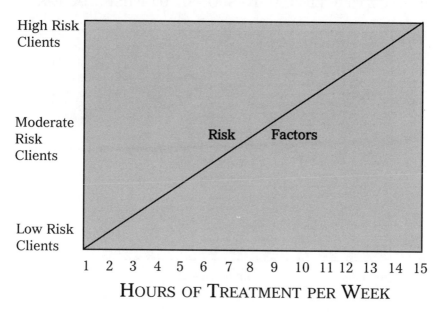

HOURS OF TREATMENT PER WEEK

FIGURE 4.2
IMMEDIACY OF CLINICAL RESPONSE TO MISBEHAVIOR

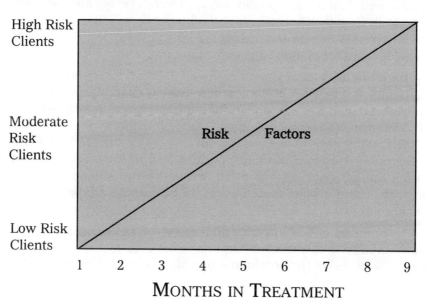

MONTHS IN TREATMENT

FIGURE 4.3
IMMEDIACY OF CLINICAL RESPONSE TO MISBEHAVIOR

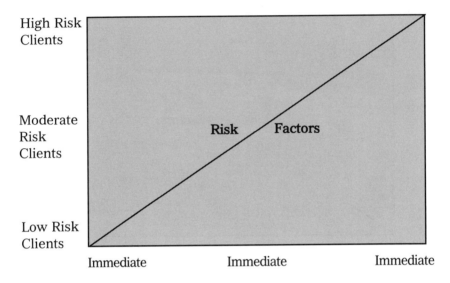

Specialized Drug Offender Program (SDOP) for the Colorado Judicial Department", Grant Johnson and Robert M. Hunter (1992) say, "probationers with severe drug problems who got extra supervision were more likely to succeed than those who did not. . . . Overall revocation rates are 41.7 percent in Regular Probation, . . . 25.5 percent in SDOP Cognitive. But rate differences among treatments are considerably larger for high-risk clients . . . and for clients with very high drug or alcohol problems."

The third intensity of treatment is shown in Figures 4.3 and 4.4. This pertains to how immediate the clinical response to client misbehavior is, both in the treatment program and in the community and how severe the clinical response is. Figure 4.3 shows how immediate the response should be. And this should be the same for low, moderate, and high-risk clients. Response to clients' misbehavior must be immediate. Being silent or ignoring the behavior, as was discussed under the section on rules, reenforces the clients' belief that they are above the rules of the program and the community.

The second part of this intensity discussion refers to how severe the response should be to misbehavior. As Figure 4.4 shows, this will depend on the client's place on the continuum or risk factors. It will depend on how the client has been responding to treatment, and it will depend on the client's prior misbehavior while in treatment. "Sanctions must be swift, or occur shortly after the behavior at issue. The sanctions schedule increases in severity as the offender continues to persist in violating treatment and supervision rules" (Montague, 2001). See the subsection on praise for a discussion on the clinical response to good conduct and the rules and sanctions in the appendix. Figure 4.4 shows the severity of clinical responses to misbehavior.

FIGURE 4.4
SEVERITY OF CLINICAL RESPONSE TO
CLIENT MISBEHAVIOR

chapter 5

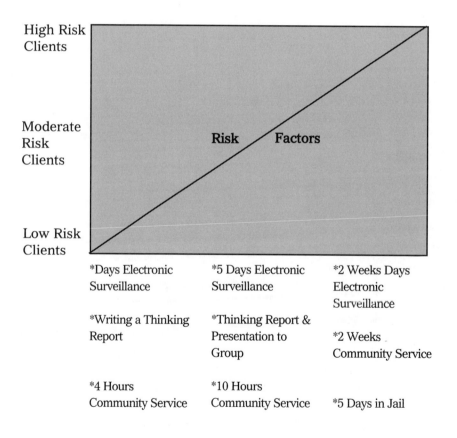

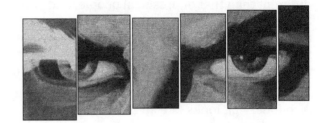

CHANGE AGENTS: STANDING TALL

Readers of *Becoming a Model Warden: Striving for Excellence* (Bartollas, 2004) are impressed with its emphasis on being a proactive warden. The author says "survival is a reactive term; it is much like crisis-oriented management practices. One does not feel good and energized by the job or view the career in positive terms if survival reactions are the way in which one views the responsibility of the warden. What is far more desirable is to view what is needed for wardens to thrive in their jobs." Though this book is addressing the conduct of wardens, the title could have just as well have been "Becoming a Model Correctional Officer or Treatment Staff: Striving for Excellence." The term "standing tall" is borrowed from chapter six of this book, "Standing Tall: A Person of Integrity."

This book outlines a positive approach to working with criminals. It actually shows how to change their thinking and behavior while not sugarcoating the behavior of the criminal, either in a prison or while on probation or parole and while not trying to downplay the stress on correctional officers, treatment staff, and other people, who work with criminals.

Hopefully, by now you understand that the criminal's thinking is far different than that of prosocial people, and you agree that because of that thinking we need to have a different approach to be effective in treating and changing the thinking and behavior of criminals so that they can be law-abiding and productive citizens. And, at this point, you expect that the criminal can and will change under this approach.

Our job can be compared to finding a thunder egg in the mountains. A thunder egg looks like an old volcanic rock, but when you split it open, you find an agate. As you polish the agate, it begins to shine; so with the criminal. Granted, there are some thunder eggs that have crystallized, but most have not.

"When you change the way you look at something, the thing or person you look at will change" (Dyer, 2004). ~~If you view criminals as animals, pukes, children, scum, and no goods, you will get what you view. However, if you view criminals as changeable and with dignity and respect,~~ if you set expectations and follow through, and if you expect them to meet those expectations, then you will get that also. You get what you put your mind on. No idea or goal was ever accomplished by contemplating (thinking) of its opposite. So, you are urged to view the client as an uncut thunder egg.

We now come to the most difficult and exacting area of working with the criminal: being an effective change agent. This takes the greatest skills needed in any profession. It demands that we keep the passion for working to keep our cities, towns, and streets safe and secure while remaining serene and tranquil. It requires us to hold the criminal responsible and accountable and yet remain detached from the outcome of our efforts. The challenge is how one can be cursed, manipulated, and abused—yet remain firm, friendly, and fair. This is the subject of this section.

What do we want to do in working with criminals, whether as inmates, parolees, or probationers? First, we want to keep our citizens safe from their predatory behavior. However, we want to rehabilitate them so that they do not reoffend again. Francis J. Schweigert (2002) says, "Merely returning like for like, in punishment or in reparation, is acting under compulsion and equivalent to going only the one mile; creative restitution calls upon offenders to go further than this and redeem the situation . . . there are three dimensions of justice, retribution, reparation, and redemption."

You can do this by changing their thinking; then, their behavior will change. We want to assist them in changing how they perceive the world and themselves—to move their perception point on the thinking-pattern continuum from self-centered/self-absorbed and competitive to not thinking so highly of themselves and to being more cooperative. We want to move their perception point from greed and ownership to appreciation and generosity. We want to move them from being forceful in their behavior to having authentic power. We want to assist them in "walking down another street."

Hawkins (1995) lists 140 contrasting low-energy versus high-energy responses to life. He says "reflection on the many contrasting pairs of qualities can initiate a consciousness-raising process." Listing a few of the contrasts provides some insight. On the left are the high-energy patterns and on the right are the low-energy patterns. If criminals' thinking will change from the right to the left, they will change.

Admitting-Denying	Detached-Removed
Accepting-Rejecting	Agreeable-Condescending
Allowing-Controlling	Attractive-Seductive
Honest-Illegal	Truthful-Lying
Choosing to-Having to	Concerned-Judgmental
Constructive-Destructive	Contending-Competing

DETACHMENT

The first step to accomplishing this and remaining a healthy change agent is to detach yourself from the outcome of your efforts. "Only the person who is utterly detached and utterly dedicated," Gandhi says, "is free to enjoy life" (Easwaran, 1985). We should do everything we can to change the criminal thinking and behavior, work with a passion for the desired outcome, and then become unattached to the outcome. Dan Johnson, superintendent of the Powder River Correctional Facility, in discussing the writing of a misconduct report, always instructed his staff to write the report on misconduct and then walk away from the results. Leave the decision on findings and consequence up to the hearings officer and be satisfied with the outcome. "We have to view the outcome of our actions with a sense of complete detachment. This means we can't get involved with the idea of succeeding or failing" (Abelar, 1992).

After one correctional program won a national award, the clinical director became possessive of the program. He felt he should have received the accolades. He refused to co-accept an award given to the executive director. This attachment to being seen as the creator caused a gulf between him and the executive director. Detachment means giving up the need to keep score on how well we are doing. It means forsaking setting a quota. "[Our] judgments will be better and [our] vision clearer if [we] are not emotionally entangled in the outcome of what [we] do" (Easwaran, 1985).

The Dallas Cowboys won two Super Bowls in a row and then Jerry Jones fired Jimmy Johnson, the coach. Why? They both had become attached to receiving the credit for the success of the team. Jones, as the owner, felt he should be given the most credit for spending the money to put the team together. Johnson felt he should be given the most credit for having coached the team and getting them to give their all. So, both had to go their separate ways because they were so attached to the outcome— the keeping of score over who was the most responsible for the success. "It is not that such people have acquired too much wealth, fame, or attention; it is that these influences distort their egos. Whether it uplifts or destroys us depends not upon success itself, but on how it's integrated into our personalities" (Hawkins, 1995). The story is told of a king who asked his engraver to inscribe on the inside of his ring something that would sustain him, both in victory and defeat. The engraver inscribed: "This too will pass."

Detachment is not indifference, giving up, or resignation. It is a choice to not have an ego that depends on the outcome of our efforts. "The inner self has no best to perform, it simply listens and knows and goes about its business in a purposeful manner, with no concern for how everything turns out" (Dyer, 1995). It means not using "force" to get the criminal to do our bidding. "Staff who fall prey to a successful con are encouraged to walk away" (Elliott and Verdeyen, 2002), to become detached from the episode, reflect on the situation, and come back the next day with a clean slate.

There were three friends: Carl, Dean, and Bill. Dean died of an unexpected, sudden and massive heart attack. When Bill called Carl to inform him of the death of their friend, Carl replied "Aw shucks." Bill's immediate reaction was one of astonishment. What an understatement, he thought. After further thought, Bill came to appreciate the response.

What a way to respond to the world, whether good or bad comes our way. "Aw shucks" is a good response in our business of being unattached to the outcome of our work. When we hear that an inmate, probationer, or parolee has reoffended or an alcoholic has had a relapse, responding with an "aw shucks" might just be the correct response. Instead of berating the offender or saying, "I didn't think he would make it," or becoming disillusioned or even worse, getting down on ourselves, we take it in stride and move on with an "aw shucks."

Another example of detachment comes from Dan Millman (1984). Millman was consoling his friend as they watched the friend's restaurant burn to the ground. The friend told Millman the following story.

> In a small fishing village in Japan, there lived a young, unmarried woman who gave birth to a child. Her parents felt disgraced and demanded to know the identity of the father. Afraid, she refused to tell them. The fisherman she loved had told her, secretly, that he was going off to seek his fortune and would return to marry her. Her parents persisted. In desperation, she named Hakuin, a monk who lived in the hills, as the father.
>
> Outraged, the parents took the infant girl up to his door, pounded until he opened it, and handed him the baby, saying "This child is yours, you must care for it."
>
> "Is that so?" Hakuin said, taking the child in his arms and waving good-bye to the parents.
>
> A year passed and the real father returned to marry the woman. At once they went to Hakuin to beg for the return of the child. "We must have our daughter," they said.
>
> "Is that so?" said Hakuin, handing the child to them.
>
> "An interesting story," Millman said, "but I don't understand why you're telling it to me now. I mean, your café just burned." "Is that so?" his friend replied.

Whether the inmate makes it or not, our response, "Is that so?" may be just the right response to keep us from becoming so invested in the outcome of our work that we loose the perspective of what, how, and why we are doing what we are doing.

"Striving to do your best for the joy of expressing all that you have to contribute is a satisfying experience that does not depend upon the outcome" (Zukav and Francis, 2001). "The danger, of course, of a life of active engagement in the world of [corrections] is that [we] will get caught up in [our] actions and begin to act out of selfish motives" (Easwaran,1985).

Let us look at detachment versus attachment. Bartollas (2004) discusses power versus force as put forth by Hawkins in *Power Versus Force* (1995). Dyer also discusses power versus force and compares it as we saw in a previous section. The *Bhagavad Gita* (Easwaran, 1985), the ancient Hindu scripture, is devoted to the idea of detachment and its characteristics. Zukav and Francis (2001) discuss authentic power, and *The Tibetan Book of Living and Dying* (Rinpoche, 1993) confronts the reader with the idea of detachment. People who are detached from the outcome often do not look any different from the people who are attached to the outcome. However, if you spend a few moments in conversation with these people who are detached, you see how unique they are (Dyer, 2004). If we use the idea of detachment as authentic power and attachment as force, we can see some significant difference between the two.

DETACHMENT = POWER

Authentic personal empowerment

Motivated by ethics, and serenity

Focuses on what he is for

Has responsibility

Has forgiveness

Has a peaceful countenance

Is compassionate

Is kind

ATTACHMENT = FORCE

Demands external power

Motivated by achievement and performance

Focuses on what he is against

No sense of responsibility

Holds grudges, seeks revenge

Is in turmoil, disharmony

Is angry

Has a need to be right

Empowers others	Must always win
Has humility	Is arrogant and proud
Believes in freedom	Believes in bondage
Is a gentle person	Is aggressive
Is honest in his dealings	Is manipulative
Overlooks slights	Is easily offended
Believes in equality	Feels superior
Gives others credit	Must keep score and compare
Looks at others' point of view	Is argumentative
Is in a state of appreciation	Is a depreciator
Is not a fault finder	Complains about everything
Is self-assured	Feels threatened
Has gratitude for what he has and does	Brags about their achievements
Feels good no matter what	Feels bad no matter what
Is highly inspired and inspires people	Is disillusioned and negative
Has infinite patience	Has knee-jerk reactions
Is open to new ideas	Is closed minded
Is harmonious	Is competitive

In summary, detachment means holding clients, inmates, parolees, or probationers accountable and responsible for their behavior without judgment, without vengeance, without malice, without revenge, rejection, condescension, anger, or righteousness. "Detachment relieves [us] of the self-appointed job of being judge and jury" (Zukav, 1990).

THINKING PATTERNS OF THE COUNSELOR

Prosocial	Prosocial	Erroneous	Problem	Criminal	Chronic
Internal	External	Thinking	Thinking	Thinking	Psychopathic
Thinking	Thinking				Thinking

In Father Martin's film, *Chalk Talk* (1972), he states that in assessing a person's drinking problem, the person does not have a problem if his drinking pattern matches that of the person completing the assessment. It seems that it is important to also say that when working with criminals and assessing their behavior, if our thinking pattern matches their thinking pattern, then we will not be so inclined to think they have a problem. If we have procriminal thoughts or sympathies, we will be less likely to hold criminals accountable and responsible for their thinking or behavior. If our views concerning management, the system, fairness, police supervisors, and so forth are similar to the criminals, then we will be much less effective in getting them to change. "Only when we have removed the harm in ourselves do we become truly useful to others" Rinpoche (1993). Thus, it is vital that we assess ourselves to determine where we fit on the thinking-pattern scale. "Corrections is a fascinating but emotionally demanding line of work and not everybody can do it" (Walsh, 2005).

Take the following test. With which items do you agree?

The police are overbearing or even abusive.

Criminal behavior has causes.

Many innocent people go to prison (discussed further in the section "Innocent Until Proven Guilty").

You have a need to hug a thug.

You must punish.

You need vengeance (a Chinese proverb says that if you seek vengeance, then you should dig two graves).

You need to be the police, judge, and jury.

You like to become involved in an inmate disturbance. (We have seen a majority of the officers leave their post to get in on quelling a disturbance while their area was left unsupervised).

If you checked any of these items, then your thinking may be closely matching the criminals, and your effectiveness will be greatly limited.

ZONES

What other characteristics do counselors and other staff need to be successful when working with criminals? People working with criminals seem to get into three zones: the white, the red, or the yellow zone. Though, at times, all change agents (counselors, case managers, volunteers, parole/probation officers, and others) will be in all three. However, to be successful, it is important to consistently be in the yellow zone.

White zone. The white zone is when change agents have on their blinders. They do not really see what is going on around them. They are so caught up in what they are thinking about or doing that they do not see the things that a criminal is doing, the criminal's misbehavior, or the breaking of rules. In this zone, the change agent often misses the nuances of the criminal's thought pattern. These people are called Pollyannas (Walsh, 2005).

Staff people in the white zone are predictable, sympathetic, and gullible. They accept, at face value, what the client says. Often, they are indecisive and permissive. This zone will get the change agents in trouble because they do not observe enough and respond enough. This can happen when they get comfortable with the treatment progress. The criminal will try to lull the change agents into a false sense of comfort and acceptance to get them into this white zone.

Elliott and Verdeyen (2002) illustrate several things including disclosure and shaky boundaries, a con and manipulation. Also, those in the white zone are not aware of what is occurring. An inmate overheard a new correctional officer saying he had been inadequately trained to do his job. (He overheard this by listening at a partially closed door). The inmate introduced himself and said "Don't worry, Boss. Just tell me what you want done and I'll make it happen." The officer began to rely more and more on the inmate because the unit was running well. He had no idea what was going on in the unit and the fact that all communication from him were being run through the inmate. On a surprise shakedown, weapons, alcohol, and drugs were found on the unit. The new officer was terminated, but his final question to the inmate was, "Why didn't you tell me about all that stuff that the guys were warehousing?" The inmate smile and replied, "Because you never asked me?"

Red zone. The opposite of the white zone is the red zone. This is where the change agents are so suspicious that they always are questioning or challenging the criminals. They come down hard on everyone. Walsh (2005) calls these staff members Cassandras. Everything seems to be a crisis and is interpreted as failure, as not working. They view the clients as hopeless, pukes, and so forth. Change agents in the red zone are harsh, critical, and negative. They assume that the clients never will make it. They get into an adversarial position with the clients and are aggressive. These staff persons have tunnel vision about the clients. We had a maintenance supervisor whose opinion was that the inmates were always tearing things up on purpose. So, when a toilet would plug up or break, he would wait days to fix it. He said he was teaching them a lesson. Of course, there were many complaints to management, unruly inmates and tension on the unit (a self-fulfilling prophecy). His behavior resulted in his being terminated.

Yellow zone. The middle zone is the yellow zone, where change agents are not always criticizing everyone, but they also do not ignore everything. In this zone, the clients are accepted for whom they are without unrealistic expectations being placed on them. In this zone, the change agents are rational, candid, and empowering. In the yellow zone, the change agent has passion as opposed to mayhem in the red zone or resignation in the white zone. In the yellow zone, the change agent has detachment as opposed to attachment in the red zone or indifference in the white zone. This is the zone where the staff people should be. Each staff member should help all other staff members to see which zone they inhabit. Yet, to maintain this balance is difficult. It is much easier to be in the red zone or the white zone.

Being in the yellow zone means creating a working environment that allows staff to not only support each other, but to be able to address each other's slippage into either the red or the white zone. Most times, other staff members can see our tendencies to become a Pollyanna or a Cassandra. When staff is empowered to create a working environment that is respectful of everyone, where staff is detached from the outcome and supportive of all, then it becomes possible to give and receive feedback that enriches and improves our effectiveness. In the yellow zone, we are maximizing each other's strengths and minimizing each other's weaknesses.

This is not about "hug a thug" day or "bleeding heartism" (Walsh, 2005). There will be times when we do not act as we plan. We will loose it on occasion, but stop and say, "That is not like me" (Graham and

Hyrum, 1999). Our objective is to keep our intention focused on the yellow zone, not the white zone or the red zone, but to keep our focus on authentic power and not on force.

Chart 5.1 (on next page) is a fuller list of change-agent behavior and attitudes for each zone. Assess yourself. How many times does your behavior fall into the yellow category? What can you do to keep it in this zone?

DO NOT NEED ANYTHING FROM THE CLIENT

"If the correctional worker has unresolved needs, the counselor/offender relationship is not the place to attempt to satisfy them" (Walsh, 2005). Staff should not need or want anything from their clients. "A good looking, fast-talking psychopath (criminal) and a victim who has weak spots is a devastating combination" (Hare, 1993). Staff cannot get hung up on trying to change the clients; again, we must be detached from the outcome. Instead, we must work with criminals because we want to, not because we need to for personal fulfillment.

That sounds so right; yet, in working with the criminal, staff needs become too apparent. A film that illustrates the needs of change agents is *The Silence of the Lambs*. Here, the difference between two counselors becomes apparent. Hannibal Lecter's psychiatrist was portrayed as needing something from Lecter. Clearly, Lecter took advantage of him. The other counselor, who was attempting to stop a crime, got caught up in Lecter's seduction, yet was able to remain outside his con to fulfill her mission. She could accomplish this because she did not need anything from Lecter.

The Institute for Integral Development lists *Some Considerations in Interviewing Hostile and Resistant Clients* (Samenow, N.D., workshop handout). We will discuss six of these points.

1. Do not put a premium on getting the client to "like" you; rather, you must try to earn his/her respect.
   The staff must respect the client. We are not talking about their behavior or attitude. We are just talking about treating them as human beings. Do not call them low-lifers or use terms of that sort. Do not call them "children" or otherwise label them. We demand respect from them, and they also should be

CHART 5.1 ZONES

WHITE ZONE	YELLOW ZONE	RED ZONE
Soft	Firm	Hard
Predictable	Unpredictable	Predictable
Friends	Friendly	Adversarial
Fix it	Advocate	Judgmental
Sympathetic	Empathic	Antagonistic
Consents	Deflects	Argues
Ignores most of what is said	Acts as a sponge	Reacts to everything that is said
Withdraws	Is open	Power thrusts
Proscribes	Guides	Manipulates
Gullible	Wise	Cynical
Unaware of many errors in thinking and behavior	Alert to errors in thinking and behavior	Polices errors in thinking and behavior
Indirect	Direct	Provocative
Accepts everything client says	Time will tell	Plays detective (searches for lies)
Courts the client	Accepts the client	Rejects the client
Enables the client	It is his/her life	Controls the client
Makes excuses	Realistic expectations	Sets too high expectations
Trusts	Expects	Distrusts
Submissive	Assertive	Aggressive
Believes all clients will succeed	Is neutral—again time will tell	Sees most clients failing
Role model	Teacher	Police officer
Wants clients to be like him/her	Lets clients find own standard	Forces clients into a mold
Ambiguous	Candid	Opinionated
Indecisive	Rational	Concrete
Permissive	Reasonable	Restrictive
Demoralizing	Dispassionate	Sarcastic
Silent	Enlightens	Ridicules
Gives personal data	Turns personal data requests back on client	Angrily responds to request for personal data
Discourages by repetition	Is willing to continually repeat	Only states something once
Placates	Sincere	Contemptuous
Accommodates	Stipulates	Battles
Unsure	Confident	Overbearing
Fragmented	Focused	Tunnel vision
Gives up	Patient	Exasperated
Timid	Assured	Overpowering
Excitable	Composed	Stoic
Complacent	Searching	Dictatorial
Vague	Clear/detailed	Dogmatic
Scattered	Flexible	Rigid
Appeases	Open minded	Prejudicial
Not resolute	Resolute	Not resolute
Phoney	Empowering	Puts down clients
Wants clients to like him/her	Fair	Biased

respected. We have a better chance of treating criminals if we treat them with respect.

At the same time, the staff is not out to be the criminal's friend. "If a staff member measures his or her competency through perceived liking by an inmate, he or she will be disappointed time and time again" (Elliott and Verdeyen, 2002). It is important to be friendly but not his or her friend. Be firm, friendly, and fair. The criminal is always looking for hooks or ways to manipulate staff. The criminal will come up to a staff member and give a compliment or do something that will make the staff member feel warmer to him or her. It is important that staff tell the criminal what that individual is doing.

> [W]orkers make use of the authority inherent in their position without engaging in interpersonal domination (in other words, they are "firm but fair"); they demonstrate in vivid ways their own anticriminal-prosocial attitudes, values, and beliefs; and they enthusiastically engage the offender in the process of increasing rewards for noncriminal activity. The worker exposes and makes attractive the alternatives to procriminal attitudes, styles of thinking, and ways of acting. The worker does not depend upon the presumed benefits of a warm relationship with the offender and does not assume that offenders will self-discover these alternatives (Andrews and Bonta, 1998).

2. Do not think that you must manipulate or do things that are contrived to court the client's favor; for example, using street language or dressing a certain way. "It is . . . important that staff avoid using manipulative tactics in their own efforts to assert or regain power over inmates" (Elliott and Verdeyen, 2002). We often have film companies call us to sell their latest treatment film. When describing films geared toward the criminal population, they talk about how realistic the film is. When questioned, what they mean is that the film uses graphic street language. Their belief is that you have to get down to the clients' level to relate to them. Some staff or volunteers may adopt "con talk" to get closer to the clients (Andrews and Bonta, 1998). Our belief is that this is counterproductive with the criminal. One of our rules is that there will be no cussing in the treatment program. We feel it is important to raise the level

of consciousness in the criminal. Thus, it is important to understand our own thinking and "distinguish between anticriminal and procriminal expression" (Andrews and Bonta, 1998).

Do not court the clients' favor in any way or attempt to help the client in a personal way. One evening in the prison program, a client approached his counselor and said it was his anniversary. He said he did not have the means to make a call home to his wife. The client expressed real sadness at not being able to call home. A short time later, another of the counselor's clients came to him saying that it was his wife's birthday and he wanted to call her, but did not have any money.

The counselor thought both clients were doing well in treatment. He wanted to reward them for their effort. He genuinely felt their calling home would be a good thing. So, he told them that they could come into his office and he would use his telephone calling card to let each of them make one call home. The counselor placed the calls himself and allowed each client to talk to his wife.

The next morning at 11:00 AM, the phone company called the counselor to inform him that there had been $1,500 worth of calls placed on his phone credit card. They asked if he was aware of this. Of course, he was not. The two clients had memorized his calling number as he placed the calls. They went on to give the number out to all fifty clients, other inmates in the prison system, and their families and friends. What seemed like a nice gesture by the counselor turned into a situation whereby he was compromised by the clients. His effectiveness with the criminal population was diminished. We had to transfer him to a prosocial program. "The criminal interprets kindness as weakness" (Yochelson and Samenow, 1977).

Another example illustrating the firm boundaries needed in this area concerns a client who could not give a urinalysis (U.A.). The policy was that after the clients' names were posted they had a certain timeframe in which to contact a staff person and give a U.A. For a variety of reasons, clients seem not to be able to produce urine samples—shy bladders; forgetting; urinating and then remembering, "Oh I was supposed to give a urine sample," and not the least being because they will produce a positive U.A. Therefore, we have a policy that if they do not give a urine sample within two hours, they will be considered as having a positive U.A.

One day, a client kept going to a staff person to give his urine sample and each time, he could not or would not produce any urine. The counselor worked with him, having him drink water and so forth. Eventually, as the client did not produce a urine sample, the counselor felt the client had made a sincere effort. Against policy, he agreed to allow the client to wait and give a sample the next day.

When this was addressed with the client, he said, "We had done everything we could to produce a urine sample, but we were unable to pee." We then brought the staff person in so that he could hear the client talk about how "we could not produce a urine sample."

In subsequent discussion with the counselor, we pointed out how his efforts on behalf of the client, in getting the client to produce a U.A., became enabling. Setting aside the policy, the counselor's role was perceived by the client as a "we" thing. For the client, the boundaries became nonexistent. This is what happens if we court clients' favor or need anything from them.

3. **Avoid the twin pitfalls of gullibility and cynicism.** In the section on zones, we suggested that you not be gullible nor cynical. It is a balance. Again, it is important to understand that from the moment you meet the criminal, he or she is trying to set you up. It is important to remember that no matter how the criminals behave, they are trying to set you up. Their goal is to make you gullible and to try and get you to believe them. Make sure you are aware of this. One way criminals will try to do this is to gather information about you through your body language. They will try to see when you are nervous and what subjects make you nervous. As mentioned earlier, your manner of dress may be an area on which they center. They observe whether you make eye contact and under what circumstances. How do you respond to threats from them?

Staff should remember not to talk about other staff or other clients around the criminals. Criminals will use this information to their best advantage and always against you. In the case mentioned in the white zone, the inmate gathered the information that the new correctional officer felt untrained to run the unit, by listening to him talk on the phone through an open door. They will try to peg whether you are soft or hard. Also, it is important not to bring problems from home into the work-place. As difficult as it is, these need to stay at home.

Once criminals gather personal information, they begin try-ing to spin you. They will try to build up your ego. They will try to pledge loyalty or devotion to you. They will have empathy for you if they hear something bad has happened to you. They will do anything to try to bond with you and establish a "you and me" feeling. Be cautious of this.

The video made for home viewing, *My Blue Heaven*, is about a criminal in the FBI witness protection agency. He is relocated to a rural town and has an FBI manager. This criminal portrays most of the thinking errors and tactics previously discussed. In addition, it also portrays the needs and wants of the change agents surrounding the criminal. We see a criminal who manipulates himself through all of their rules, guidelines, and beliefs.

He lies, blames, redefines, manipulates, refocuses, displays ownership, and takes down the boundaries between himself and the change agents. The change agents vacillate between really caring for the criminal and hating him based on which of their needs are getting met. The film displays a master criminal in action, and the audience sees how people around him get sucked into his manipulation.

The following are things to look for in this film. When were the first lie and the first con? Look immediately for excuses, blaming, lying, redefining, and refocusing. How does he feed the change agent? What set ups does he use on change agents and how does he get the change agents to identify with him? How does he get staff members to disagree and thus defocus off of him? When does he display the first sentimentality and how does demonstrate ownership? How does he gather infor-mation about others to use against them? These are only a few things to watch for as you view this film.

We have discussed the fact that whether in the institution or in the community, criminals have a tremendous network where they interact with one another. Many of these individuals may know who you are and things about you before they ever walk in and sit in a chair and talk to you. They may know what some of your vulnerabilities are. They may know what interests or hobbies you may have. "Seated across the interviewing table was Casey. His face and mannerisms displayed hate and anger. I knew that he knew about me from his own sources" (Walsh, 2005).

The following is an illustration of how inmates accomplish this. In Powder River, five clients sat at a table playing cards. They did not see the observing staff member; however, he could hear what they were saying. The clients were discussing another staff member who was at the other end of the building. They were conspiring about how they were going to get to know this staff member. They decided they would have each client, individually, go up to the staff member and ask a question or make an observation. In other words, they were going to find his buttons. They were getting ready to set him up. We observed this process as one client would get up, go down and interact with the targeted staff person. The client would come back and report to the other four clients. They would share information on how the staff member responded to their questions or what his observations were. Then, another client would go to the staff person and repeat the process. Their goal was to "spin the therapist" to see what it would take to get the therapist upset or frustrated. We confronted them with their behavior in a community meeting after this event.

4. **Be prepared to terminate interviews when anger stands in the way of receptivity, disclosure, and a dialog, and most certainly if the client is directly threatening or intimidating.** In the discussion on tactics, we mentioned how criminals use anger to control situations and other people to get their own way and to avoid responsibility and accountability for their actions. "The agent of change (A.C.) has no hope of being successful if he allows a criminal to set the conditions of a meeting. Nor can an agent of change who is permissive later establish himself as a firm authority. The A.C. must have the confidence and strength to assume control of the interview right away" (Yochelson and Samenow, 1977). "One should not hesitate to exit a potentially dangerous situation and/or ask for help from other staff. . . . Moreover, a staff member should not remain in a room alone with an agitated inmate, the employee should call for assistance and wait for help to arrive" (Elliott and Verdeyen, 2002).

5. If you use a confrontational style, be sure to be direct and firm without being provocative and forcing the client into a corner where an attack is his only way out. Often, we have seen staff get into a power-thrusting situation with a client. The client always will win these efforts. Remember, the client's whole life is based on gaining and losing power and control. We may imprison clients, suspend them from treatment, give them a learning experience, but the clients believe they have won.

We will not accomplish anything in treatment if the criminals feel as if they have to fight us. If we get into a power thrust with clients, we should apologize to them and tell them that was not our intention. Tell the criminals that you are ending the session because you feel that you are in a power struggle with them and you do not feel comfortable with this. You could go on to say that when you feel more in control of yourself, you will have another session with them.

Early on in the Powder River Program, as this philosophy was being developed and implemented, a supervisor observed a client misbehaving. He asked another staff member to come with him and ordered the client to come to the office. While the supervisor was reading the riot act to the inmate, a power thrust began. The supervisor escalated and the inmate escalated. After a few minutes, the inmate sat back with a large smile. When he was questioned about this he said, "I knew I could get you angry." The supervisor also sat back and replied, "You certainly did. That is not how I choose to act. Please leave while I calm down and then come back. Let's say you will be back in ten minutes."

"Firmness and strength should not be confused with harshness. Cornering a criminal and interrogating him, to get him to talk breeds either silence or contests" (Yochelson and Samenow, 1977). "Directly challenging an inmate . . . can easily lead to a power struggle, from which staff seldom comes away a winner. . . . It is crucial that correctional employees understand that engaging in power struggles with an inmate, especially a psychopathic one, is risky business" (Elliott and Verdeyen, 2002). This was addressed previously, but it needs to be emphasized. Remember, criminals spend their whole life, seven days a week, perfecting their technique. They always will be better at this than we will. Often times, they are even better at what they do than we are at what we do. But, be assured they are better at what they do than we will ever be at what they do. "You are never going to intimidate or threaten inmates and get them to say that staff are tougher then they are. . . . what you face is that you will eventually be in a courtroom or the inmate will injure or kill a staff member" (Bartollas, 2004).

Also, we most often get into a power thrust because we feel we have been disrespected by the inmate and we become offended. In one instance, a security manager rushed to the treatment dorm to set things right because he felt his staff had been disrespected. He was offended that this had happened. The treatment director was running right behind him, trying to reason with him that this was going to undermine the treatment staff's credibility and would only escalate the situation. Thankfully, this manager was mature and able to stop before he reached the dorm. A more thoughtful solution was agreed upon and a power struggle avoided. Staff "cannot allow themselves to be provoked." They "must remain true even when inmates may swear at the warden or insult staff members" (Bartollas, 2004).

Dyer (2002) said, "There are no justified resentments. . . . All the time you hear people say: 'I have a right to be upset because of the way I've been treated. I have a right to be angry, hurt, and resentful.'" Carlos Castaneda said it this way: "Self-importance is our greatest enemy. Think about it—what weakens us is feeling offended by the deeds and misdeeds of our fellow men. Our self-importance requires that we spend most of our lives offended by someone" (from *The Fire Within* by Carlos Castaneda. Copyright 1984 by Carlos Castaneda. Reprinted by permission of Simon & Schuster Adult Publishing Group). A person in the corrections field, working with the clients we do, can find a multitude of reasons to be offended. "Just about anything will do if you are looking for an occasion to be offended" (Dyer, 2001). You will never find a mature correctional change agent engaging in this kind of behavior. "A power struggle does not depend on behavior. It depends on intention. The intention to manipulate and control creates a power struggle when it meets the same intention. A power struggle collapses when you withdraw your energy from it," (Zukav and Francis, 2001). You must give yourself the permission to not always be right or to win or to be offended.

6. **Expect to have to repeat the same point in different ways.** Repetition will be necessary. You may have to keep repeating the same instruction to criminals for four or five months before they can come to understand and accept the point you are trying to make. It is much like working with chronic mentally ill clients. Expect baby steps from this population. It takes an average of three times longer to get an idea across to the criminal than it does to a prosocial client, according to the author's personal observation. Many counselors get discouraged because it takes so long to see movement with the criminal clients.

Staff often set objectives by their prosocial standards and then bemoan the fact that the client is not progressing as rapidly as they want. As mentioned before, successfully treating criminals is a time consuming task. You cannot rush the criminal through treatment. "How many times is it necessary to hit bottom before a lesson is learned? Perhaps thousands, which may account for the sheer quantity of human suffering, so vast as to be incomprehensible. Slowly, by inches, does civilization advance" (Hawkins, 1995). And inch by inch, we assist the criminal to move to become a responsible member of society. Sometimes it is more exciting watching grass grow than to watch a criminal grow. "They knew that it is a long process that has to be carried out little by little at a snail's pace" (Castenada, 1984). "What works is not doable in piecemeal, grab-bag or fast and easy fashion" (Porporino, 2005). Programs of this type are seen as programs with "high program-attrition rates . . . leading to labeling of the program as 'too long,' 'too difficult,' or 'too structured and too inflexible'" (Porporino, 2005).

Another area to consider here is to use as many object lessons as possible. Write diagrams or use role plays. Illustrate by using something that is visual. Assign tasks that have to be physically carried out. In this regard, see Jacobs and Spadaro (2003). It is helpful to use a chalkboard during treatment sessions to draw diagrams or write down what you are saying. Though many of these clients can talk your ear off about something and write beautiful abstract concepts, their talk and abstracts have no meaning to them. There is no connection between what they say and what they mean. They are masters at feeding the change agent what they think the change agent wants to hear.

We use the phrase "time will tell" (from Samenow) repeatedly with the client. This approach and attitude assists the staff person from setting expectations that are too high. You see growth one day and are excited by it. Then, the next day it is gone and you have to begin again on the same subject.

HOME/COMMUNITY RELATIONSHIPS

Your home and community life generally will determine how well you do as a competent correctional change agent. If most of your friends are fellow correctional people, it becomes very easy to get a jaundiced view of the world. People often begin to see everyone else in the same light as they see the criminal, including family members. So, it is imperative to cultivate a healthy lifestyle outside of the correctional setting (Cornelius, 2005). Getting involved in community groups such as service clubs, church, synagogue, or mosque can be quite empowering. Donating time to worthy community endeavors often is a great release from the constant grind of corrections. "Some people clearly focus on other aspects of their personal life and their fulfillment comes from contributions to their community that enhance the quality of life for their children and community" (Bartollas, 2004).

Insurance of a healthy family life, also, lends itself to a more stable work attitude. Staff "cannot be a model of integrity if they beat their spouse and children or have problems with substance abuse" (Bartollas, 2004). Of course, it is vital that one does not bring any home or community problems into the workplace.

SET UP

We have discussed the inmate's efforts at manipulating the change agent, but this is not the sum and total of what we are about. However, it is important to avoid the con games sprung on us by the inmates.

From the very first moment criminals meet us, they are trying to set us up. They need to manipulate us, get something over on us, control us, and push our buttons to be able to escape being held accountable and responsible for their behavior. They do this in the many ways we already have discussed. "Many inmates are seeking to compromise the integrity of the institution in some way that they can use or to exploit this information to position themselves to compromise institutional security. There is no limit to the scenarios" (Bartollas, 2004).

"Unfortunately for staff, the good con (the successful duping of prison officials) simply requires careful thought and knowledge of the person being deceived" (Elliott and Verdeyen, 2002). Remember the previous story of the new correctional officer who felt unprepared to run the unit. Elliott and Verden go on to say, "Testing refers to an effort to create a situation in which an inmate can gather information about a staff member or a group of staff . . . . In most cases, the inmate bears no particular malice toward the employee whom he or she attempts to discredit; rather, the offender merely seeks to achieve a sense of superiority over the staff member." Remember the previous illustration about the five inmates at Powder River gathering information about a new staff member.

Criminals will compliment, accidentally touch, ask for small favors that are not warranted, suggest that some rules be set aside for them, and so forth. They will cajole, empathize, sympathize, and express concern. They will build up our egos, offer to help, pledge faith and devotion, share similar problems, create a you/me syndrome (they don't understand you, but I do; they're wrong about you; they're treating you like they treat us), confess how much they need us, and so forth. It is important to understand this and be alert to it.

This is from an essay signed, "A psychopath in prison" (Hare, 1993):

> He will choose you, disarm you with his words, and control you with this presence. He will delight you with his wit and his plans. He will show you a good time, but you will always get the bill. He will smile and deceive you, and he will scare you with his eyes. And when he is through with you, and he will be through with you, he will desert you and take with him your innocence and your pride. You will be left much sadder but not a lot wiser, and for a long time, you will wonder what happened and what you did wrong. And if another of his kind comes knocking at your door, will you open it?

Earlier we talked about excitement and mentioned the film *The Outside Woman*. The woman in this film, who commandeered the helicopter to break the men out of prison, is a good example of how the change agent's needs get used by criminals to their advantage.

When you watch this film, look for the following. What did Joyce (the change agent here) need from the criminal? How did Jesse (the criminal) go about setting Joyce up? What was the first set up and what other acts of setting Joyce up did Jesses do? What was the second hook used by Jesse and what was the final hook? Where was the excitement evident in the movie and when was the good guy displayed? What do the following statements from the movie mean? "You have her on the hook—use her up." "People use people until they use them up—it's all about using and being used." "Don't waste time on things free men waste time on—do you have time to waste?" "If you play it right, it is a kick."

The following episode illustrates this. One of our recovering staff attended local self-help meetings. Sometime in the past, a present client also had attended the same self-help group (this is a common problem in small rural communities). While working for us and when this client was in treatment, a former significant other of hers died. The following is a letter that the male client gave to this female counselor.

Come Away

When theres a time of need that has a healing from the hidden side of your loss. Wishing that I could real be able to comfort you as real as I'm being held by you now. Learning that you need support. My sincerity is as real as I may be able to speak it. I've worked at how I care. You need the courage to see that a man is very real. That a man can be very caring. Come away with me as you listen to a real giving man. Take what is inside as we can both come away together. I may not be able to hold you but my thought of holding you is reaching to pull you threw. Come away and let me be real comfort. A lot of what is written, as you can feel my words. Heal what you feel is hidden. Come away an see that I still care about who you are. A friend in my eyes is what I see in you take my friendship. Because I really care.

In this note, there are many set ups and thinking errors. Read through it before you continue and identify as many of the errors as possible. Then, continue reading. The errors include "feed the change agent," "pretentiousness," "good person," "rationalization," "criminal pride," "grandiosity," and "uniqueness," to name some.

We repeatedly have discussed the need not to discuss personal matters in front of clients, as they are searching for this kind of information. In our jail program, one of the women staff members was going through difficulty with her husband. She and another woman staff member were free in telling sexual jokes with each other and making sexual remarks to each other. The woman was surprised one morning, on coming to work, to be presented with a papier-mâché of male genitals by a male inmate. She was shocked and could not understand why he would have done this. She was unaware of how her sexual discussion, being overheard by inmates, gave them what they thought was permission to become much more familiar with her. "An obvious example of familiarity is discussing any kind of personal or financial problem with or in the vicinity of inmates" (Elliott and Verdeyen, 2002).

THE FINAL ANALYSIS

We leave you with these final thoughts from two well known and wise people. The first is part of the poem "If" by Rudyard Kipling.

If you can keep your head when all about you
Are losing theirs and blaming it on you,
If you can trust yourself when all men doubt you
But make allowance for their doubting too,
Or being lied about, don't deal in lies,
Or being hated, don't give way to hating,
And yet don't look too good, nor talk too wise:

If you can meet with Triumph and Disaster
And treat those two impostors just the same;
If you can bear to hear the truth you've spoken
Twisted by knaves to make a trap for fools,
Or watch the things you gave your life to, broken,
And stoop and build 'em up with worn-out tools:
If neither foes nor loving friends can hurt you;
If all men count with you, but none too much,

If you can fill the unforgiving minute
With sixty seconds' worth of distance run,
Yours is the Earth and everything that's in it,

And what's more you will be a model correctional change agent.

The second, "The Final Analysis," comes from Mother Theresa of Calcutta.

The Final Analysis

People are often unreasonable, illogical and self-centered;
Forgive them anyway.
If you are kind, people may accuse you of selfish, ulterior motives;
Be kind anyway.
If you are successful, you will win some false friends and some true enemies;
Succeed anyway.
If you are honest and frank, people may cheat you;
Be honest and frank anyway.
What you spend years building, someone may destroy overnight;
Build anyway.
If you find serenity and happiness, they may be jealous;
Be happy anyway.
The good you do today, people will often forget tomorrow;
Do good anyway.
Give the world the best you have, and it may never be enough;
Give the world the best you have anyway.

You see, in the final analysis, it is all between you and your conscience, you and your ethics, you and your morals, you and the Universe, and you and your higher power. It was never between you and the inmate anyway.

chapter 6

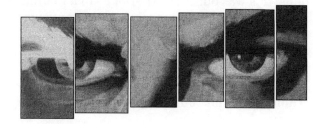

COGNITIVE RESTRUCTURING PROGRAMS

ORIGINS OF THE POWDER RIVER PROGRAM

We arrived at the ideas for the antisocial model after much deliberation, research, trial, and error. This search began at the Powder River Correctional Facility Alcohol and Drug Program in Baker City, Oregon. Our ideas continued to be solidified in the Klamath Falls Treatment and Corrections Provider's Consortium in Klamath Falls, Oregon.

When the Powder River Correction Facility was built in 1989, the Oregon Department of Corrections authorized a fifty-bed alcohol and drug therapeutic program. We outline the beginnings of the Powder River Alcohol and Drug Program (PRAD) and the research that was developed in 1990. This chapter describes the changes that have occurred in the past several years.

WORKING WITH CRIMINALS: SOME INITIAL SHOCKS

When we began at Powder River in the alcohol and drug program, we thought we knew something about how to work with criminals. We quickly found out that we did not. The staff really did not know anything about how to work with criminals, especially not with criminals within a

175

prison setting. We were developing a therapeutic community. For most of us, this was our first experience in a therapeutic community. It took us a year to develop the program and antisocial model discussed in the book. It took another two years for us to become comfortable with the dynamics. Ever since that time, it has been an evolving process.

VARIANCES FROM CORRECTIONAL POLICY

In the Powder River program, we obtained many variances to correctional policy and procedures because we were the first alcohol/drug therapeutic program inside an institution in Oregon. Cornerstone, a thirty-five-bed correctional alcohol and drug program, had existed for some time in Oregon outside an institution. In Cornerstone, people are taken outside the institution to another building, a lock-up.

We examined several things to see what worked and what did not. We negotiated many items with the Department of Corrections. One area was the development of a therapeutic community inside a prison. In Oregon state correctional institutions, inmates do not tell other inmates what to do. However, in any type of therapeutic community, you need a hierarchy where the residents have responsibility to instruct other inmates or residents on what to do. This was the topic of our first discussion.

Other negotiations addressed such issues as treatment staff being able to take residents outside the facility to self-help groups, community services, and so forth. Family therapy was another issue. Visitor's rights were not granted to recent past felons and especially to drug-related felons. We had to get waivers to allow family members to attend family therapy inside the facility. Another concern was to develop a structure where the program could hold these residents accountable without using the quasi-legal proceedings of the corrections department. We developed a disciplinary system for the program within the department's system, and the Consortium modified this.

PROGRAM DESIGN

The Powder River program was six to fifteen months long, on average at least nine months. Inmates were awakened at 6:00 AM and went to bed at 11:00 PM. Throughout the day, we kept them busy.

Alcohol/drug staff arrived at 6:00 AM and stayed until 10:00 PM when a correctional officer came in, remaining through the evening until the alcohol/drug staff returned in the morning. The inmates slept during the hours the correctional staff supervised the program, except for one hour.

ADMISSION CRITERIA

Inmates admitted to the Powder River program had from six to fifteen months to serve and were free of detainers. This meant that inmates were not eligible if they had a pending county or city charge for which they would have to return to court upon release. We discovered that it is best to discharge people from the program directly into an aftercare program in their community. We did not want them to go back into the general prison population. We spent the duration of program time addressing their thinking errors, getting them to rethink and confront the criminal code. If they were to return to the general prison population or go back into a jail setting, they immediately were going to pick up the criminal code for their own protection. So, we did not want them to have any detainers, which could send them back to court, to jail, or into the general prison population. The third requirement was that they had no severe medical problem because the facility did not have a major medical facility. If people had to have teeth extracted or some kind of operation, we sent them to a prison facility equipped with the proper facilities. Once they went to another facility, because of transportation problems, they often were back in the general prison population for two or three weeks. That required us to start over. Thus, they had to be medically capable of completing the program.

The fourth requirement for admission was that they had no mental problems. Since the criminal was a dually diagnosed client, we did not want any other diagnoses such as schizophrenia or manic/depressive illness that required medication because we used no medication in the treatment program.

The final requirement was that patients not be sentenced sex offenders. However, three-fourths of the clients had committed sex offenses. They just were not caught or had plea bargained down to something else. Suffice it to say that for most of our residents, sex offense was not their crime of record. However, as we worked with them, we found that they had committed sex offenses.

177

PROGRAM INGREDIENTS

The Powder River facility was built on the idea of the therapeutic community. Every room opened out into a community or common area. All the bedrooms, group rooms, and offices opened into this common area. When people came out of any of the offices or bedrooms, they had to come into a common area. This promoted the therapeutic idea of everyone being together. The entire community ate together at Powder River. Clients went to self-help groups together, conducted recreation together, attended community meetings as an entire group, and conducted accountability group meetings together.

GOALS FOR RESIDENTS

When residents/clients came into the program, they came into the pretreatment unit at Powder River and into level I at the Consortium. In the first two months in treatment, we wanted the residents to accomplish four major goals. First, we wanted the residents to accept that they were an alcoholic and/or an addict and work through any denial concerning this. Secondly, we wanted the residents to accept the idea that they were criminals and to work through any denial about this as well. The third thing we wanted them to do was to buy into the therapeutic community where other residents gave them instructions, and they gave other residents instructions.

They confronted residents and had residents confront them. This was probably the biggest hurdle in terms of the assessment and level I. The convict code is that you do not rat, narc, or squeal on each other. You do everything you can to get one over on the man, and that is what the game is all about for the criminal. As we have stressed, criminals are out to set up the therapist/change agent from the day they meet him or her.

The fourth goal was that the residents had to accept the whole idea of treatment. If they accomplished this within the first two months, then we moved them into treatment at Powder River and level II at the Consortium. If they did not accomplish these goals, we terminated them from the program.

THE SCHEDULE

The schedule, shown in Appendix B, provides a sense of the intensity of the program. We held at least two groups each day. Generally, criminals attended an individual session each week. In addition, the day consisted of meditation, self-help meetings, and a criminality class for most residents. More than half of the residents attended school on a daily basis at Powder River. Some classes included English as a second language, work toward the general equivalency degree, and continuing education. Some who entered the program could not read or write English, and when they left the program, they could read and write English at a third or fourth grade level. We felt this was a strong area of the program.

DEPARTMENTS

We organized all facets of the department and the program. The Powder River program had five departments: the beautification/inspiration department, the recreation department, the education department, the orientation department, and the coordinating council. All clients, as they entered the treatment phase of the program, were assigned to one of these departments and their responsibility was to help in managing it. The system was highly organized. The departments managed what we did in the therapeutic community except for the counseling.

The education department was responsible for getting residents into formal education, Alcoholics Anonymous meetings, and for scheduling all of the treatment program education groups, such as values clarification, grief, anger, nutritional class, sexuality class, and the codependency group. All these groups were in addition to the two daily therapy groups.

At Powder River, clients were assigned to the departments either as a crew member, a crew chief, a department head, or a coordinator on the council. We developed descriptions for all of the positions. Clients made weekly written reports to staff. These reports focused on their assigned responsibilities at Powder River. They were being taught how to work together and how to take and give instructions. This was important because often criminals cannot take or give instructions in an acceptable way.

UPDATED POWDER RIVER ALCOHOL AND DRUG TREATMENT PROGRAM INFORMATION

Because of the success of the Powder River Program, there have been significant expansions to the program. One change was that during the late 1990s, Baker County Council on Alcohol and Drugs, Inc. changed its name to "New Directions Northwest" (NDN). The following information comes from NDN's website with the permission of Bart Murray, Executive Director, from Oregon State Archives, from Chapter 464 Oregon Laws 2003 and from the Truthought's website with permission from Rogie Spon.

Oregon State Legislative action has greatly influenced the program. An expanded number of beds available for treatment at the Powder River Correctional Facility was one of the direct effects of the legislation. In September 2003, the alcohol and drug program bed capacity was expanded from 50 beds to 178 beds by the Oregon Department of Corrections. Renamed the New Directions Alternative Incarceration Program at Powder River (AIP), its goal was to continue the same effective correctional treatment. The Oregon Law as activated by a very progressive and treatment-oriented legislature stated:

The Department of Corrections shall establish an intensive alternative incarceration addiction program. The program shall:

1. Be based on intensive interventions, rigorous personal responsibility and accountability, physical labor and service to the community;
2. Require strict discipline and compliance with program rules;
3. Provide fourteen hours of highly structured and regimented routine every day;
4. Provide for cognitive restructuring to enable offenders participating in the program to confront and alter their criminal thinking patterns;
5. Provide addictions treatment that incorporates proven, research-based interventions; and
6. Be at least 279 days' duration.

This State legislative body mandated cognitive restructuring into its prison-based programs. In addition, it recognized that treatment is a long-term process and legislated a minimum of nine months of treatment.

"Clients who stay in treatment longer and who complete the program regime are more likely to have better outcomes. And findings indicate that drug offenders who receive twelve-to-fifteen months of treatment in prison followed by an additional six months of drug treatment and job training in the community were more than twice as likely to be drug-free as offenders who received prison-based treatment alone" Montague (2001).

The law also established admission criteria and stated that "Offenders participating in the program and successfully completing the program are eligible for a transitional leave of up to ninety days."

The Department of Corrections' Administrative Rule #291-062 established the following admission criteria:

1. Must have no less then 10 months and no more than 36 months left on their sentence
2. Have a minimum-security classification
3. Must not have an escape conviction on his record [only males were eligible]
4. Must not have a detainer for his return to a city or county jurisdiction;
5. Must have no other legal charge qualifications to do with severity of crime and mandatory sentencing guidelines;
6. The inmate must submit a written request to participate with a signed statement stating he is physically and mentally able to withstand the rigors of the program
7. The inmate must agree to comply with each of the program requirements

The administrative rule also states that "because alternative incarceration program participants who successfully complete their program will effectively receive a reduction in their incarceration term, they will be held to a higher standard of behavior on transitional leave than other inmates on short-term transitional leave."

The administrative rule covered many of the variances initially required when the program was first developed such as grooming, canteen operations, food service, internal processes for staff and inmates outlining the applicable requirements and/or restrictions specific to these programs. Now they are law. Some of these variances meet the needs of the therapeutic community.

NDN's website says:

> This concept saves taxpayers money, provides quality treatment to the most high risk offenders, and increases the possibilities of ending the prison cycle that is taxing the resources of every state in America. The firm commitment to alternative motivation strategies (early release), on a voluntary basis, creates an opportunity for treatment professionals to refine correction interventions and treat only those criminals who have a genuine interest in changing their lives. The core treatment values of New Direction Alternative Incarceration Program are not complex. Alcoholics Anonymous and Narcotics Anonymous provide established introspective and spiritual tools. Cognitive behavioral groups and individual therapy provide an arena for self-criticism, humility, and a change through moral growth, and the "therapeutic community" provides a safe and accountable environment to rehearse pro social and community building skills. The therapeutic community concept makes the program one of the safest places in the Oregon prison system.

In fourteen years, there have only been two fights, no sexual assaults, no hospitalizations due to violence, no staff has been assaulted, and only one escape.

HORTICULTURE PROGRAM

Five years ago, Oregon passed legislation that mandated every inmate work. The Oregon Department of Corrections was struggling to create jobs that could provide real work, not just "make work." The Oregon Department of Employment, indicating a sustained need for workers in the growing Oregon horticulture industry, prompted staff at Powder River to investigate a horticulture skills program.

The idea was to integrate cognitive-behavioral alcohol and drug treatment with the sobriety of working with plants. Horticulture therapy had proven successful in one correctional facility in Florida, where staff was experiencing 50 percent fewer disciplinary problems after "lifers" were introduced to gardening. We felt horticulture could be a valuable addition to clinical recovery work.

In the spring of 1998, with the support of the Department of Corrections Inmate Work Programs and Department of Corrections Correctional Treatment Services, we were able to hire a horticulturist, build a greenhouse, and purchase tools. It was the beginning of an extraordinary journey.

Initial reaction to the project was mixed. Security staff saw numerous risks and more monitoring of tools and areas. The Department of Corrections administration questioned spending money for horticulture therapy when the legislative mood was more "bricks and bars construction." In the end, an alliance of work programs, clinical practice, security realities, and administrative risk taking allowed Powder River to proceed as a pilot horticulture program.

In September of 1998, the Horticulture Program came together with a sixteen-week course in basic horticulture skills. The core curriculum included plant anatomy and physiology, growing structures, plant propagation, integrated pest management, landscape design, and vegetable gardening. Each inmate had his own greenhouse table of seedlings and cuttings. They were responsible for the success, or failure, of their table. The personal growth and nurturing connections were made with little effort. Inmates were responding:

- "This is like trying to stay out of jail, you keep your table clean, fertilize, feed, keep the environment just right and things grow . . . no effort, no growth."
- "This is the first time I have done something that has succeeded, all by myself, I'm getting a feeling that I can do anything if I slow down and pay attention to details."
- "It gets heavy when you lose a plant you have been trying to save. It sounds crazy from me, but I can relate to loss. I can relate to what I have done to people. They looked at me the way I look at these plants. Don't do it, please hang in there, don't give up . . . it's so clear it is hard to handle."
- "I can have some real craziness going on in group, or on the unit. . . . I come out here and start digging and fussing, I forget about it, I begin to relax. I begin to see things in a less threatening way. I go back, I'm OK, I figure out, it is me just wanting my way or being bull-headed again."
- "I grew dope for years. I never saw myself growing anything legal. I can see growing things that people like to look at, like to see in their garden, I can see running a greenhouse. I never saw anything like that before."

As we complete our third full season, the program has stabilized and our initial vision is becoming reality. Our program has a work crew that has turned our facility into an island of hanging plants, vegetable gardens, rose gardens, bedding plants, indigenous flowers, trees, shrubs, and lawns. We have graduated more than 100 men with the skills to go directly into the horticulture trade. We provide food for the facility and community programs in need. In our next season, we plan to enter a contract with the Department of Transportation to bring indigenous plants back to the roadsides, parks, and rest areas of eastern Oregon. Our horticulturist is now consulting with two other Oregon facilities to expand horticulture programming in other eastern Oregon prisons. Perhaps the most important aspect is that men who complete the Horticulture Program complete the treatment program at a 20 percent better rate than those who do not get involved with the program.

PROGRAM SUCCESS

Since 2004, four research projects are affiliated with our program: In November, the University of California Los Angeles Integrated Substance Abuse Programs began a two-year study of our graduates, and Alex Millkey, a graduate student at Pacific University, will complete a doctoral thesis on our effectiveness on clients while in treatment in 2005. Oregon Department of Corrections' Research is also studying the effectiveness of treatment versus a control group of inmates who do not receive treatment. Results are expected in 2007. Currently, we are 79 percent successful with our current population staying out of prison for ninety days after their release, according to the Oregon Department of Corrections. This figure coordinates with the Alternative Incarceration Program Oregon Legislature Bill passed in 2004, which allows a sentence reduction if an inmate completes our program and ninety days of close supervision in the community. We treat the most difficult addiction cases in the state. Several evaluative studies completed on the program consistently revealed the program as successful.

The January 1995 study considered three-year criminal activity outcomes on 163 subjects. These are shown in Table 6.1 below.

TABLE 6.1. RATES OF AVOIDING ARREST, CONVICTION, OR PRISON INCARCERATION FOR THREE YEARS AFTER PRISON RELEASE FOR POWDER RIVER ALCOHOL AND DRUG PROGRAM PARTICIPANTS

	No ARRESTS	No CONVICTION	No PRISON TIME
Drop-Outs (N=44) (less than 60 days)	11%	20%	27%
Partial Treatment (N=52) (60-150 days)	27%	46%	52%
Treatment (N=67) (more than 150 days)	43%	54%	63%

The report goes on to say, "Based on three-year follow-up data, the program appears to be reducing criminal activity of program participants as measured by arrest, conviction, and reincarceration rates. Offenders who completed five months of the program show a 54 percent decrease in arrests and a 66 percent decrease in convictions following treatment."

In December 1992, the program submitted data on its program participants to the 1992 Search for Excellence in Chemical Dependency Treatment competition sponsored by the JM Foundation and the Scaife Family Foundation. Although the submitted sample included data on only eighty-four participants—fifty-five who completed the program and twenty-nine who did not—the findings were significant. The program scored as follows:

TABLE 6.2. EXCELLENCE REPORT

Primary Treatment in Chemical Dependency
1992 Search for Excellence (Walker and Associates, 1992)
Overall Excellence Ranking, your program: Top 10 percent.

Excellence Factor	All Residential Program Applicants			Your Program	
	25%	50%	75%	Data	%
% Total abstinence maintained through six-month follow-up	26%	35%	49%	65%	94%
% Total or limited abstinence	38%	50%	60%	76%	93%
% Completing Treatment program	45%	63%	75%	65%	57%
% Active in self-help group at follow-up	19%	36%	50%	46%	64%
% Employed, in school or training	28%	44%	63%	44%	51%
Average program cost per person completing program	$15,500	$6,600	$3,400	$10,657	33%
Average program cost per person achieving total or limited abstinence	$18,600	$9,200	$4.800	$9,159	51%
Average severity level of persons served, "scores" range from 3.8 to 9.0	5.3	6.1	7.1	7.5	85%

The program won first place in the competition and a cash prize of $25,000.

In January 1996, the program again was evaluated (Oregon Department of Corrections, 1996). This study was based on 262 clients who entered the residential program since its conception and who were released from prison before April 1994. They were in the program thirty-one days or more. In this evaluation, two methods of analyzing program outcomes were used: matched comparison group approach and base-expectancy modeling. The case-by-case matching approach selected a "best fit" comparison group of untreated inmates.

Comparing the recidivism of treated inmates with statistically weighted average rates of reincarceration and conviction for new crimes, the program showed some reduction in prison return and a reduction in new convictions. The reductions in incarceration are greater at one or two years after parole, and are relatively small after three years. Using the other approach, when treated inmates are compared with matched untreated inmates, the program demonstrated reductions in incarceration and conviction for the first two years after release from prison. Overall, depending on the measure and the period of observation, inmates treated in the program had recidivism rates between 5 and 40 percent lower than comparable untreated offenders. Two years after release from prison, clients had 33 percent fewer convictions, and 24 percent fewer revocations than their matched comparison group.

Longer treatment generally appears to reduce recidivism. Clients who had longer stays in treatment tended to have lower postprison rates of conviction and incarceration. Reductions seem to occur after 120 days or more of treatment.

THE KLAMATH FALLS CONSORTIUM CENTER DAY TREATMENT PROGRAM

PROGRAM DESIGN

This section describes the initial design of the Consortium program followed by the changes initiated during the past ten years. Several of the changes already have been noted, such as the reward system and the development of the thinking error and tactic clusters.

The Consortium program had a dual track. Many clients were working or going to school in the daytime. For them to participate in treatment, an evening track was necessary. The program was open from 7:30 AM to 11:00 PM Monday through Friday. This allowed a day reporting/day treatment program to accommodate clients in an evening program. A benefit of parallel programs was that it allowed clients from each track to make up sessions in the other track. Clients could be moved between the two tracks for a variety of reasons, including program violation. Some clients were assigned to several days or weeks of both day and night treatment as a learning experience for misbehaving.

The Consortium program was designed as a year-long program with clients moving through four levels of treatment. However, some clients took much longer to accomplish all of the tasks of each level. Often, clients were demoted a level for misbehavior and required to begin over at an appointed level. Level I was eight weeks; level II was fifteen weeks and further intensified level I treatment, addressing criminal thinking and addiction issues. The twelve weeks of level III moved into more of the traditional alcohol and drug treatment, addressing issues such as stress management, communication skills, feelings, and so forth. In the nine-week level IV, aftercare and relapse prevention planning occurred.

ADMISSION CRITERIA

The Consortium program provided treatment for nonincarcerated, alcohol and other drug-abusing offenders (criminals) with five or more drug-related arrests. In contrast with the other programs, sex offenders and people with posttraumatic stress disorders and mental illness were admitted.

PROGRAM INGREDIENTS

The Consortium building, unlike the Powder River program, was not ideal for the therapeutic community idea, or for that matter, not ideal for an antisocial-model treatment program. It did not have enough room, and the layout was not security friendly. In the Consortium, we provided microwaved meals three times a day for all clients who were present.

THE SCHEDULE

At least two groups were held each day. Generally, there was an individual session each week. In addition, the day consisted of meditation, self-help meetings, and criminality or alcohol/drug class for most clients. The Consortium's evening program was abbreviated to two on-site groups. In the Consortium program, many clients were referred out to classes, job training, mental health treatment, sex offender treatment, posttraumatic stress syndrome treatment, and so forth.

DEPARTMENTS

The departments were modified at the Consortium because of the day reporting/day treatment format to include the food, the inspiration/beautification, the orientation, and the cleaning departments. Only selected clients were assigned to these tasks. The Consortium clients were either crew chiefs or crew members. Job descriptions for all of the positions were developed in the Consortium program similar to the Powder River program.

PROGRAM CHANGES OVER THE PAST TEN YEARS

Several dynamics necessitated changes in the program over its years of existence to allow the program to respond to new research and client-response information. This resulted in the development of the reward system and the clustering of the errors and tactics.

The grant for the project ended in September of 1998. Many people in the community thought with the end of the grant, the program would not continue. However, an outpouring of the community partners, such as judges, adult family services, corrections, the college, United Way, police, and others clearly indicated that the Consortium filled a community need and should be continued. Funds to continue the program were provided by the local mental health clinic, the state alcohol and drug agency, services for children and families, the local correction department, United Way, and a contract with the two Oregon Health Plan contractors.

However, this meant that the program shortened the daytime track to begin at 1 PM rather than 8 AM. The evening track was continued. The food service portion of the program was eliminated, along with the housing opportunities. The beautification/inspirational, orientation, and cleaning departments were continued.

STAGES OF CHANGE

Oregon statutes recently dictated the use of the American Society of Addiction Medicine (ASAM) continued stay and discharge criteria and the stages of change format. With this mandate, the Consortium in 2001 changed its stages of treatment to be more client driven. Clients proceeded at their own pace through each of the following stages, and in some cases a client could complete treatment in as little as six months. In addition, clients could enter the treatment regimen at any of the first three stages, depending on their past treatment and current status. For example, clients leaving prison, who had completed a program at Powder River, most likely would enter treatment at stage III. Also, a client completing a community residential treatment program could enter at stage III. The components of treatment addressing the thinking process remained constant with all the changes.

STAGE I: ENGAGEMENT

At this stage of treatment, the client does not have a working relationship with a counselor. The client does not have an understanding of the program or therapy used by this facility. Goals of the engagement stage are to establish a therapeutic relationship and gain information to break through the walls of denial. The objective was that clients must demonstrate at least 20 percent progress in each of the six ASAM dimensions to advance to the next stage of treatment. Clients had fourteen activities to assist them in achieving the goals.

STAGE II: PERSUASION

In Stage II of treatment, clients have a working relationship with a counselor and the program. The goal of this stage is to help the clients see that substance use and criminal thinking and behavior have produced negative results that interfere with their achieving personal goals and that treatment can help empower them to achieve their goals. The objective was that the client must demonstrate at least 40 percent progress in each of the six ASAM dimensions to advance to the next stage of treatment. Again, there were fourteen activities to assist the client to achieve this.

STAGE III: ACTIVE TREATMENT

During this active stage of treatment, having recognized that substance abuse and the individual's thinking process are problems, the client takes an active part in recovery. The desire to pursue abstinence now comes from the client. The goal is to establish interventions for chemical use and criminal thinking and behavior. The objective is for the client to demonstrate at least 60 percent progress in each of the six dimensions to advance. Sixteen activities are available to help this process.

STAGE IV: RELAPSE PREVENTION

During this stage, the client has discontinued substance use and has abstained from criminal thinking and behavior. The goal is to establish ongoing plans to ensure continued abstinence of substances and criminal thinking and behavior. The client continues to address other areas of functioning, such as social relationships and work. This sometimes requires referral to community service. Some referrals are made to the Consortium Alumni, the Community Resource Center, Work Connection, and Clean/Sober Support Groups. Clients successfully complete treatment while in this stage during a ceremony with their peers, family, and staff. At the conclusion, clients are presented with a medallion and a graduation certificate. There are thirteen activities for this stage.

During this time, a jail treatment program was initiated through an Edward Byrnes Memorial Grant (this program is described in more detail later). An additional pod was built to house jail treatment, outpatient treatment, and the county parolee and probation offices, but no funds became available to provide the full spectrum of treatment. This reduced the size of the Consortium Day Treatment program.

CONSTRAINING INFLUENCES, DETERMINING PARTNERS, AND CONTRACTING

By Steve Berger, Klamath Falls Community Corrections Manager
Edited by Boyd Sharp

During the construction phase of the Community Corrections Center, it became clear there would be insufficient funding from the state or county to operate the work-release program incorporated into the design of the facility. This initiated significant debate by the Local Public Safety Coordinating Council on the fate of this facility, specifically on what would be done with the first floor.

At the same time, state funding for alcohol and drug treatment and other counseling services was significantly reduced, forcing many local providers to evaluate their ability to remain in operation. Committed to maintaining the spirit and design of the Community Corrections Center, community corrections staff and directors of local treatment programs began seeking cooperative partnerships to maintain the established continuum of services.

The concept of co-location and service integration—establishing "one stop" style corrections counseling services were a product of this effort. While this concept was explored, it appeared to promise many desired outcomes, including shared overhead and facilities costs. Based on research and evidence-based best practice principles, we believed co-location and service integration of community corrections and community counseling agencies would enhance offender participation, successful completion of counseling, and probation and parole supervision.

Participants in the local Public Safety Coordinating Council's "brainstorming" process were determined to identify three primary treatment components to be pursued in establishing services within the Community Corrections Center: Substance Abuse, Domestic Violence and Sex Offender Treatment, and Cognitive Restructuring.

Klamath County Community Corrections historically has chosen to contract out the primary services. The significant difference was the fact Klamath County Community Corrections had no funds to purchase the services. However, in exchange for services, the department provided office space and group treatment classrooms. To determine an equitable exchange, Klamath County and the providers determined a prorated space rent according to use and related that to predetermined fees for treatment services.

Two proposals from the substance abuse providers were an encouraging start. Both of these providers were facing significant financial losses from the state and possible closure. The potential loss of these providers would be a blow to our rural community in that there are only three providers countywide. Thus, all parties were motivated to make the relationship work.

Ultimately, both substance-abuse counseling providers and the county came to contractual terms and set forth how services would be provided and integrated. The secondary educational services (employment services, parenting, literacy, and cognitive restructuring) were identified in the contract negotiations with the substance-abuse providers. Both providers and community corrections staff could collaborate in developing a satisfactory program.

PROGRAM DEVELOPMENT, SERVICE INTEGRATION, AND DESIRED OUTCOMES

With the partnerships identified, the administrators of Community Corrections, Klamath Alcohol and Drug Abuse (KADA) and the Consortium, began a series of meetings to begin the development process. Items initially identified for potential co-case management and service integration included combined file documentation (a shared MIS system), joint release of information, and treatment co-facilitators (probation officers and providers). Potential obstacles included scheduling, multiagency policies and procedures, communication, and trust within the administrative team (all agencies involved).

Desired outcomes included increased offender retention; an increase in the percentage of offenders engaging in treatment; enhanced communication and partnerships between probation officers and treatment staff; a lower offender arrest and sanction rate while in treatment and under probation or parole supervision; and reduced drug use while in treatment and under probation or parole supervision.

CHANGES WHEN WE MOVED INTO THE CORRECTIONAL POD

By Barbara Down, CADCC II, R.N., Consortium Treatment Center Counselor

Edited by Boyd Sharp

Treatment is very individualized now. We only have one track in the evening, but two groups are held every night. Clients attend whichever group seems appropriate for them at the time. There are no longer any "stages" of treatment. When clients come in, we discuss with them what they believe they need in the way of treatment. If they choose two days per week, we say "fine." We tell them that as long as they follow the rules and do what is expected of them, they will stay at two days a week. However, we explain, "If you have a positive UA, treatment will go up a day. If you are a 'no show,' it goes up a day. So, if you stay at two days a week, good for you! By the same respect, if you are attending five days a week within a month, that is up to you. We gave you the chance, so you have no one to blame but yourself if you end up going to treatment five days a week."

Promotions are still discussed and announced, but because they can be promoted every time they complete a group, there are more of them, giving them more frequent praise than before. Sometimes a promotion is announced, but they do not get a decrease in treatment—they are switched from one group to another-but it is not handled as a promotion.

"It's Up to Me" is the most basic of groups and is required for everyone. It teaches the "language" ("Words Mean Things"), Franklin Reality, the Power Pendulum, and how to do thinking reports. Alcohol and Drugs and Criminality I (Hazelden lecture groups) are also two early basic groups that clients attend as soon as possible.

The two medium-intensity classes are less intense than the "hard-core criminal classes" we have had in the past. These were especially instituted for the drug court medium-intensity clients we now take.

Retention of women has increased tremendously with our gender-specific groups. These started out as an experimental "Women's Anger Management" group for the drug court. They chose to let it lapse after the time period was up, but we saw our retention numbers go up so dramatically, so we kept it on. Women frequently are placed here immediately if it appears they are the type who will not be able to remain in treatment long enough to even get to detox. The group consists of one hour or so to discuss their personal issues; then, they have an hour to learn some sort of craft or relaxation technique-something fun.

The old relapse—prevention group is still the final phase before leaving. Changes in it include the most recent Gorski (1993) methods.

Another change centers around dual diagnosis, especially fetal-alcohol effected adults. We treat them very differently than our usual antisocial model. Because they crave attention and approval, they are praised for the slightest thing they do right. They consistently get extra time and attention. They are told the minute they walk through the door how glad we are to see them. This was a difficult transition for most of us, but it appears very effective. Other than these changes, our treatment remains basically as it had been originally created.

REVIEW OF OUTCOME DATA—FIRST PROGRESS REPORT AFTER REORGANIZATION

Once we identified the initial obstacles for co-case management and desired outcomes, representative staff from each agency was assigned to a work group. This work group was tasked with the implementation of the outlined goals and desired outcomes.

For the first six-month progress report period, the work group provided the following general summary on three of the five desired outcomes. First, communication and partnerships between probation officers and treatment staff increased significantly. Co-location within the same facility has helped and is the main factor but additional contributing factors identified by staff include monthly "all-staff" meetings between community corrections and treatment agencies, weekly work group meetings focused on daily operations between community corrections and treatment agencies, and development of a joint agency release-of-information format.

To determine if co-location and service integration lowers offender arrest and sanction rates while in treatment and under probation or parole supervision, we studied the arrest and sanction records of all fifty clients who had been in the program for at least thirty days as of January 1, 2004. We began one year before program entry, and followed them from then until January 1, 2004. No new arrests occurred among this total group. Further, combined arrest and sanction rates were down 97.5 percent, and 98 percent of all clients lowered their combined arrest and sanction records. Data on changes in arrest and sanction rates are represented in Table 6.4.

We also conducted a study on the extent to which the fifty clients in the program decreased their drug usage as determined by urine sample testing. We studied the number of urine sample records of all fifty clients who had been in the program for at least thirty days as of January 1, 2004. We began one year before program entry, and followed them from then until January 1, 2004. For all fifty clients, there was a 21 percent decrease in urine samples testing positive for drug use. At the same time, there was an average increase of 3.68 urine collections per client during this time period. Urine sample collection and positive drug use rates are represented in Table 6.3.

TABLE 6.3. ARREST AND SANCTION RATES

	0-6 Months
Number of clients*	50
Arrest rate 1-year prior to admission	1.14
Sanction rate 1-year prior to admission	.5
Combined arrest and sanction Rate 1 year prior to admission	1.64
Arrest rate after entry in treatement and supervision	0
Combined arrest and sanction rate After entry in treatment and supervision	.16
% decrease in arrest and sanction rate	97.5%
% of offenders with lower arrest and sanction rates 98%	
*minimum 30 days in treatment and probation/parole supervision	

TABLE 6.4. URINE COLLECTION AND POSITIVE DRUG USE RATES

	0-6 Months
Number of clients*	50
UA** rate 1 year prior to admission	1.98
Positive UA*** rate 1 year prior to admission	.32
UA rate after admission	5.66
Positive UA rate after entry in treatment and probation supervision	.11
Increase in UA rate after entry in treatment and supervision	3.68
% decrease in UA rate	21%

  * Minimum 30 days in treatment and probation/parole supervision

** Urinalysis—urine sample collection

***Urinalysis—urine sample testing positive for drug use

CONCLUSION AND RECOMMENDATIONS

When the Klamath County Board of Commissioners approved the concept of community counseling service co-location and integration, Community Corrections initiated a semi-annual review process. This is the first review after only six months. Although the numbers of clients and length of time in this study are small, the numbers are encouraging. As noted above, the trend for three of the five desired outcomes appear to be going in the right direction in the short term:

- Enhanced communication and partnerships between probation officers and treatment staff
- Lower offender arrest and sanction rate while in treatment and under probation or parole supervision

- Reduced drug use while in treatment and under probation or parole supervision

The other two desired outcomes—increased offender retention and increased percent of offenders engaging in treatment—still need to be studied.

After considering our experiences thus far, we make the following recommendations:

- Continue monitoring offender arrest and sanction rate for two years following admission to treatment and probation or parole supervision.
- Continue monitoring offender drug use rates for two years following admission to treatment and probation or parole supervision.

Further, to determine actual program outcome measures, two-year results should be measured against arrest, sanction, and drug-use rates two years prior to inception of community counseling services with community corrections.

CONSORTIUM OUTPATIENT DAY TREATMENT PROGRAM SUCCESS (FIRST THREE YEARS AND NINE MONTHS)

The Consortium Final Report begins with this abstract:

How did the Consortium perform during the three years and nine months (December 1994 to June1998) of support provided by CSAT (Center for Substance Abuse Treatment)? The average Consortium client [had] dropped out before high school graduation, earned $100/month legally, had seven previous arrests, and had spent twenty-six months in jail at program entry. The majority of clients met two-thirds of their treatment goals. Clients who remained in treatment for six months or more lowered their arrest rate during and after treatment. One-hundred percent of six-month clients attended self-help groups, 92 percent improved their employability, and 86 percent did not abuse substances as indicated by random drug testing. The cost of $5,000 to $6,000 per client per year was far less than the cost of incarceration. This data suggests that the Consortium model is effective with criminal substance abusers. (Pohl, 1997, p. 1).

Pohl used three studies to specifically examine the question of reduced arrest rates after treatment. All three studies examined clients in treatment for at least six months. The first study reported that 78 percent of clients had lower arrest rates after leaving the program than they did before entering it. The second and third studies show that more than 90 percent of clients were arrest-free and that the reduced arrest rate existed for as long as data is available (about one year). Thus, all three studies suggest that the Consortium's treatment program reduced arrests after clients left the program.

Arrests in all three studies were taken from the "booking number" obtained from the Klamath County Regional Detention Center. Figure 6.1 shows the average reductions in arrest rates reported in all three studies from before entry compared to the time they were in the program

A further study was done of the original program (*The Consortium Day Treatment Program: Its Effects on the Number of Arrests Following Treatment*, Kristi A. Mabou, Oregon Institute of Technology, August 4, 2000). The arrest rates of clients who have gone through the Consortium Day Treatment Program significantly decreased in comparison to their arrest rates prior to treatment.

As shown in Figure 6.2, there was a significant decrease in post-treatment arrests, from a mean of 2.120 arrests prior to treatment to .554 arrests following treatment for Sample 1.

As shown in Figure 6.3, there was also a decrease in posttreatment arrests for Sample 2 (N=59), from a mean of 2.46 prior to treatment to 1.73 following treatment. Examination of the descriptive statistics between the two samples reveals a significant difference between the length of treatment and the reduction of arrests.

This shows that there is a significantly greater reduction in the number of arrests once a client has been in treatment for 120 days as opposed to being in treatment for less than sixty days. Also, there was no significant difference between women and men in terms of reduction of arrests (which is good news in terms of treating both men and women in this model).

FIGURE 6.1.
AVERAGE REDUCTION IN THE ARREST RATE

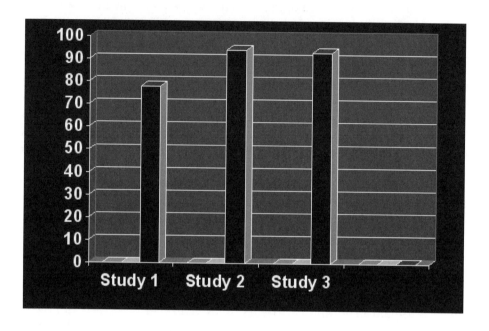

THE KLAMATH FALLS CONSORTIUM JAIL TREATMENT PROGRAM

THE BEGINNING

The original intent of the Klamath Falls community in 1991 was to secure funding and to develop a program for treatment in the jail. In the fall of 1991, a staff meeting of probation and parole officers employed by the Klamath County Department of Corrections occurred. Jacquelyn Hoffmann, a nurse employed by the sheriff's office at the Klamath County Jail, presented some astonishing and disconcerting information. She presented statistics on repeat offenders arrested five or more times since the establishment of a new local jail in the fall of 1989. The statistics made it quite clear that an overwhelming proportion of local crime was being committed by the repeat-offender population.

FIGURE 6.2. MEAN ARRESTS 180 DAYS PRIOR VERSUS 180 DAYS POSTTREATMENT

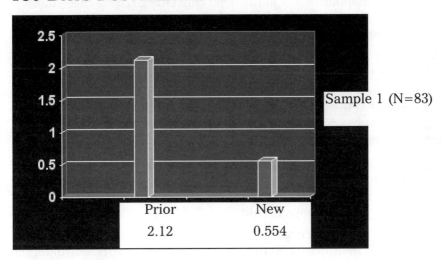

FIGURE 6.3. MEAN ARRESTS 180 DAYS PRIOR VERSUS 180 DAYS POSTTREATMENT

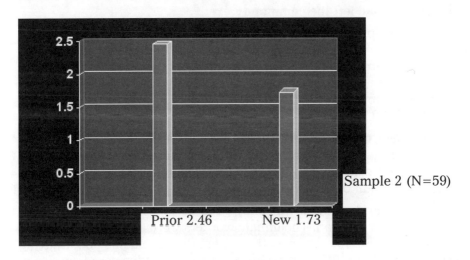

The consensus of the corrections staff was that more than 90 percent of the identified repeat offenders had histories of drug and/or alcohol abuse and/or dependence. Local financial capacities to treat these offenders were inadequate to cover more than one-quarter of actual treatment costs for correction clients.

For a full year, the planning group met at least monthly to discuss and plan a project intended to "Positively impact the target repeat offender population through treatment, improve local sanctioning capacities, especially at the county jail, and increase funding to local treatment providers to enhance their capacity to treat the target population" (Sharp, Clarke, and Pohl, 1996).

When federal funding for jail treatment programs dried up and funding for outpatient treatment became available, the community switched its attention to an outpatient program. Thus, the Consortium Day Treatment Program became a reality.

However, in 1998, Edward Byrnes Memorial Grant funds became available for jail treatment, and the community once again came together to apply for these funds. The Community Correction office and the Consortium nonprofit corporation were awarded a four-year grant in October of 1998 to develop and implement an alcohol/drug jail treatment program. This was the realization of a seven-year dream. As the development and implementation began, the jail nurse had also left the community, so there was little support from this area. Two treatment directors also had left the community.

The initial program clients were housed in an overflow pod in which the kitchen, facility, and yard workers were housed. Of course, the inmates were protective of their turf. In addition, the correctional officers supported those inmates. The officers viewed the treatment staff as outsiders and as volunteers. They were given no keys, no rights, and were barely tolerated.

Treatment of the initial twelve clients was conducted outside the prison in a trailer. They were marched to and from the facility, and staff had no say in the management of the pod. The rat picture, shown previously, was a result of this mixed group.

A year later, treatment was allowed to occur within the facility, but with the same restriction. The inmate workers were not to be deprived of their comforts. So, for instance, there were disagreements about having the television shut off during group. Staff was still considered outsiders.

Nothing could be placed on the wall, or if it were, it had to be taken down each night.

However, as the staff slowly initiated a quasi-therapeutic community as previously discussed and used the effective treatment methods noted at Powder River and in the Consortium Day Treatment program, jail staff began to warm up to the program. They began to see that there were fewer discipline problems and that the pod ran more smoothly. They began to rely on treatment staff to be in the pod alone and to manage the pod. This allowed them more staff coverage in other areas of the jail. The client population went from twelve to twenty-four. Agreements were made to allow staff more authority in the pod and to curtail other pod inmates' activities while treatment was in progress.

By the end of two years, the pod had completely become a therapeutic treatment community, with all forty-two inmates a part of the treatment program. If an inmate wanted to be part of a work crew, he had to have successfully completed Stage I of treatment. Also, treatment staff were given full range of the facility and were made team members in determining work assignment, discharge questions, and admittance criteria.

WORK CREW POLICY AND PROCEDURE

POLICY:

Clients entering treatment in the Consortium Jail Program have an opportunity to earn work-time credit as a result of successful participation and achievement in treatment. Jail staff has agreed to accept Consortium clients on work crews and allow work-time credits to be earned by eligible clients assigned to work crews. For a Consortium client to be considered for work crew duties in and about the jail premises, he must have completed Stage I of Consortium Treatment. For a client to be eligible for consideration for work crew duties away from the jail premises, he must have completed Stage II.

Work crew positions can be revoked by jail staff and/or treatment staff for improper client behavior (any violation of jail and/or treatment guidelines). Clients choosing to leave treatment against staff advice or leaving for disciplinary reasons will be considered ineligible for work crew and may lose work-time credits earned.

Current work crew members will be retained on the work crew. It is intended that in time, all work crew members will have completed at least Stage I of the Consortium Treatment. This may not always be possible or practical. Adjustments to and/or changes in work crew assignments are solely at the discretion of jail staff. No right to work crew assignment is gained merely by participation in or completion of Consortium Treatment, nor does time in the treatment program create any right of seniority or privilege over any other inmate for work crew consideration.

The Consortium Jail Treatment Program is divided into three stages as follows:

Stage I is designed to assist clients in facing and overcoming denial of addiction and criminality. Stage I allows for the clients' introduction into the therapeutic community. Each client is expected to be an active participant in the therapeutic community, as evidenced by periodic evaluations by staff and peers.

Stage I Requirements:

Alcohol/Drug 1st Step

Criminality 1st Step

Alcohol/Drug Autobiography

Cognitive Restructuring Phase 1

Complete four Alcohol/Drug Thinking Reports

Complete Hazelden A and D and Criminality

Klamath/Lake Employment Training Institute (K.L.E.T.I.) Screening for eligibility

Peer/staff rating of 4 or more

Upon completion of Stage I, the client's name will be presented to staff for consideration for promotion to Stage II. During Stage II, the client is expected to be involved in the Client Council work, K.L.E.T.I. participation (if applicable) and day work crews (on jail premises). Client's staff and peer evaluations and overall behavior are contributors to this consideration.

Stage II Requirements:

Completion of all Stage I requirements

Alcohol/Drug Steps II and III and a Criminality Autobiography

Identify and Present Five Criminal Masks

K.L.E.T.I. involvement and participation (if applicable)

Participation in jail premises work crews

Breaking Barriers

Relapse Prevention Aftercare Plan

Cognitive Restructuring Phase II

Client Council involvement/participation

Peer/staff rating of 6 or more

Upon completion of Stage II, the client's name will be presented to staff for consideration for promotion to Stage III. Upon promotion, the client will enter the Continuing Recovery Group and be placed on an eligibility list for an outside work crew assignment. Any client on the outside work crew list, who is not working on that day, will present himself for treatment. Clients who work that day will attend treatment from 1800-1900 Monday through Thursday. Clients on the work crew roster will receive work-time credit, as determined by jail personnel. Clients will perform mentoring duties as assigned and/or appropriate. Clients will provide the Client Council with weekly reports concerning their work crew duties and treatment participation.

Stage III Requirements:

Work crew eligible

Completion of all Stage II requirements

Complete a continuum of criminality

Attend 1800-1900 hours Monday thru Thursday (AA, NA)

Submit weekly reports to client council

Commence work on Step IV

Perform mentoring roles as assigned/appropriate

Attend treatment functions if not working that day

CONTINUING RECOVERY GROUP

The Continuing Recovery Group provides tools for the client prior to leaving the Jail Treatment Program, which help clients remain abstinent from crimes and chemicals when reentering the community. Continuing recovery is objective oriented, identifying target behaviors within individuals who will learn to identify and apply interventions as well as brakes to prevent relapse on alcohol/drugs and criminal behavior.

To enter this group, the client must have satisfied the following criteria:

1. Completed Stages I and II
2. Maintained a score of 6 or more on Peer I Staff evaluations
3. Demonstrated the ability to complete a thinking-error report
4. Show evidence of acceptance for criminality and addiction
5. Demonstrate responsibility for own behavior
6. Identify and apply interventions to criminal tactics

The success of the Consortium Jail Treatment Program is similar to that of the Day Treatment Program. Specific outcome data is available from the author.

IN CONCLUSION

Some concluding comments concerning the correction field in general and specifically the programs and concepts presented in the foregoing are appropriate. In this mid-decade of 2000, the American correctional field enjoys an unprecedented level of integrity, reliability, and quality. This is due to people like Frank Wood as described by Bartollas (2004), Elliott and Verdeyen (2002), Samenow (1976 to 2004) and the writers of the articles in *Restorative Justice* as edited by Perry (2002) to name a few. This, of course, is not an exhaustive list; however, these individuals are representative of the myriad of correctional workers who are concerned, dedicated, and functioning at a very high level of credibility.

Francis J. Schweigert (2002) seems to sum up the direction the field is moving. He says, "merely returning like for like in punishment or in reparation, is acting under compulsion and equivalent to going only the one mile; creative restitution calls upon offenders to go further than this and redeem the situation." There are "three dimensions of justice:

retribution, reparation, and redemption. . . . This is justice that goes beyond retribution to redemption."

The correctional field today is exhibiting flexibility and a realistic appraisal of the problems. There is not the drive to be right and having to get one's own way. It is being replaced with a sense of inner confidence and power. The field is much more able to roll with the ups and downs. There is a sense of well-being and capability. Workers are interested in creating a safe workplace and less interested in conflict, competition, or guilt. There is a greater desire to redeem the criminals we are charged with overseeing. At no other time in our history has there been such a plateau of creative opportunity as there is at this moment.

The forgoing evidence presented in this book attests to the viability and profitability of developing programs along the lines suggested. The Powder River program began in 1990 and has been expanded from 50 beds to 178 beds and encompasses the entire facility. The cognitive approach outlined here now has been mandated by the Oregon Department of Correction for its operation. The data suggests that there is significant reduction in rearrests and incarceration.

The Consortium program was developed in 1993 using a Center for Substance Abuse Treatment four-year grant. The community was of the opinion that when the grant ended, the program would also end. However, it is still in operation, although in a smaller form, some twelve years later. The data from both the outpatient and jail treatment program also suggest significant reductions in rearrests and incarceration.

Both programs have been dynamic in that each has changed as new information has been generated, and staff is constantly adapting their programs to incorporate new information. This has made them strong dynamic programs. It is important to note that all three programs (Powder River, Consortium Day Treatment, and Consortium Jail) were faced with difficulty in terms of initial acceptance by the environment in which they were attempting to operate. However, they each overcame these obstacles. Leaders of the programs made changes to accommodate the changing needs. Though all three took about two years to become viable programs, they were able to operate at a highly acceptable level. The key here is to continue to have dialog, build teams, educate yourself and your partners, and build programs that employ the ingredients suggested above.

In addition, the cognitive-restructuring therapy increasingly is being discussed in the literature. Walsh (2005) in the fourth edition of his best-selling book, *Correctional Assessment, Casework and Counseling,* includes a chapter on this therapy. Two courses using *Changing Criminal Thinking*, as a text are taught each year in the Applied Psychology program at Oregon Institute of Technology. One course of Breaking Barriers (Graham and Smith, 1999) is being taught at the Oregon Institute of Technology. Cognitive restructuring also is being employed to assist people with weight loss and smoking cessation.

What this means is that you can develop quality programs to significantly reduce recidivism by using the suggestions in this book. You are applauded and supported in your efforts to begin a program or change your program to employ these dynamics.

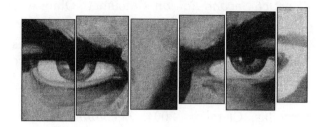

Bibliography

Abelar, Taisha. 1992. *The Sorcerer's Crossing: A Woman's Journey*. New York: Viking Arkana.

Allen, Tim. 1994. *Don't Stand Too Close to A Naked Man*. Hyperion, New York: Boxing Cat Production, Inc.

American Psychiatric Association. 1980. *Diagnostic and Statistical Manual, Third Edition*. Washington, D.C.: American Psychiatric Association.

——. 1989. *Diagnostic and Statistical Manual, Third Edition Revised*. Washington, D.C.: American Psychiatric Association.

——. 1994. *Diagnostic and Statistical Manual, Fourth Edition*. Washington, D.C.: American Psychiatric Association.

____. 2000. *Diagnostic and Statistical Manual of Mental Disorders, Fourth Edition*. Washington. D.C., American Psychiatric Association.

Andrews, D. A. and James Bonta. 1998. *The Psychology of Criminal Conduct, Second Edition.* Cincinnati, Ohio: Anderson Publishing Co.

Anthony, Ted. 1998. "Thrill Burglar Leaves Police Scrounging for Victims." *The Register Guard*, Eugene, Oregon: Associated Press. October 11.

Bartollas, Clemens. 2004. *Becoming a Model Warden: Striving For Excellence.* Lanham, Maryland: American Correctional Association.

Bennett, Robert F. with Hyrum R. Smith. 1987. *Gaining Control: The Franklin Reality Model.* Franklin International Institute, Inc. PO Box 25127, Salt Lake, Utah.

Boss, Suzie. 1994. "Talking Tough," *Oregonian*, Portland, Oregon.

Brickey, Dean. 2004. "Dad Who Slit Son's Wrist Headed to Prison." *East Oregonian.* Pendleton, Oregon. November 9.

Brodenhamer, Gregory. 1983. *Back in Control.* New York: Simon and Schuster.

Brooks, Terry. 1994. *The Tangle Box.* New York: Ballantine Books.

Browne, Chris. 1994. Hagar the Horrible. Cartoon. King Features Syndicate.

Bush, John M. 1993. Counseling the Criminal Client. *The Counselor.* March/April.

Bush, John M. and Brian Bilodeau. ND. *A Cognitive Change Program*, Eastern Oregon Correctional Institution. Revised by: Lee A. Warren, assisted by Risa Umbarger and Ralph S. Taylor. Document prepared under an Interagency Agreement with the U.S. Navy, consultant contract for program number 93-N4301, and the National Institute of Corrections.

Carey, John. 2002. Summary of Powder River Alcohol and Drug Program (PRAD) Graduate Statistics. Truthought Website, www.tru thought.com. Reprinted by permission of Rogie A. Spon.

Castaneda, Carlos. 1972. *Journey to Ixtlan: The Teachings of Don Juan.* New York: Simon & Schuster.

——. 1984. *The Fire From Within.* New York: Washington Square Press.

Clancy, Tom. 1989. *Clear and Present Danger,* copyright © by Jack Ryan Enterprises Ltd. Used by permission of G.P. Putnam's Sons, a division of Penguin Group (USA) Inc.

Cohen, K. A. and M. Stitzer July 23, 2002 "Contingency Management-- The Evidence and Issues." Workshop by the Northwest Institute of Addiction Studies, Inc., Portland, Oregon.

Cornelius, Gary. 2005. *Stressed Out: Strategies for Living and Working in Corrections, 2nd edition.* Lanham, Maryland: American Correctional Association.

Cornerstone Program Manual. 1977. Oregon State Hospital, Oregon Department of Corrections, Salem, Oregon.

Craig, John. August 24, 1996. "Man gets 18-year sentence for raping teen," *The Spokesman Review,* Spokane, Washington.

De Mello, Anthony. 1991. *The Way of Love.* New York: Doubleday.

Down, Barbara, CADCC II, R.N., Consortium treatment center counselor. 2002. *Words Mean Things.* Klamath Falls, Oregon. Used with permission from Down in unpublished paper.

——. 2004. Program Update. Klamath Falls, Oregon. Used with permission from Down.

Dyer, Wayne W. Ph.D. 1976. *Your Erroneous Zones.* New York: Avon Books.

——. 1992. *Real Magic.* New York: Harper/Collins.

——. 1995. *Your Sacred Self.* New York: Harper/Collins.

——. 2001. *10 Secrets for Success and Inner Peace.* Carlsbad, California: Hay House, Inc.

——. 2001. *There's A Spiritual Solution to Every Problem.* New York: Harper/Collins.

——. 2002. *It's Never Crowded Along the Extra Mile.* Tapes. Carlsbad, California: Hay House, Inc.

——. 2004. *The Power of Intention.* Carlsbad, California: Hay House, Inc.

Easwaran, Eknath,Translator. 1985. *The Bhagavad Gita.* Tomales, California.: Nilgiri Press.

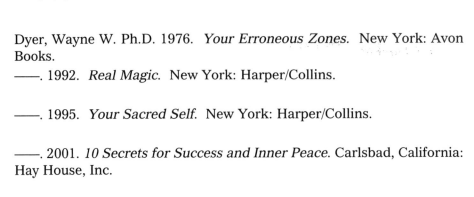
Elliott, Bill and Vicki Verdeyen. 2002. *Game Over: Strategies for Redirecting Inmate Deception.* Lanham, Maryland: American Correctional Association.

Estrich, Susan. 1993. Op Ed. October 26. "Don't Blame Me—Defense Can Get Guilty Off Hook." *Oregonian,* Creator's Syndicate.

Field, Gary. ND. Preliminary Outcome Study of the Powder River Alcohol and Drug Program, and Addendum #1 and #2. Oregon Department of Corrections, Salem, Oregon.

——.1998. "Continuity of Offender Treatment: Institution to the Community." Paper prepared for the Office of National Drug Control Policy.

Fogg, Vern. 1992. "Implementation of a Cognitive Skills Development Program," *Perspective*, Winter, pp 23-26.

Gadsden, Vivian L., ed. 2003. *Heading Home: Offender Reintegration into the Family.* Lanham, Maryland: American Correctional Association and International Community Corrections Association.

Gendreau, Paul.1994. *What Works in Community Corrections: Promising Approaches in Reducing Criminal Behavior.* Speech given at IARCA's Research Conference, November 3, Seattle, Washington.

———. 1996. Offender Rehabilitation: What We Know and What Needs to Be Done. *Criminal Justice Behavior.* 23, 1.

Gendreau, P., F. T. Cullen, and J. Bonta, 1994. Intensive Rehabilitation Supervision: The Next Generation in Community Corrections? *Federal Probation.* 58:173-84

Gorski, Terence T. No Date. "Relapse Prevention Therapy with Chemically Dependent Offenders." The CENAPS Corporation, Homewood, Illinois.

Graham, Gordon. July 16, 2004. "Navigating Change: Charting Your Own Course," workshop. Pendleton, Oreon.

Graham, Gordon and Co. 1991. Rev. 1993. *A Framework for Breaking Barriers.* Seattle, Washington: Graham Gordon and Co.

Graham G., S. Hyrum. 1999. *A Framework for Breaking Barriers; A Cognitive Reality Model.* Bellevue, Washington: Grodon Graham and Company, Inc.

Hare, Robert D.1993. *Without Conscience: The Disturbing World of the Psychopath Among Us.* New York: Guilford Press.

Hawkins, David R. 1995. *Power vs Force: The Hidden Determinants of Human Behavior.* Veritas Publishing, WWW.veritaspub.com.

The Hazelden Foundation. 1993. *Design for Living—Criminality and Substance Abuse: A Cognitive Intervention for Substance Abusing*

Offenders. Hazelden Correctional Services, Center City, Minnesota: The Hazelden Foundation.

Herald and News, September 29, 1996. "Klaas Slayer's Outburst." San Jose, California. AP byline.

____. Nov. 1996. "Neighbors Set Suspect's Home Ablaze in Anger." Fort Lauderdale, Florida. AP byline.

Higgins, Jack. 1966. *Angel of Death.* New York: Berkeley Books.

Higgins, S.T., N. M. Petry, November 2, 1999. Contingency Management. *Alcohol Research and Health,* Vol. 23.

Houtz, Jolyanne. 1993. "Judge Lets Shoplifter Off the Hook, Chastises Store for Selling Cigarettes." *Oregonian.* Reprinted from the Seattle Times.

Jacobs, E. and N. Spadaro, 2003. *Leading Groups in Corrections: Skills and Techniques.* Lanham, Maryland, American Correctional Association.

Johnson, Grant and Robert M. Hunter. 1992. "Evaluation of the Specialized Drug Offender Program (SDOP) for the Colorado Judicial Department." Center for Action Research, University of Colorado at Boulder, January.

Kane, Bill. April 14, 1994. Dunagin's People. Cartoon. North American Syndicate.

Keane, Bill. February 12, 1995. Family Circus. Cartoon. Distributed by Cowles Syndicate, Inc.

Kipling, Rudyard. 1910. "If" and "Rewards and Fairies." A.P. Watt Ltd, Literary Agents, London WCIN 2DR.

Kraemer, Kristin M. November 3, 2004. *"Man Accused of Killing Wife Won't Face Death." Tri-City Herald,* Kennewick, Washington.

Levy, M. and B. Sharp. January 20, 2000. Klamath Falls, Oregon. *Effects of the Jail Treatment Program on Number of Arrests Following Incarceration: Predictions and Analysis: Six Month Pre/Post Data.* Unpublished

____. April 5, 2000. Klamath Falls, Oregon. *Effects of the Jail Treatment Program on Number of Arrests Following Incarceration: Addendum # 1: Twelve Month Pre/Post Data.* Unpublished

Lipton, Douglas S. 1996. Prison-Based Therapeutic Communities: Their Success with Drug-Abusing Offenders. *National Institute of Justice Journal.* February. pp. 12-20.

Locke, M. 1996. "Klaas Vents Rage Against Child Killer." *Herald and News.* September 27. Associated Press.

Mabou, Kristi A. August 4, 2000. *The Consortium Treatment Program: Its Effects on the Number of Arrest Following Treatment.* Oregon Institute of Technology: Unpublished.

Marciulano, Francesco. October 24, 2004. Sally Forth Cartoon. *East Oregonian*, Pendleton, Oregon.

Martin, Father. 1992. *Chalk Talk.* Aberdeen, Maryland: Kelly Productions.

McCold, Paul and Benjamin Wachtel, 2002. "Community is Not a Place: A New Look at Community Justice Initiatives," in John Perry, ed.,*Repairing Communities Through Restorative Justice.* Lanham, Maryland: American Correctional Association.

Milkman, Harvey. July 30, 2004. "Pathways To Self-Discovery and Change: Delinquency, Crime and Substance Abuse Treatment for Adolescents;" workshop by the Northwest Institute of Addiction Studies, Inc. Portland, Oregon.

Millman, Dan. 1984. *The Way of the Peaceful Warrior.* New York: MJF Books.

Montague, Dixie, ed. April, May and June 2001. What Works for Offender Treatment. Salem, Oregon. *Addiction Messenger,* Northwest Frontier Addiction Technology Training Center.

Mother Theresa of Calcutta. 1968. "The Final Analysis,"attributed to Mother Theresa as she adapted them from Kent M. Keith, "The Paradoxical Commandments." Printed by permission of www.wowzone.com.

My Blue Heaven. 1990. Warner Brothers Studios. Burbank, California.

National Conference on Addiction and Criminal Behavior Training sponsored by GWC, Inc. September 23-26, 2001. St. Louis, Missouri

Nelson, Portia, 1994. "There's A Hole In My Sidewalk!" *The Romance of Self Discovery.* Beyond Works Publishing, Hillsboro, Oregon.

New Directions Northwest. 2004. AIP Program. Webmaster: jeidson@newdirectionsnw.Org. Website: newdirectionsnw.org. With permission of Bart Murray, Executive Director.

New Directions Northwest. 2004. The PRAD Horticulture Program Webmaster: jeidson@newdirectionsnw.Org. Website: newdirectionsnw.org. With permission of Bart Murray, Executive Director.

Ocean's Eleven, 2001. Warner Brothers Studios, Burbank, California.

Ocean's Twelve, 2004. Warner Brothers Sudios, Burbank, California.

Oregon Department of Corrections. 1996. *Evaluation of the Powder River and Turning Point Alcohol and Drug Treatment Programs.* Research Unit. Salem, Oregon.

The Outside Woman. 1989. Green/Epstein Productions. Studio City, California.

Perry, John, ed. 2002, *Repairing Communities through Restorative Justice.* Lanham, Maryland: American Correctional Association.

Petry, Nancy M. February 2002. Contingency Management in Addiction Treatment. *Psychiatric Times,* Vol XIX, Issue 2.

Pohl, Richard. 1977. *Consortium Final Report.* 324 Mountain View Blvd., Klamath Falls, Oregon 97601, September 20.

Porporino, Frank J., 2005. Revisiting "Responsivity": Why What Works? Isn't Working! In *What Works and Why: Effective Approaches to Reentry.* Lanham, Maryland: American Correctional Association and International Community Corrections Association.

Pressfield, Steven. 1995. *The Legend of Bagger Vance.* New York: Harpertorch.

Puzo, Mario. 1985. *The Sicilian.* New York: Bantam Books.

Rinpoche, Sogyal. 1993. *The Tibetan Book of Living and Dying.* New York: Harper/Collins Pub.

Rhodes, Richard. 1999. *Why They Kill: The Discoveries of a Maverick Criminologist.* New York: Alfred A. Knopf.

Robinson, Ken. July 29, 2004 "What Works in Treatment: Research Based on Cognitive Models and Their Use in Substance Abuse Treatment ("Moral Reconation Therapy (MRT)" workshop by the Northwest Institute of Addiction Studies, Inc. Portland, Oregon.

Ross, Robert R., Elizabeth A. Fabiano, and Crystal D. Ewles. 1998. "Reasoning and Rehabilitation" *International Journal of Offender Therapy and Comparative Criminology,* pp 29-35.

Samenow, Stanton. 1991. "Understaning the Anti-Social Personality," workshop, May 2 and 3. By the Institute for Integral Development, featuring Stanton E. Samenow, Ph.D., San Francisco, California.

——. 1994. *Before it's Too Late: Why Some Kids Get Into Trouble and What Parents Can Do About it.* New York: Times Books.

——. 1994 and 2000. *Commitment to Change.* Two series of three videotapes with accompanying workbooks. Carpenteria, California. FMS

——. 1998. *Straight Talk about Criminals.* Livingston, New Jersey: Jason Aronson.

——. 2004. *Inside the Criminal Mind.* New York: Times Books.

——. ND. Workshop handout for Institute for Integral Development. Colorado Springs, Colorado.

Schweigert, Francis J. 2002. "Moral and Philosophical Foundations of Restorative Justice," in *Repairing Communities through Restorative Justice*, Lanham, Maryland: American Correctional Association.

Sharp, B. D. and K. J. Beam. 1995. Treatment Perspectives on Criminal Personalities in a Rural Setting. *In Treating Alcohol and Other Drug Abusers in Rural And Frontier Areas.* Technical Assistance Publication (TAP) Series, No. 17. DHHS Pub. No (SMAO 95-3054. Rockville, Maryland. Center for Substance Abuse Treatment.

Sharp, B. D., R. Clarke, and R. Pohl. 1996. In Rural and Frontier America, It Takes A Whole Community To Habilitate a Substance Abusing Criminal. In *Bringing Excellence To Substance Abuse Services in Rural and Frontier America.* Technical Assistance Publication (TAP) Series, No. 20. DHHS Pub. No (SMA) 97-3134. Rockville, Maryland, Center for Substance Abuse Treatment.

The Silence of the Lambs. 1991. MGM/United Artists. Santa Monica, California.

Spon, Rogie A. 1995. *Lifestyle Choices: Curriculum for Responsible Living.*

Truthought's "Charting a New Course." N.D. Roscoe, Illinois.

Stanger, Catherine. April 2003. Contingency Management in the Treatment of Adolescent Marijuana Abusers. *Counselor: The Magazine for Addiction Professionals.* Deerfield Beach, Florida.

Stay'n Out Drug Treatment Program. 1977. Therapeutic Communities, Inc. New York City, Aurthurkill Correctional Facility, New York, N.Y.

St. Clair Correctional Facility. July/August 1988 and revised February 1990. *New Outlook Therapeutic Community Handbook.* St. Clair Correctional Facility, Alabama Department of Corrections.

Stewart, Lynn and Natalie Gabora-Roth. 2003. "What Works in the Treatment of Family Violence in Correctional Populations: Issues and Directions," in Vivian Gadsen, ed. *Heading Home: Offender Reintegration into the Family.* Lanham, Maryland: American Correctional Association and International Community Corrections Association.

Szal, G.A. and D. D. Simpson, June 2002. Contingency Management and Treatment Engagement in a Sample of Cocaine-using Methadone Patients. Poster presented at the 62nd Scientific Meeting of the College on Problems of Drug Dependence (CPDD), San Juan, Puerto Rico. Institute of Behavioral Research, Texas Christian University.

Taxman, F.S. 1999. Unraveling "What Works" for Offenders in Substance Abuse Treatment Services. Alexandria. Virginia: National Drug Court Institute Review pp. 93-134.

Thelma and Louise, 1991. MGM/United Artist. Santa Monica, California.

Tri-City Herald. December 14, 2004. "Jury calls for execution of Scott Peterson. Kennewick, Washington. *Washington Post* by-line.

Volunteers of America of Oregon. *Brakes to Errors.* 1993 Multnomah County Department of Community Corrections. Portland, Oregon.

Walker and Associates, Inc., 1992. *Excellence Report: Primary Treatment in Chemical Dependency Search for Excellence.* No. 103. Minneapolis, Minnesota.

Walsh, Anthony. 2005. *Correctional Assessment, Casework and Counseling*, *4th ed.*, Lanham, Maryland: American Correctional Association.

Wambaugh, Joseph. 1987. *Echoes in the Darkness*. New York: Bantam Books, Inc.

Watterson, Bill. 1992. Calvin and Hobbes. Cartoon. Universal Press Syndicate. DATE

White, Casey. November 2, 2004. Rettman Pleads Guilty. *East Oregonian*, Pendleton, Oregon.

Yochelson, Samuel and Stanton E. Samenow. 1976. *The Criminal Personality: A Profile for Change*. Livingston, New Jersey: Jason Aronson.

____. 1977. *The Criminal Personality: The Change Process*. Livingston, New Jersey: Jason Aronson.

____. 1987. *The Criminal Personality: The Drug User*. Livingston, New Jersey: Jason Aronson.

Zukav, Gary. 1990. *The Seat of the Soul*. New York: Fireside Books.

Zukav, Gary and Linda Francis. 2001. *The Heart of the Soul*. New York: Simon and Schuster.

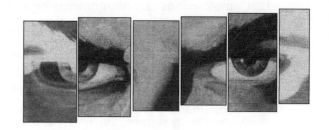

Appendix A: Program Expectations

Every client will comply with the following guidelines and rules while involved in the Consortium Criminality, Alcohol and Drug Treatment Program. These guidelines ensure the safety and health of the community.

CODE OF CONDUCT

Every client agrees to conduct himself or herself in a way that is a positive role model for his or her peers. He or she agrees to:

1. Not use drugs or alcohol
2. Refrain from committing new crimes
3. Refrain from physical violence
4. Respect other people's property
5. Not get involved in sexual relationships with other group members (except significant others)
6. Not intimidate, harass, or threaten others
7. Present himself or herself for urinalysis or breath test, as scheduled
8. Not engage in any gambling activity
9. Only enter authorized areas
10. Smoke only in designated areas

11. Attend all appointments and be on time
12. Complete jobs and assignments on time
13. Use furniture appropriately
14. Be appropriately dressed
15. Treat others with respect, concern, and dignity
16. Obey all verbal instructions from staff
17. Sign in and out for all activities or when entering and leaving the facility
18. Work the program, have a positive attitude, participate in group, and be accepting of directions and instructions and input from staff and peers

GROUP EXPECTATIONS

I voluntarily agree to follow all these rules and to help the rest of the group follow them by not enabling, supporting, and rescuing. I further agree to help keep all group members accountable for following these rules.

1. I agree to be free of alcohol and all other drugs for the entire time I am in the program.
2. I will arrive on time so that I will not interrupt or disturb the group.
3. I will not have anything in my hands during group unless instructed to do so.
4. I will dress modestly.
5. I will not wear clothing with insignias, advertising, or that supports a criminal lifestyle or drug/alcohol use.
6. I will not eat anything during group.
7. I will not wear a hat or sunglasses during group.
8. I will not become involved in sexual relationships with other members of the group (unless a significant other).
9. I will not get involved in any verbal or physical abuse.
10. I will be attentive to the group.
11. I will not leave the group without permission of staff.
12. I will not use suggestive words, language, or actions.
13. I will use socially acceptable language.

14. I promise to keep everything I hear, everything we say, and everything we do confidential within this program. I will not reveal names to anyone else and this includes my spouse, family, friends, and sponsor.

Client signature   Staff signature

Date _____   _____

_____

CLIENT DRESS CODE

POLICY

An important part of recovery takes place in learning new behaviors. One new behavior is learning to dress appropriately for the situations in which clients will find themselves. These situations may include job sites, schools, training programs, or social services. To help clients' learning in this area, the following guidelines for dress while in treatment at the Consortium are established.

Procedure

Clients will wear clothing that is appropriate for treatment. The following list is a guideline for both male and female clients. Staff may address individual client's dress as deemed necessary.

1. Clients will wear no clothing or jewelry with messages or themes involving drugs and alcohol or of a sexual or sexually exploitive nature.

2. Clients will wear no shorts or skirts more than two inches above the knee.

3. Clients will wear no "cut-off" shorts.

4. Clients will wear no halter tops.

5. Clients will wear no bare-midriff clothing.

6. Clients will wear shoes or sandals.

7. Clients are expected to wear underwear.

8. Clients will wear clothing that generally is in good repair.

LEARNING EXPERIENCES AND CONSEQUENCES FOR RULE VIOLATIONS

In treatment, social and physical safety is needed for trust. Consequences and learning experiences are invoked against behavior that threatens the safety of the therapeutic environment and/or interpersonal growth and change. For example, a cardinal rule such as violence, or threats of violence, can bring immediate removal from the therapeutic community and program until a client has notified his or her probation officer of the situation and arranged to resolve the situation with program staff. Breaking less serious rules and infractions are also addressed through the use of learning experiences and homework assignments, such as thinking-error reports to be presented to staff and group. At times, status and level may be changed due to infractions such as relapses or other noncompliance with program rules and/or treatment expectations.

Though often seen as punishment, consequences and learning experiences offer an opportunity for clients to see their own behavior as others do, to think about their own motives, to feel some regret for what they did, and to consider different ways of thinking or acting under similar situations in the future.

Consequences and learning experiences also have important community/group functions. The entire group will be aware of clients' consequences and learning experiences to discourage misconduct. They provide learning opportunities for others and help assure that the program is a safe place to be and strengthens positive peer cultures, pride, and therapeutic community togetherness.

The degree of consequences and learning experiences depends on the severity of the misconduct and an individual's history of misconduct. The staff, group leaders, and community agency representatives may assign any of the following consequences and learning experiences when there has been misconduct in any area of treatment.

It is important to know that a progress report may be written by staff instead of consequences or learning experiences whenever there is misconduct. Such reports may be written when there are several separate misbehaviors. Clients will be expected to report any serious violations to their probation and parole officers as part of any other consequences and learning experiences. There will be no secrets about violations between this agency and probation and parole.

MISCONDUCT VIOLATIONS AND LEARNING EXPERIENCES

Major Rule Violation

A. Physical Violence:
Removal from program; reported to parole and probation; recommendation for sanction time: referral to in-jail treatment: continuation in in-house program after staffing. All assigned work must be completed.

B. Learning Experiences for Positive Urine Analysis/Breathalyzer Results:

1. First Confirmed Positive: If the use of chemicals is spontaneously admitted prior to a request for testing, the client will be required to:
    a. Self-disclose to group
    b. Self-report to probation officer with staff confirming report. There will be no loss of level.

    If the use of chemicals is admitted after a request for testing and before the test is given, a client will be required to write a thinking report and present it to group. The probation officer will be notified and the possibility of sanction time will be discussed.
    If the use of chemicals has not been admitted prior to receiving results, or after the test has been given, the sanction time recommended to the probation officer will be two days.
    Work will be completed, as assigned, while in sanction. The individual will participate in the jail program while sanctioned. The individual will present a Thinking Report to group when released from sanction. A power staffing will be held to determine other consequences, such as a loss of level.

2. Second Confirmed Positive: If the use of chemicals is spontaneously admitted prior to a request for testing, we will recommend a sanction time of one day to the probation officer. The client will be required to: complete work as assigned while

in sanction; participate in jail program while sanctioned; present a thinking report to group when released from sanction. We will hold a power staffing to determine other consequences, such as a loss of level.

If the use of chemicals is admitted after a request for testing and before the test is given, we will recommend a sanction time of two days to the probation officer. The client will be required to complete work as assigned while in sanction, participate in the jail program while sanctioned, and present a thinking report to the group when released from sanction. There will be a power staffing to determine other consequences, such as a loss of level.

If the use of chemicals has not been admitted prior to receiving results, or after the test has been given, we will recommend a sanction time of four days to the probation officer. The client will be required to complete work as assigned while in sanction, participate in the jail program while sanctioned, and present a thinking report to the group when released from sanction. There will be a power staffing to determine other consequences, such as a loss of level.

3. Third Confirmed Positive: Whether client has admitted use or not: The sanction time recommended to the probation officer will be five days. The client will be required to complete work as assigned while in sanction, participate in the jail program while sanctioned, and present a thinking report to the group when released from sanction. There will be a power staffing to determine other consequences, such as a loss of level.

4. Fourth Confirmed Positive: Whether client has admitted use or not: We will recommend termination from the program and report to the probation officer. The circumstances of each individual may determine termination prior to the fourth offense. Refusal to submit to a urine analysis will be considered the same as a positive result and will be reported to probation and parole immediately. In addition, it will be considered major noncompliance with the program. First Refusal:

    1. Sanction time of two days will be recommended to the probation office.

2. Client's work must be completed, as assigned while in sanction.
3. Clients must participate in the jail program while sanctioned.
4. Client will present a thinking report to group when released from sanction.
5. There will be a power staffing to determine other consequences, such as a loss of level.

Second Refusal:
1. A sanction time of four days will be recommended to the probation officer
2. Client will complete work, as assigned, while in sanction.
3. Client will participate in the jail program while sanctioned.
4. Client will present a thinking report to group when released from sanction.
5. There will be power staffing to determine other consequences, such as a loss of level.

Third Refusal:
1. A sanction time of five days minimum will be recommended to the probation officer.
2. Client will complete work, as assigned, while in sanction.
3. Client will participate in the jail program while sanctioned.
4. The client will present a thinking report to group when released from sanction.
5. There will be a power staffing to determine other consequences, such as a loss of level.

Fourth Refusal:
1. We will recommend termination from the program and report to the probation officer
2. Circumstances of each individual may determine termination prior to the fourth offense.

C. Stealing from Staff or Other Clients: The probation officer will be notified. We will recommend a sanction. The client's program continues while in jail. There will be a staffing prior to client's continuing the in-house program.

227

D. Violating Confidentiality Outside of the Consortium

First Offense:

1. A sanction time of two days recommended to probation officer.
2. Client will complete work as assigned while on sanction.
3. Client will present a thinking report to the group when released from sanction.
4. There will be a power staffing to determine other consequences, such as a loss of level.

Second Offense:

1. Sanction time of four days recommended to probation officer.
2. Work will be completed as assigned while on sanction.
3. Thinking report will be presented to group when released from sanction.
4. Power staffing will determine other consequences, such as a loss of level.

Third Offense:

1. Sanction time of ten days recommended to probation officer
2. Client will complete work as assigned while on sanction.
3. Client will present thinking report to the group when released from sanction.
4. Power staffing will determine other consequences, such as a loss of level.

Fourth Offense:

1. We will make recommendation for termination from the program.
2. Circumstances of each individual may determine termination prior to the fourth offense.

E. Disobedience of Verbal Request from Staff or Group Leaders:

First Offense:

Client will present thinking-error report to group within forty-eight hours, or as assigned prior to return to group activities.

Second Offense:

Report to probation officer informing of noncompliance. Client will present thinking report plus one week (minimum) journal exercise on resistance to authority.

Third Offense:

Report to probation officer with recommendation for two-day sanction: The client's work will be sent to jail. There will be a staffing prior to the client's return.

SUBSEQUENT INCIDENTS: AS ABOVE.

F. Intimidation/Harassment/Threats:

First Offense:

Client will write a thinking report. Client will be restricted from group for twenty-four hours. Client will do work on grounds.

Second Offense:

Report to probation officer Client will write a thinking report, do journal exercise (minimum one week) on use of intimidation and consequences or we will make recommendation for sanction time of two to five days.

BASIC RULES

1. Failure to do tasks as required:

   Verbal reprimand and reminder to do assignments on time with thinking report: Accountability and responsibility restriction from group activities until assignments are complete. Possible report to probation officer if behavior continues, staffing to determine other consequences.

2. Tardiness:

   First Offense:

   All unexcused tardiness will report to on-duty staff. There will be thinking report make-up time. Restriction from group if entry would distract from others.

   Second Offense:

   Tardy as above

   Third Offense:

   Report to PO. Possible recommendation for sanction time of one day.
   Staffing to continue in house.

3. Unexcused Absences:
   a. All unexcused absences require a urinanalysis on return.
   b. All unexcused absences reported to probation officer

   First Offense:

   There will be a review of client attendance. Client will write a thinking report, do journal on attendance, discuss barriers to attendance.

Second Offense:

> We will recommend sanction time. Client will continue to work in jail.

Third Offense:

> As above: Recommendation for staffing to discuss progress/performance in program and barriers.

Medical Absences:

> All medical absences require a doctor's verification. Client will be given verification forms to take to all medical appointments. Clients must ask for one prior to going to the doctor's unless an emergency exists. Clients must sign a release of information for all doctors they see. Clients must bring in all prescriptions (bottle and prescription notes for documentation).

It is the responsibility of clients to clear all absences other than medical emergencies and illness prior to the absence. This includes all court dates and appointments with social services or corrections. This also includes any changes in work schedules. Clients may not decide on their own that they will switch programs. Clients will be held accountable for providing verification for any and all absences and tardies.

4. Disrespect to Staff, Volunteers, or Clients:

> Thinking reports. Restriction from group participation until learning experience and thinking report complete. Journal on disrespect. Noncompliance reported to probation officer

5. Taking Food Without Approval:

> *See* stealing: Client will be assessed for needs. Application for assistance will be encouraged.

6. Disruption of Program Services: Not working the program, having a poor attitude, displaying negativity, nonparticipating, being critical and blaming, using sarcasm, putting program down:

    a. Restriction from program group activities
    b. Thinking reports
    c. Group evaluation and staffing
    d. Possible report of noncompliance to probation officer

7. Miscellaneous Infractions: These include: horseplay, smoking in a nonsmoking area, being in unauthorized area, gambling, inappropriately using furniture/materials/supplies, dressing inappropriately, and not following group rules.

First Offense:

Verbal reminders with thinking reports

Second Offense:

Restriction from group, make-up work, thinking report

Third Offense:

Report to probation officer, power staffing

Possible recommendation for sanction.
Contract of commitment to follow all rules.

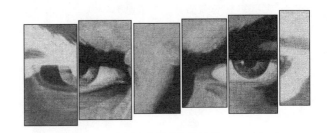

APPENDIX B: SCHEDULE

6:00 AM	Wake up, shower, shave, mop rooms, make bed, prepare rooms for inspection, and start chores
6:45 AM.	Breakfast
7:30 AM	Chores
8:00 AM	Meditation
8:30 AM	Morning therapy group
10:30 AM	Recreational therapy
12:00 PM	Lunch
1:00 PM	1-1, Group, modules, spirituality groups, educational classes, a/d groups, physical activity or homework
2:30 PM	Afternoon therapy group
4:30 PM	Count, followed by free time, homework, telephone calls, study time, laundry, and so forth
5:45 PM.	Dinner
6:30 PM.	A.A./N.A., Big Book, Twelve-By-Twelve, Step Study
7:15 PM.	Swimming in community (Mondays only)
9:00 PM	Chores
11:00 PM	Lights out

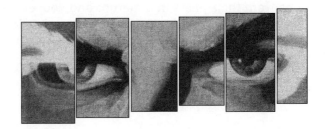

APPENDIX C

GUIDELINES FOR CLIENTS IN THE JAIL TREATMENT PROGRAM

GOALS

The goals of the Consortium Jail Treatment Program are to assist its clients to reach their fullest potential by promoting a substance-free lifestyle, enhance their self-dignity and independence, and to assist the individuals in achieving self-reliance. To accomplish this goal, the program has structured a therapeutic environment that is designed to meet the needs of the people served. The motivation for change comes from the clients themselves. In their treatment responsibilities, groups, meetings, recreation, personal and social times, it is clients who continually transmit to each other the main messages and expectations of the program.

An important part of the program is the involvement of the clients. This is demonstrated by providing opportunities for clients themselves to have an impact upon the system.

PURPOSES

There are many purposes for the organization of client-treatment responsibilities. It will teach people to work together responsibly and safely. It will break down the convict code by having clients follow directions from their peers in a mature and cooperative attitude and manner. It serves to expand the client's horizons, develop poise, instill self-confidence, promote discipline, and it teaches positive regard for authority.

ORGANIZATION/RESPONSIBILITY/AUTHORITY

Each client in the treatment unit is assigned to a treatment responsibility that has certain duties, privileges, and responsibilities. The position is part of a peer group that in turn belongs to a higher peer group that is led by individual staff. There is an ordered network of others who share mutual responsibility at various levels of the program. The operation of the community itself is the task of the clients, working under staff supervision.

Clients are assigned to treatment responsibilities that require them to give direction to peers. These assignments are positions of prestige and responsibility.

The clients are encouraged to be aware of the atmosphere of the community, of each other's strengths and weaknesses, and to resolve any problem areas whenever possible. The community itself serves as a teacher and mentor. But the responsibility to follow the directions always falls back on the individual client. He must decide to support and comply with the larger community's code of conduct. Voluntary conformity to the expectations of the community is the desired goal.

The staff expects clients in positions of responsibility to keep the staff informed of individual, departmental, or community problems. They do this through daily and weekly departmental status reports, discussion with staff, and by bringing issues to the group. Through these, and direct observation, staff will be aware of the status and atmosphere of the community, the departments, and the individuals.

The final responsibility and authority for the community, the departments, and the individuals belongs to the staff. They monitor and evaluate client status, supervise client groups, assign and supervise client treatment responsibilities, and oversee program operations. Clinically, staff conduct all therapeutic groups and provide individual counseling. They decide matters of client status, discipline, promotion, graduations, removals from the program, and treatment planning.

ASSIGNMENTS

Newly admitted clients will be assigned to the cleaning department as crew members. As clients demonstrate their acceptance of the therapeutic-community philosophy and move beyond their denial about their alcohol/drug addiction and their denial about their criminality, they will become eligible to transfer to the one of the other departments as crew members. As they satisfactorily serve in that role, they then will become eligible for promotion to a position on the coordinating council. Client status and functions will be determined, by staff, based on a client's seniority, individual progress, and participation in the program. Clients may apply for promotions and higher treatment responsibilities when they become eligible. However, there must be an opening at a higher level. Staff make all promotions and appointments. A client may be demoted and his status reduced if his performance and behavior fall below program expectations as indicated by his behavior and conduct.

Assignments are made on a monthly basis, at the first of every month. Adjustments for people leaving the program or demotions will be made, as required

COORDINATING COUNCIL

This department consists of the senior coordinator, program mentor, page, and crew leaders from the orientation department, the education department, the inspirational and beautification department, and the cleaning department. The senior coordinator is responsible for this department. The department is responsible for room and facility cleanliness, community meetings, coordinating council meetings, group attendance, and group punctuality.

The purpose of the Coordinating Council is the coordination and completion of all activities pertaining to the community and the assignment of ongoing responsibilities to others. The Coordinating Council members are the pulse of the community and are therefore the "go-between" for staff and clients. They are the eyes and ears of the entire community and, therefore, facilitate the smooth operation of all departments. They are responsible for knowing the status of all clients and departmental units, and are also responsible for recording and reporting all significant occurrences to the staff.

They help clients resolve difficulties that the community finds a problem. They are responsible for minimizing or resolving difficulties that may occur with a client or department.

The Coordinating Council members constantly evaluate the atmosphere, the attitude, and the performance of the clients and departments to be prepared for possible problem situations. They inform the staff of their periodic evaluations along with their suggestions and recommendations.

Clients assigned to the Coordinating Council must be responsible and positive clients who have related to various structural positions in the therapeutic community setting. They must exhibit a consistent attitude in personal growth as role models. They are persons who the clients trust, respect, and feel they are committed to the treatment program and its concepts. They must conduct themselves in a responsible manner at all times.

SENIOR COORDINATOR

The senior coordinator is responsible for this department. He submits weekly reports from all departments to staff, schedules all work of subordinate clients, secures and maintains a cohesive unit atmosphere, requisitions unit needs and supplies, is aware of all departments and knows how they function, and periodically evaluates subordinate clients, and department and community meetings.

The senior coordinator must be a mature individual who is easygoing, able to communicate effectively, is firm but friendly, and is able to understand where people are coming from. He must be a person who others trust and have confidence in. He must respect others' rights and be respectful of their property. The senior coordinator must be assertive and not someone who is easily intimidated or angered.

CREW LEADERS

Crew leaders assist the senior coordinator and are responsible for each of the four departments of the program. They report directly to the senior coordinator and the staff person responsible for each department. The crew leaders submit weekly reports to the senior coordinator. They evaluate the performance of the departments.

The crew leaders always must be aware of the activities, attitudes, problems, and plans of their departments. They should anticipate issues and solutions and be prepared to make appropriate recommendations. The clients appointed to this job function have demonstrated a high degree of responsibility in performing all of the inter-unit job assignments.

The crew leaders must be confident in their ability to organize and express themselves. They must be able to function within a business-like setting, maintaining a positive attitude, and have good manners and behavior. Crew leader must be mature individuals who are easygoing, able to communicate effectively, are firm but friendly, and are able to understand where people are coming from. They must be persons who others trust and have confidence in. They must respect others' rights and be respectful of their property. The crew leaders must be assertive and not easily intimidated or angered.

PROGRAM MENTOR

The purpose of the program mentor assignment is to help clients resolve difficulties. The program mentor is responsible for minimizing or resolving difficulties that may occur with a client or department. Preferably, he will not act independently, but in cooperation with the crew leaders and senior coordinator. He should let the departments solve their own difficulties whenever possible.

The program mentor will attend all meetings and participate in all scheduled activities and be prepared to provide feedback to the staff, as needed. He will submit a weekly progress report that will include a description of problems and difficulties with his suggestions or solutions. This report will be submitted to the senior coordinator with a copy for the counselors. The program mentor is to constantly evaluate the atmosphere, the attitude, and performances of the clients and the departments, to be prepared for possible problem situations. He will inform the staff and the senior coordinator of his periodic evaluations along with his suggestions and recommendations. He should have an attitude of total program commitment with knowledge of the concepts used.

The program mentor must be a mature individual who is easygoing, able to communicate effectively, is firm but friendly, and is able to understand where people are coming from. He must be a person who others trust and have confidence in. He must respect others' rights and be respectful of their property. He must be assertive and not someone who is easily intimidated or angered.

The program mentor is one of the most important client jobs and requires an awareness of all unit departments and knowledge of how they function. He reports directly to the senior coordinator.

THE PAGE

The page is responsible to record client, council, and community meeting minutes, submitting all client requests to staff, promoting group activity, attendance and punctuality, reminding council members of meeting times, reminding clients of group time, posting community meeting notices, and generally keeping the community informed of all activities, groups, information, and plans.

The page must be a mature individual who is easygoing, able to communicate effectively, is firm but friendly, and is able to understand where people are coming from. He must be a person who others trust and have confidence in. He must respect others' rights and be respectful of their property. The page must be assertive and not someone who is easily intimidated or angered. The page is directly responsible to the senior coordinator.

CLIENT-TREATMENT RESPONSIBILITIES

ORIENTATION DEPARTMENT

The crew leader is responsible for this department and its crew members, and department plans. He coordinates and conducts an orientation for all new clients.

Orientation is provided to each new client on rules, procedures, activities, and concepts of the program. The crew leader is acquainted with the facility and introduced to other clients. Crew leaders work 1:1 with clients. New clients must be made aware of the program's expectation that each client will share in treatment responsibilities, as well as the workload.

Orientation most often will consist of several sessions over the first two weeks after a client arrives in the program. Each new client will be assigned a sponsor from this department who will guide him through his assessment phase, help him settle in, and act as a big brother.

The crew leader must keep an ongoing list of who has been assigned as a sponsor, who has been assigned to complete orientation sessions with new clients, and how many orientation sessions have been conducted, and submit a weekly report to the coordinator on activities. The crew leader evaluates the performance of each crew member and reports directly to the senior coordinator.

EDUCATIONAL DEPARTMENT

The crew leader is responsible for this department and its crew members. The department plans and conducts or arranges the activities of the department, which include: morning meditation, evening meetings, AA/NA meetings, Step Study, Big Book study, audio tapes, spiritual groups/church/Bible study, and special group subjects such as department of motor vehicle classes, communication classes, HIV lectures, transitional group, and so forth.

The crew leader must keep an ongoing list of all clients involved and those who are not and must submit a weekly report to the coordinator on activities and requested needs, and so forth. The crew leader evaluates the performance of each crew member and reports directly to the senior coordinator.

INSPIRATIONAL AND BEAUTIFICATION DEPARTMENT

The crew leader is responsible for this department and its crew members. The department is responsible for house beautification boards, slogans, posters, concepts, structure boards, organization of special events, graduations, cultural activities, birthdays, calligraphy projects, and plants.

The crew leader must keep an ongoing list of all clients involved and must submit a weekly report to the senior coordinator on activities and requested needs, and so forth. The crew leader evaluates the performance of each crew member and reports directly to the senior coordinator.

CLEANING DEPARTMENT

The crew leader is responsible for this department and its crew members. The department is responsible for the cleanliness of the facility. The crew leader is responsible for the crew members during cleaning times. He is responsible for the safety, cleanliness, and for work being completed within the facility. He will evaluate the performance of crew members, will count, record, and dispense all supplies and equipment used on a daily basis and forward information to staff, along with a weekly report on activities and requests for needs.

The cleaning crew leader will assign each crew member a cleaning duty, which must be done daily. Clients will receive alternate jobs weekly. At the end of the day on Friday, the cleaning crew leader will write all the names on the board in the group room for next week's cleaning chore. The next week, the client will complete the duty assigned to him. The crew leader will check off the names of each client as his duties are completed. It is his responsibility to ensure the cleaning job is completed "thoroughly." If a client chooses to not complete the cleaning duty assigned to him, the group and/or staff will decide a learning experience.

All clients must keep in mind that this is their treatment program. If guests or volunteers come to share the day with us and see a dirty treatment room or area, this is their first impression of us. First impressions are key no matter who the person may be. The crew leader reports directly to the senior coordinator.

ORGANIZATIONAL CHART

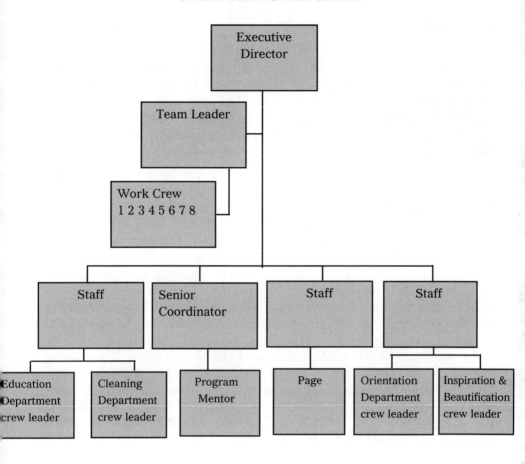

BEHAVIORAL ASSESSMENT RATING
LEVEL SYSTEM

Client status and functions will be determined by staff based on the following behavioral-assessment scores. These forms will be completed on each client at least every thirty days. For crew members, the evaluation will be completed by the client's crew leader, the senior coordinator, the program mentor, the staff members in charge of the department, and the client's counselor.

For crew leaders, the evaluation will be completed by the senior coordinator, the program mentor, the page, staff members in charge of the department, the client's counselor, and the team leader. The program mentor will be evaluated by the senior coordinator, the page, the crew leaders, the treatment team, and the team leader. The page will be evaluated by the senior coordinator, the program mentor, the crew leaders, the treatment team, and the team leader. The senior coordinator will be evaluated by the program mentor, the page, the crew leaders, the treatment team, and the team leader. Laundry, kitchen, and utility workers will be evaluated by all clients on these crews, the Klamath/Lace Education Training Institute education facilitator, continuing recovery group facilitator, client's counselor, and the team leader. The outside work crew will be evaluated by all clients on the outside work crew, Klamath/Lace Education Training Institute education facilitator, continuing recovery group facilitator, client's counselor, and the team leader. The composite scores of these evaluations will determine the work opportunities and privileges for each client.

TREATMENT RESPONSIBILITIES, WORK OPPORTUNITIES, AND PRIVILEGES

Behavioral Assessment 1 & 2   Janitorial crew.

Behavioral Assessment 3 & 4   Are eligible to be promoted to educational, orientation, and inspiration and beautification departments as crew members.

Behavioral Assessment 4   Upon completion of Stage I are eligible for advancement to Stage II.

Behavioral Assessment 5 & 6   Are eligible to be promoted to the position of crew leader.

Behavioral Assessment 6   Upon completion of Stage I are eligible to be placed on eligibility list for outside work crew, laundry, kitchen and utility worker. Upon completion of Stage II are eligible for advancement to Stage III.

Behavioral Assessment 7 - 10   Are eligible to be promoted to the positions of senior coordinator, program mentor, and page.

A client may be demoted and his status reduced if his performance and behavior fall below program expectations as indicated by the behavioral ratings and conduct.

1. Work Crew Participation: All work crew tasks have been accomplished promptly. Little or no supervision is needed. Tasks are completed well.   1 2 3 4 5 6 7 8 9 10

2. Follow Orders: Person completes tasks as explained. Requests information during tasks for clarification.   1 2 3 4 5 6 7 8 9 10

3. Fulfills Obligations: Person completes tasks he agrees to do. He does not attempt to renegotiate if the task is too hard. In other words, he contracts, and completes verbal agreements.   1 2 3 4 5 6 7 8 9 10

4. Accepts Responsibility: Person accepts responsibility for his actions. He avoids victim stance. Accepts ownership for his failings.

1 2 3 4 5 6 7 8 9 10

5. Receptive to Criticism: Person is able to accept comments about himself that may not be to his liking Person does not have to agree with criticism to accept it, though the intensity of the disagreement is important.

1 2 3 4 5 6 7 8 9 10

6. Respectful to Others' Rights: Person is able to respond to other person in appropriate ways. He listens to opinions by others, accepts other's individualities, and takes turn speaking.

1 2 3 4 5 6 7 8 9 10

7. Manipulation of Others: Person does not take advantage of other persons or staff. He does not use gambling, blackmail, power to control, or intimidation.

1 2 3 4 5 6 7 8 9 10

8. Assertiveness: Person assumes assertive posture. He does not allow exploitation. He avoids situations where "bigger" more manipulative persons can control. He does not have a "puppy dog" personality.

1 2 3 4 5 6 7 8 9 10

9. Honesty: Person uses honest means for personal gains. He avoids false reporting, lying by omission, half-truths,or assent.

1 2 3 4 5 6 7 8 9 10

10. Delays Gratification: Person does not insist on immediate action for the things he wants; in other words, success in program, privileges, appointments, head of the line, top man.

1 2 3 4 5 6 7 8 9 10

11. Slang: Person does not use criminal, psychological, or profane slang.

1 2 3 4 5 6 7 8 9 10

Date:_____

Client's Name:_____

Rated by:_____Position:_____
[One is low and ten is high]

1. Conduct Expectation: The person has not received any summonses, misconduct reports, papers, or warnings.

1 2 3 4 5 6 7 8 9 10

2. Room Cleanliness: The person has not received any room inspection infractions.

1 2 3 4 5 6 7 8 9 10

3. Response in Groups: Person offers information in group meetings about himself, other members, unit operations, his thinking, and feelings.

1 2 3 4 5 6 7 8 9 10

4. Honest Disclosure: Person is
   able to share information about
   his thinking process in keeping
   with his own history. Reports
   are accurate.

   1 2 3 4 5 6 7 8 9 10

5. Expression of Emotions:
   Person uses "I feel" statements
   and expresses emotions more
   positively than negatively.

   1 2 3 4 5 6 7 8 9 10

6. Receptive to Criticism: Person
   is able to accept comments
   about himself that may not be
   to his liking. Person does not
   have to agree with criticism
   to accept it, though the intensity of the disagreement is
   important.

   1 2 3 4 5 6 7 8 9 10

7. Self-criticism: Person is able to
   criticize his own actions, thinking, and behavior. Self-criticism
   must be followed with self-
   improvement to be effective.

   1 2 3 4 5 6 7 8 9 10

8. Realistic Expectations: Person
   has obtainable goals for himself. Behavioral contracts are
   realistic and obtainable.

   1 2 3 4 5 6 7 8 9 10

9. Honesty: Person uses honest
   means for personal gains. He
   avoids false reporting, lying, by
   omission, half truths, or assent.

   1 2 3 4 5 6 7 8 9 10

10. Delays Gratification: Person
    does not insist on immediate
    action for the things he wants.

    1 2 3 4 5 6 7 8 9 10

11. Fulfills Obligations: Person completes tasks he agrees to do; does not attempt to renegotiate if the task is too hard.

1 2 3 4 5 6 7 8 9 10

12. Respectful of Others' Rights: Person is able to respond to other person in appropriate ways. He listens to opinions by others, accepts other individualities, and takes turn speaking.

1 2 3 4 5 6 7 8 9 10

13. Manipulation of Others: Person does not take advantage of other persons or staff. He does not use gambling, blackmail, power to control, or intimidation.

1 2 3 4 5 6 7 8 9 10

14. Accepts Responsibility: Person accepts responsibility for his actions. He avoids victims' stance. Accepts ownership for his failings.

1 2 3 4 5 6 7 8 9 10

15. Slang: Person does not use criminal, psychological, or profane slang.

1 2 3 4 5 6 7 8 9 10

16. Assertiveness: Person assumes assertive posture. He does not allow exploitation. He avoids situations where "bigger" more manipulative persons can control. He does not have a "puppy dog" personality.

1 2 3 4 5 6 7 8 9 10

17. Work Crew Participation: All
    work crew tasks have been
    accomplished promptly. Little
    or no supervision is needed.
    Tasks are completed well.

1 2 3 4 5 6 7 8 9 10

STAFF BEHAVIORAL ASSESSMENT RATING

Date: _____ Client's Name: _____

Rated by: _____ Position: _____

COMMENTS:

_____
_____
_____
_____
_____
_____
_____
_____
_____
_____

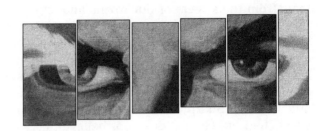

ABOUT THE AUTHOR

Boyd Sharp has more than thirty years of clinical and management experience in the alcohol/drug treatment field, with the last twelve years dedicated to working with high-risk, antisocial repeat offenders. In 1994, he became the executive director of the Consortium, a community-based correctional day treatment program and a jail-based program in Klamath Falls, Oregon. Prior to that (1990-1994) he was the clinical supervisor for the award-winning Powder River Correctional Alcohol and Drug treatment program in Baker City, Oregon.

Mr. Sharp received his bachelor's degree from Whitworth College in Spokane, Washington and his master's degree from Oregon State University, Corvallis, Oregon. He is an Oregon State Licensed Professional Counselor. Mr. Sharp is currently an active board member of six associations concerned with alcohol/drug problems, solutions, and treatment at local, state, and northwest levels.

Mr. Sharp has authored numerous articles and uses this book in the applied psychology classes he teaches at the Oregon Institute of Technology in Klamath Falls, Oregon. He also has taught at a community college and has conducted numerous training sessions in Oregon and Idaho.

This book is based on Mr. Sharp's practical experience and research. The passion for what is written comes from his concern about the ever-increasing incidence of crime in America and the world.

This is the same as the passion of those who want to remove all crim-inals from the streets of our towns and cities and keep them locked up forever, or at least, for a very long time. They desire this because they want the streets safe for their families. They want to be able to have their children walk down the street to school without fear of being kidnapped, raped, or molested. They want their children and themselves to be able to play in the park or run on the running path without fear of being attacked. Mr. Sharp wants this, too. He too wants the streets safe for his grandchildren. He just does not believe this will come about by locking people up and throwing the key away. These people will get out of prison. Therefore, he is committed to promoting the ideas in this book because he believes this is the most promising solution to reducing the crime in America and the world.

Mr. Sharp retired in 2001, a year after the first edition of this book was published. Though he has retired from actively directing treatment programs, he continues to teach courses in criminal behavior at the Oregon Institute of Technology. He serves on the Board of the North West Institute of Addiction Studies and is a member of the Umatilla County Local Alcohol and Drug Planning Committee. You may contact him at bsharp@oregontrail.net